THE BURLINGTON STRIKE

THE BURLINGTON STRIKE

ITS MOTIVES AND METHODS

INCLUDING

THE CAUSES OF THE STRIKE

COMPILED BY

C. H. SALMONS

[1889]

REPRINTS OF ECONOMIC CLASSICS

AUGUSTUS M. KELLEY · PUBLISHERS

NEW YORK 1970

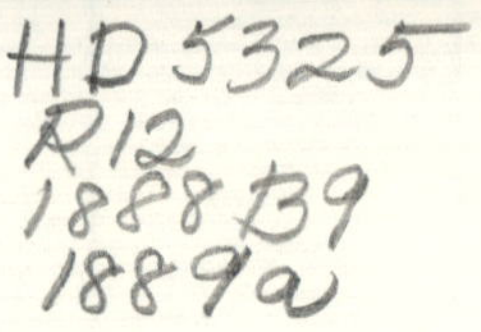

First Edition 1889

(Aurora, Illinois: Press of Bunnell & Ward, 1889)

Reprinted 1970 by
AUGUSTUS M. KELLEY · PUBLISHERS
REPRINTS OF ECONOMIC CLASSICS
New York New York 10001

S B N 678-00552-4
L C N 67-30470

Printed in the United States of America
by Sentry Press, New York, N. Y. 10019

C. H. SALMONS.

THE BURLINGTON STRIKE:

ITS MOTIVES AND METHODS,

INCLUDING

THE CAUSES OF THE STRIKE,

REMOTE AND DIRECT,

AND

THE RELATIONS TO IT, OF THE ORGANIZATIONS

OF

LOCOMOTIVE ENGINEERS,

LOCOMOTIVE FIREMEN,

SWITCHMEN'S M. A. A.,

AND

ACTION TAKEN BY

ORDER BROTHERHOOD R. R. BRAKEMEN,

ORDER RAILWAY CONDUCTORS,

AND KNIGHTS OF LABOR.

The Great Dynamite Conspiracy;

ENDING WITH

A SKETCH BY C. H. FRISBIE;

Forty-Seven Years on a Locomotive.

FROM AUTHENTIC DOCUMENTS AND LIVING WITNESSES.

COMPILED BY C. H. SALMONS.

AURORA, ILL.:
PRESS OF BUNNELL AND WARD,
1889.

TO

The Brave Men whose Adherence to Principle

INVOLVED THE POSSIBLE

SACRIFICE OF HOME AND MEANS OF LIFE,

IN THE LABOR CONTEST

WITH

THE CHICAGO, BURLINGTON & QUINCY R. R. COMPANY,

DURING THE YEAR 1888,

This Book is Affectionately Dedicated

IN DEEP SYMPATHY WITH THE FAMILIES OF THOSE

WHO LOST THEIR LIVES

AS A RESULT OF THE MADNESS

OF A COMPANY WHICH BROUGHT UPON THEIR

FAITHFUL SERVANTS

THIS MOST INIQUITOUS CONTEST.

By their Sincere Friends

THE COMMITTEE OF PUBLICATION.

CHAS. H. SALMONS,

COMPILER.

CONTENTS.

CHAPTER XXXV.

CHAPTER XXXVI.

CHAPTER XXXVII.

CHAPTER XXXVIII.

CHAPTER XXXIX.

CHAPTER XL.

CHAPTER XLI.

CHAPTER XLII.

CHAPTER XLIII.

CHAPTER XLIV.

CHAPTER XLV.

CHAPTER XLVI.

CHAPTER XLVII.

CHAPTER XLVIII.

CHAPTER XLIX.

CHAPTER L.

CHAPTER LI.

INDEX TO ILLUSTRATIONS.

*Reproductions of pencil sketches by Priest, Frisbie, and other old employes, who were present to view the wrecks.

PREFACE.

The relations between capital and labor, along the Burlington system in 1888, attracted the attention of employers and employes in all parts of the world. The causes which led to dissatisfaction on the part of the laborers, and their ineffectual efforts to remedy notable evils, ought to be as widely known. The power which a great company has to coerce, or to punish, has hardly been known in this country until the great Burlington strike brought it out. The labor organizations have a right to know what kind of a foe a railroad company may become, what are its aggressions in time of peace, and what its tactics in time of strife.

It is not likely that any of the parties who are conspicuous in the contest had any thought that they were making history. None of the actors in the struggle between capital and labor had any thought that they were speaking into a phonograph, which some day would reproduce their words; or that a camera was beside them which would some day restore in unerring light the relationships and attitudes of moments of blinding passion.

Strangely enough, records were preserved, letters were copied, telegrams were stored away, and many persons have vivid recollections of the events just passed.

The world has seen a new instance of the selfishness and relentlessness of capital; and legislators have come to the new tasks of regulating internal commerce, and protecting labor. Laboring men have come to see how varied and how vital are their relations to the prosperity of the country. They understand now better than ever before that the condition, resources, and aims of the laborer have more to do with the progress of any nation than the achievements of its arms, or the successes of its diplomacy.

An increasing number of people desires that the history of the greatest labor contest of all time, should be put in permanent form, while the witnesses yet live. Accordingly, during the last few months, a few men located on the line of the Burlington system, have undertaken to print the record of the Burlington strike. This may guide other corporations into safer policy than that one madly chosen by the Burlington, and it may throw a light upon the relationships of the laborer that will make him a wiser and more potent factor in defining the destinies of our country.

The men who have undertaken this history were participants in this contest. The association is composed of J. C. Porter, Div. 32., President; J. W. White, Div. 32, Treasurer; C. H. Salmons, Div. 79, Sec. and Compiler; George Minot, Div. 32; Geo. Goding, Self-Help Lodge No. 80; C. H. Frisbie, and others.

The labor Orders mentioned in this book, are in no way responsible for its publication. Grateful acknowledgments are tendered to P. M. Arthur, G. C. E. B. of L. E.; to F. P. Sargent, Grand Master B. of L. F. James L. Monaghan, Grand Master S. M. A. A.; S. E. Wilkinson, Grand Master B. of R. B.; Ed. F. Oshea, Grand Sec. B. of R. B.; to A. R. Cavner, S. G. A. E.; Geo. W. Wheatley, B. of L. E.; and to other and valued correspondence for material assistance.

C. H. Salmons, Compiler.

P. M. ARTHUR.

GRAND CHIEF ENGINEER B. OF L. E.

CHAPTER I.

THE BURLINGTON STRIKE.

On February 27th, 1888, at 4 o'clock A. M., the locomotive engine-men, on their own motion, terminated their connection with the Chicago, Burlington & Quincy Railroad Company. To prevent any needless damage to property, all the trains in transit at that hour went on to the nearest terminal station, but as nearly as possible to the stroke of the clock, the two thousand locomotive engineers and firemen quietly severed themselves from the Burlington system. It was not the work of a tumultuous assembly. The movement was well considered and cordially approved, and notice of intention was duly given to the company. As late as at 2 o'clock on the preceding day, a committee had waited upon the authorities of the company to implore any concessions consistent with their obligations to stockholders and duties to employes, that would avert the impending strike.

The importance of the step which severed the engineers and firemen from the Burlington system can hardly be over-estimated. That great road extends through the states of Illinois, Missouri, Iowa, Kansas, Nebraska, Colorado, Wisconsin and Minnesota. It passes through more than fifteen hundred cities, towns and villages, all of which are more or less dependent upon its facilities for freight and travel. In some of these states competing and intersecting lines of road are numerous, so that the calamity of a blockade would not be everywhere disastrous. In the various states traversed there are hundreds of small stations entirely dependent on the Burlington, and situated from fifteen to fifty miles from any other road. In case of a scarcity of coal among hundreds of prairie villages, the effect of a suspension of railroad traffic would be serious. To all the stations along a railroad track the company offers the convenience of transportation, and agrees to take in return the favor of patronage. The employes cannot be a party to this agreement, but the company is bound to the fairness and the foresight which will always prevent a suspension of its work.

The methods pursued by the engineers were peaceable. With a delicate sense of honor they regarded the right of property in the company with which they could no longer agree. The fifteen hundred engineers surrendered their engines with not a bolt, or screw, or valve out of order. The matters of complaint, with the unquestionable facts which underlay them, with dates and names, and records, were laid before the chief officers of the company by calm, dispassionate men. Timely warning of the day and hour of the strike, with the causes compelling it, were fairly and fully given. The determination reached was not that of a tumultuous assembly, nor of an inflammable mob. The principles involved had been under public discussion for years, and their correctness in the main had been conceded by various of the great Railroad Companies. It could be no trifling affair that thrilled with a single impulse the men of the footboard along the six thousand miles of the Burlington lines. It is difficult for any one to estimate how much it meant when so many intelligent and practical men left their places, unfitted for any other skilled labor, and with the probability that similar doors of employment would be closed to them upon other roads.

Who is the Locomotive Engineer ?

He is a man of bone and brawn, equal to the hardest work. He inherits from a robust ancestry great bodily vigor, as well as clearness and accuracy of eye and ear. He reaches a locomotive only after preparatory years of untiring study and toil. In his probation he acquires a quickness to detect danger and a promptness to avert it. He cannot be an engineer unless he can command his tired nerves to work on in the face of rain and storm, or in defiance of sleet and cold. Higher than commanding the obedience of muscles and nerves, he must know the anatomy of his engine, and the remedy for all its maladies. On his soul is the responsibility for the safety of the precious freight of hundreds of passengers, and of hundreds of thousands of dollars. No other calling of civil life records such bravery in the face of peril, or such noble sacrifice of self to save others. The locomotive engineer's craft is the drum over which every band of the country's business gains its speed; it is the master-wheel of the world's progress.

We lie down in our sleeper and rest as we do at home. And yet we know that all through the night the train will dash on at the rate of forty miles an hour, past beacon-lights, switches, side-tracks and bridges. Stockholders at home and passengers on board sleep the night through without a fear. It is because they believe in the engineer.

The curtain has been drawn for a moment to let the light fall on the kind of men who joined issue with the Burlington Company. They were unanimous. As when Israel left Egypt, not a hoof was left behind. There was a principle involved, for which they risked employment and support. It must have been to them a matter of no small moment that could move thoughtful men to grapple with one of the most powerful companies on the face of the earth. We shall proceed in these subsequent chapters to take up events in their order of time, and carefully and honestly look the facts in the face which occasioned, and which characterized, the great Burlington strike of 1888. It was the most momentous movement of the kind that has ever gone upon the page of history.

CHAPTER II.

WHY DO LABORING MEN ORGANIZE?

If any one can tell when it was that man first discovered that in union there is power, it will fix the date when men first combined to secure to themselves prosperity and justice. Mechanical fraternities flourished among the Romans, in which affairs of common interest were regulated by their own laws. In the eleventh century, in many cities of Italy, the people united against the rapacity of the lords, and exchanged lordly rule for the right to labor and to trade as they deemed best. Merchants' combinations were common in all the flourishing cities of Europe in the twelfth century. In the same century the drapers of Hamburg, the shoemakers of Magdeburg, and various tradesmen of Milan formed unions, or brotherhoods, that have been closely imitated by various craftsmen in modern times. Guilds, as such organizations were called among the Saxons, were not necessarily trade associations, though they protected their members from injustice, secured their recognition and provided for their employment. In general they resisted arbitrary power as affecting the interests of their adherents. In England the guilds for centuries held their rights under royal charter, and in that century very many of the ordinary occupations were organized for mutual benefit. A great many of our associations of modern times can be traced to the Saxon tendency to organize bodies of men of similar pursuits. This is the origin of our corporations of every kind, as banks, insurance, and transportation companies. Our railroad corporations, Boards of Trade, Associated Press, Knights of Labor, and many others, chartered and unchartered, all come from the same parent stock, and all bear the same family likeness, the main feature of which is combining for mutual protection and profit.

Movements in connection with labor have assumed in recent times a new importance. Once they limited themselves simply to self-protection as to employment and wages. Now they study social relations and the reciprocal obligations of capital and labor. The leading minds of the labor movement are by necessity students of political economy and of social science; and in their discussions and projects every calling obtains a hearing, and finds promotion. The equitable reward of honorable labor is the great social problem of our times. It is a reasonable prediction that from the ranks of organized labor shall come the strong writers, thinkers and statesmen of the future.

But why do the employes of railroads organize?

Let us enumerate some of the reasons:

1. It is the unquestioned usage of legislatures and of congress to grant to railroad corporations almost unlimited franchises, and in perpetuity, without any personal responsibility. On the other hand, no enactment of any importance is on any statute book to protect railroad men, whose work upon trains imperils their lives with almost every duty they perform. It is not unreasonable that trainmen should be disaffected wherever they are paid less than men are usually paid

for similar work on other roads, and wherever they are held to a company by an arrangement that compels them to stay where they are, or else be prevented from railroad work anywhere else

2. It is to be remembered also, that the life of a railroad is a perpetuity; that with time its expenses will lessen and its business will increase. In view of future incomes men will take present risks. Capital can always do this, but labor cannot. Labor represents women and children; it implies food, clothing, shelter and education; the day's work if well done should meet these demands at par. The two millions, or more, now nearly three millions, of persons in the families of railway employes have the first lien on the products of their work. When, therefore, the railway laborer demands reasonable pay, he has behind him a regiment of arguments to enforce his right. The most of the work to be done is so difficult as to require experienced, or skilled labor; it is largely of a kind to impair health and to shorten life, and it exposes the laborer to great irregularities of work, and to a frightful percentage of fatal accidents. When losses occur to a company from mismanagement they should not be made up by abatement of the wages of laborers. If the business of a year proves dull, the stockholder's dividends should not be kept up by cutting down the wages of the men. One man alone counts nothing before a powerful company; one day's work bears a poor proportion to the thousands of millions of capital invested in railroads. Unless labor combines it cannot be heard at all. It has no resort, no appeal for justice if it cannot organize a moral

force that will stand between the laborer and the relentless power of gold.

3. The conditions of the trainman's life are hard. If he develops into a man of business, or if he becomes manager of great enterprises, it is in defiance of his surroundings. He usually enters in early life upon his occupation in which there is a premium on strength, alertness and endurance, and in which there is much of both physical weariness and mental dissipation. He is commonly exposed to allurements that tend downwards. Along the line there are drinking places; if not in the station itself, then within a door or two. It is a rare thing that he finds a reading room for railway men, or a resting place away from tempting odors and sights and companions. It does not seem to be recognized at headquarters that what makes a better man makes a better workman. If there are anywhere in depots, reading rooms, and places of quiet rest for the much jolted men, it is very recent, and exceedingly rare, and even where there is considerable work of this kind it is rarely traceable to a railroad company. But almost all roads in this country have, in a very effective way, testified to the capability and the character of the railroad employe. Almost everywhere men are filling the highest positions in railroad management who have come up from the lowest round. This is very noticeable in the Pennsylvania system. President Roberts, and A. J. Cassatt, formerly vice-president, began as rodmen in the engineers' corps. Second vice-president Thompson was a machinist of Altoona; general manager Pugh began as a brakeman; general passenger agent Carpenter, and James

McCrea, general manager west of Pittsburg, both began as messenger boys. A. M. Tucker, division superintendent on the Erie, was a track laborer. C. W. Bradley, general superintendent of the West Shore, was a brakeman, then conductor, on the same road. President Caldwell of the Nickel Plate was a clerk on the Pennsylvania. The engineers and firemen have been very prolific in this direction. One Division, No. 34, of Columbus, Ohio, has on its roll of honor two railroad presidents, three master mechanics, and four roundhouse foremen. There can be no doubt that everywhere similar talent abounds among men in subordinate positions along all our great railway lines. That so many reach distinction in spite of great disadvantage is an inspiring argument in favor of organization for mutual improvement and protection. It encourages honest emulation and true pride. Its result must be to make the men sober, industrious, frugal, faithful, and self-helpful.

4. The capital invested in banks and that employed in insurance companies, though in large amounts, is yet comparatively harmless as regards labor. But when capital is pitted against labor; when the issue is Money vs. Men; when the returns upon the invested capital are in proportion to the pressure upon the laborer, then as capital is heartless, the rights of the man must go under. The greatest danger is reached when capital succeeds in holding the laborer in one hand, and grasping legislation with the other. The money invested in railroad stocks, with the addition of the amount of all the funded debts of the railway companies in this country, will soon reach the

enormous amount of ten thousand millions of dollars, ($10,000,000,000.) A very small percentage on this sum will support a lobby, the third house, in every state capital, as well as at Washington. An assessment of one-fourth of one cent on each dollar of this vast sum would produce a revenue of twenty-five millions. At present rates of increase we shall soon have in this country one million of railway laborers. A reduction of five cents per day upon that number of men would produce the sum of eighteen millions of dollars, ($18,250,000.) We do not say that any one has proposed this, but we do say that similar things have been done. Wages have been cut down to replenish a foolishly exhausted treasury. How easy a thing it would be for capital to declare war on labor and then assess upon labor the expense of it. How easy to keep up dividends to stockholders by cutting down wages; or to cover the ruinous expense of an unwise policy in the management by issuing a lower rate of payments.

Capital, controlling lobbies and newspapers, constitutes a trio for evil, before which, if it is left unchecked, the rights of the American laborer will be of as little value to him as to the toilers of Russia, or of Algiers. In Europe, when contests are on between money and labor, the appeal is to the bayonet; but in this country the appeal is to argument, to righteousness, and to the ballot. Our method of protection is not by violence, but by the peaceable combination of the endangered men, so as to make themselves felt by their moral force, their intelligence, and by their numbers.

CHAPTER III.

MUTUAL OBLIGATIONS.

We believe that there are certain great principles in equity in which both capital and labor ought heartily to agree, and beyond which the demands of either would be both unreasonable and unrighteous. There is really but one universal and unerring rule, viz: As ye would that men should do to you, do ye also to them.

Most men, given to one kind of work, become skilled in it, and unfit themselves for other employments, but at the same time increase the value of their labor to their employer. To be discharged implies the loss of the time used in acquiring the skill, and also the waste of time and money in seeking a new place. It may require a removal of hundreds of miles at great expense. If permanent employment is uncertain, it will prevent the laborer from embellishing, or even from making a home, and it tends to make of him an improvident, hand-to-mouth hanger-on upon a temporary occupation, and the education of his children becomes a most unlikely thing. He cannot identify himself with permanent interests of the community, and he sinks into a characterless wage-earner. It would not be strange if some times the fear of removal would lead men to try to keep their places by unbecoming and wrongful methods, or they may do a poor service knowing they are liable to dismissal for any cause, or for none.

Now, a corporation might arbitrarily reduce the wages, or compulsorily increase the hours of labor, or frequently require additional hours of work for the pay of ten, or compel the employe to assume the risk of damage to property, or say to the men unfairly burdened, "If you do not like our administration, go elsewhere; you are at liberty." All these methods have, here or there, been resorted to. It is obvious that they deteriorate the character of the laborer, so as not only to lessen the value of the labor, but also to abate the worth of the man as a member of the community. Certainly no corporation has a moral right to do this, for it unfits the employe for honorable and skilled work.

Self-interest alone would require of a corporation the strictest integrity and fairness, and considerate provision for the adequate support of every deserving laborer. Moral obligation would require that wages should be adequate for a little more than actual current support, for the rainy day should not be a destitute one, and comforts ought to increase in every virtuous family with advancing age. The pay for a day's work should be the unstinted remuneration for an average man, and less or greater work done than the average should have higher or lower rates. We can neither buy nor sell the moral sense that makes the workman industrious, and studious to do his work rapidly and well, and to prevent loss of material; but that moral sense has a real value nevertheless, and the man who has this quality really earns more money than the man of the same strength who has it not. It is not enough for the corporation to pay only the rate of wages that it can afford with its present rate of dividends, for that would require labor to guarantee both the honesty and the intelligence of capital. If wisdom and honesty are in the foundation of an enterprise, its dividends may be delayed for years, and then make ample compensation; but food and clothing, and comforts, cannot wait. The conclusion is inevitable that every corporation employing labor is bound by the highest law known to man, to make contented and comfortable, every worthy employe it has, and to do this before it retires to count its profits.

One fact is better than many theories. The Chicago Inter-Ocean of June 20, 1889, says;

"One thing has been demonstrated by General McNulty, while receiver of the Wabash, that the best managers are not always trained railroad men. General McNulty dropped his law practice to accept the appointment of receiver of a small railroad in southern Illinois, which was bankrupt. He built this road up, and turned it back to the stock holders as a paying piece of property. When Judge Gresham appointed General McNulty receiver of the Wabash road, the property was in a deplorable condition, and he has succeeded in placing it in a better condition than ever before, and he has himself come to be acknowledged as one of the best railroad managers of the country, so that he has received flattering offers from roads that are anxious to secure his services."

The pay of the labor of this road, while this able financier was building it up, was among the best that was paid in the United States. General McNulty evidently has both ability and honesty, and he has proven that good wages can be paid and the road still succeed; and that it is not the cost of labor, but bad management that causes the bankrupt condition of railroad property.

CHAPTER IV.

THE DAWNING OF TROUBLE.

In 1862 the engineers running between Aurora, thirty-seven miles west of Chicago, and Galesburg, one hundred and twenty-five miles farther west, were paid less than other engineers were paid for the same service on other parts of the C., B. & Q. road. They believed that the injustice was directly chargeable to the division superintendent, Mr. Hammond, and accordingly they demanded of him its correction. They appointed a committee to wait upon Mr. Hammond, to ask an advance of fifty cents per day or trip, and pay for extra time. Mr. Hammond would not grant it, and the committee returned and so reported. They then agreed to insist on their demand and to give the superintendent ten days' notice, at the end of which time they would stop work if the matter was not adjusted. This notice was given. On the day when the time would expire, a despatch came from Mr. Hammond asking the men to keep at work and he would see that they were satisfied. The men were not disposed to make a contract in so loose a way as that and declined. When this news reached Mr. Hammond by telegram, he called up a special train to take himself and party to Aurora, the seat of the difficulty, and on his arrival it was found that he had with him eighteen engineers to take the places of these men. But it was intensely cold, and the scabs he brought out would not, or could not take the engines, and superintendent Hammond acceded to the demand. Work was suspended only one hour.

It is fair to the Company to state that when a superintendent, or other high administrative officer, corrects an abuse in the administration without consulting his superiors, it is evident that he is the originator of the annoying order himself. The unanimity of the engineers in this matter, and the prompt adjustment of it by the superintendent, indicate the justness of the complaint.

RAILROAD LABORERS ORGANIZE.

CHAPTER V.

BROTHERHOOD OF LOCOMOTIVE ENGINEERS.

On the 17th of April, 1863, at Marshall, Michigan, Messrs. E. Nichols, F. Avery, D. Wheeler, John Kennedy, F. Wartsmouth, H. Higgins, B. Northrup, Geo. Q. Adams, and W. D. Robinson, believing that many evils might be remedied, and much good accomplished, by an organization of practical locomotive engineers, met and instituted a society named the Brotherhood of the Foot Board. The 17th and the 18th of the following August was agreed upon by them as the time for holding the first annual convention at Detroit, Michigan, at which convention W. D. Robinson, of Detroit, was duly elected to fill, for the first time in its existence, the very important office of Grand Chief Engineer, and O. T. Johnson, of LaFayette, Indiana, was chosen first Grand Assistant Engineer. By a provision of the original constitution, locomotive firemen and machinists were admitted to equal membership. A short deliberation, and experience, convinced the incorporators that engineers should act separately in the matter of self protection. Hence it became necessary to call a special session of the convention, which assembled on the 22nd of February, 1864, at Detroit, at which time and place this objectionable clause was changed and the locomotive engineers were possessed of an organization exclusively their own.

At the second annual convention, which was held at Indianapolis, Indiana, on August 17th, 1864, Charles Wilson, of Rochester, New York, and Robert Laughlin, of Hornellsville, New York, were chosen to fill the two highest offices of the organization, and the title originally chosen was substituted by the title which is still borne by the order, viz: The Brotherhood of Locomotive Engineers.

That a good thing was done in the organization of the order is evident from its rapid growth. This convention at Indianapolis was held at the end of its first year, when sixty-seven of its subordinate divisions had been established, with a membership of over sixteen hundred. To-day the order extends through every part of the United states, and has a footing also in Canada and Mexico. The number of divisions has reached four hundred and twenty, and the membership exceeds twenty-five thousand.

There is a Mutual Insurance Association connected with the Order and an outgrowth of it, originating in 1867. The business and the reports cover now a period of twenty-one years of the work of insurance with the most satisfactory results. There were paid out, during the year previous to November, 1888, one hundred claims of three thousand dollars each, making a total of three hundred and twenty-seven thousand dollars, ($327,000.) The entire amount paid to widows, orphans and to disabled members, since 1867, is $2,572,169.61.

During the year ending with November, 1888, the

Chief Engineer was called to interpose and to adjust between men and officers on twelve different roads, and in each instance he effected an honorable and amicable adjustment. The contest between the men and the officers of the Burlington System was the only one that has occurred in eleven years that has not yielded to satisfactory adjustment by friendly interposition. The history of the Order is made up of happy results upon individual character, inspiring men with emulation, and virtuous pride in their calling. By its refining and elevating influence upon the character of its members it adds to the efficiency and to the actual wealth of every company whose engines are run by members of the Brotherhood.

In the constitution of subordinate lodges of this Brotherhood, in article V, section II, we have these words:

"Should it come to the knowledge of any member * * * that a brother * * * is guilty of drunkenness, or keeping a saloon where intoxicating liquors are sold, or being engaged in the traffic of intoxicating liquors * * it shall be his duty to bring the matter before the Chief Engineer of his division, in writing at once, who shall immediately appoint a committee of three to investigate the charges."

Section IV. (After the testimony is all offered.) "The Chief Engineer shall order the ballot passed, and it shall require a majority vote of all of the members present to expel him, excepting those convicted of keeping a saloon where intoxicating liquors are sold; in which case it shall be the duty of the Chief to declare the offending brother duly expelled without a ballot."

Section V. Should any brother neglect his duty, or injure the property of his employer, or endanger the lives of persons willfully, while under the influence of liquor or otherwise, it shall be included in the investigation as laid down above, and be subject to the same penalty."

F. P. SARGENT.

GRAND MASTER, B. OF L. FIREMEN.

CHAPTER VI.

BROTHERHOOD OF LOCOMOTIVE FIREMEN.

The locomotive firemen effected an organization, a Brotherhood, for mutual benefit, on December 1, 1873, at Port Jervis, New York. Eleven men met to devise means of mutual helpfulness, social, moral and intellectual, to protect the interests of firemen and to promote their general welfare. It has, in these sixteen years, permeated every part of the United States, extending also into Mexico and Canada. The Order receives reports from three hundred and ninety lodges, aggregating over nineteen thousand members. Its object at first was not beyond the mutual advantages that come from close affiliation of men of similar pursuits; but in 1885 the Order extended its purposes and became distinctly a labor organization without losing its benevolent characteristics. The method of adjusting differences between the Order and the authorities of a road, is to appeal directly to the highest authority of the company complained of, and if that is not successful, then to insist upon arbitration. The organization tends to good order, to mutual beneficial influences, and it is a concentration of power which may, at almost any time, be called upon for mutual protection, or in some way in the defense of the interests of labor. There is no antagonism between the firemen and any other society of railway laborers; on the contrary, the Order works for the advantage of the laborer in the interests of fair work for fair pay.

In the constitution of the Firemen's Brotherhood for subordinate lodges, there are some provisions of general interest:

Section 188. "Any member dealing in intoxicating liquors shall be expelled."

Section 190. "Any member who shall use intoxicating liquors to excess, or shall be found guilty of drunkenness, or other immoral practice, or conduct unbecoming a member, shall be suspended for the first offense, if of a light character; but if of a serious nature, or for a second offense, the offender shall be expelled."

CHAPTER VII.

SWITCHMEN'S MUTUAL AID ASSOCIATION.

The switchmen at Chicago organized a Union, for mutual aid, intended for only local purposes, on August 18, 1877. The society had but little progress until 1884, wnen it took in new blood, and various cities began to organize similar societies. A meeting of delegates, for the object of forming a national organization, was held at Chicago, February 22, 1886. The convention deliberated eight days over a constitution, which was adopted at last with enthusiastic unanimity. The object of the Mutual Aid Society, as declared in the preamble to the Constitution, is as follows:

1st. To unite and promote the general welfare, and advance the interests—social, moral, and intellectual—of its members.

2nd. To endeavor to establish mutual confidence, and create and maintain harmonious relations between employer and employe.

The forms of benevolence undertaken were, "to relieve the distress of disabled brothers, to care for their widows and orphans, and to see to the decent burial of deceased members."

The first annual meeting was held in Kansas City, Monday, September 20, 1886, having delegates from twenty-five lodges.

The first Grand Master was James L. Monaghan, whose ill-health had driven him from the law business to the outdoor work of the switchman. He became a member of the Illinois legislature in 1888. From that time on, the Society has been fortunate in having for officers, good and efficient men. In 1888, Mr. George S. Bailey was made Grand Organizer and Instructor, who also left the law for outdoor railroading work. In 1886 he became a member of the lower house of the Illinois legislature, and carried through a bill for a State Board of Arbitration, but not in time to have the action of the Senate. The Order is a vigorous one, watching carefully the interests of labor.

CHAPTER VIII.

BROTHERHOOD OF RAILROAD BRAKEMEN.

The epidemic of organization struck the railroad brakemen in the spring of 1883. A few railroad men of all occupations, chiefly brakemen and switchmen, formed, at Albany, N. Y., a society called the Capitol City Aid Association. The object was protection by mutual benevolence. In June following, eight brakemen met in a caboose at Oneonta, N. Y., and organized the first auxiliary branch, called No. 2. This enterprising offspring withdrew from Capitol City and set itself up as Oneonta Lodge of the Brotherhood of Railroad Brakemen. This occurred in July, 1883. Its members were all brakemen. The Order was greatly indebted to Eugene V. Debs, a good man, who was eminent among the Brotherhood of Firemen. The Capitol City Aid Association, finding itself no longer followed, turned about and followed the new head and became Capitol City Lodge, No. 3.

The organization by the adoption of a constitution, bears date, Oneonta, N. Y., Sept. 12, 1883. The Order spread along the lines of iron net work with great rapidity, and it numbers now over ten thousand members. It filled a well defined want among trainmen. Their position is not too well paid, and it is full of hardship, privation and peril. The calling is so full of danger that insurance men exclude brakemen from eligibility to insurance. The constitutional limit of policy of insurance is $1,000 per member, and the treasury is a mutual one, and it is refreshed by moderate assessments.

The influence of the Brotherhood is very marked upon the mental, moral and physical improvement of its members. The average character of brakemen has much improved since the organization of the Association; it has inspired ambition, and developed talent, and has made its members a surprise to themselves by the healthful and elevating influences which they have found within it.

The preamble to the constitution contains these words:

"To unite the railroad brakemen; to promote their general welfare, and advance their interests—social, moral and intellectual; to protect their families by the exercise of a systematic benevolence, very needful in a calling so hazardous as ours, this fraternity has been organized."

Article XXII, Section I, of the constitution of subordinate lodges, reads as follows:

" Any member dealing in, or in any way connected with the sale of intoxicating liquors, shall, unless he withdraws, be expelled. Any member found guilty of drunkenness shall be suspended for the first offense. A repetition shall be punished by expulsion, and under no circumstances, shall a member so expelled, be reinstated before the lapse of six months."

CHAPTER IX.

REDUCED WAGES AND CLASSIFICATION.

In 1873, the C., B. & Q. road used only a single track in doing the company's business between Chicago and Galesburg. The volume of business was so great that trains met with many delays, often waiting for hours upon the side track, waiting for Chicago bound trains having the right of way. Trains bound west would often be many hours more than time allotted on the time-card in making the trip, and no allowance was ever made for such service. It also had been the practice to allow the men to go into the repair shops with their engines when they needed repairing, and work on them. This usage had been discontinued and the men would sometimes have to wait in idleness for months, while the engine was under repairs. Being left without work, reduction of pay and other conditions equally unsatisfactory, induced the engineers to appoint a committee, which consisted of L. E. Johnson, who is at this writing superintendent at Aurora, William Wilson, and J. C. Porter, who were instructed to draw up a paper to be submitted to the various divisions for approval, or correction, and, if approved, to be presented to the general manager, Mr Harris, with the request that the matters complained of should be investigated and remedied. The committee chosen to present this to Mr. Harris, was Irwin Alexander, of Quincy,

Barney Wagner, of Galesburg, and L. E. Johnson, of Aurora. These gentlemen addressed the following letter to the General Manager:

Galesburg, Ill., Sept. 23, 1873.

Robert Harris, Esq.,

General Supt., C., B. & Q. R R.

Dear Sir

The engineers of the C., B. & Q. R. R., and leased lines east of the Mississippi River, feeling that they are not receiving sufficient pay for the labor performed, have requested the undersigned engineers to wait upon the general officers of the road, for the purpose of requesting them to increase our pay to the standard of $4 per day, on all divisions of the road as they now are, also that the nine-tenths of full time be allowed them when not made, the same to be paid monthly, allowing all extra time made over and above. The reasons for the above are as follows:

1. The increase of responsibility placed upon them.

2. The increase of the number of hours on the road.

3. The increased amount of work performed while on duty.

4. That a transfer of engines and men from Aurora to Galesburg has largely increased their expenses, also keeping them from their homes much more than previous to the change.

5. That engines running from Aurora to Chicago on freight, are in many instances compelled to run to the stock yards and then to the Chicago yards, requiring from ten to sixteen hours for one day's work.

6. That they are required to hold themselves in

readiness for duty at all times, both night and day, frequently being called upon for certain hours, and after remaining in yards waiting for trains from two to six hours, on their engines, then being obliged to make their trip for the same amount of pay.

We would also be pleased to have our firemen paid in the same proportion.

The above we most respectfully lay before you for your consideration and favor.

Yours Truly,

(Signed) Barney Wagner, Galesburg,
Irwin Alexander, Quincy,
L. E. Johnson, Aurora.

To Robert Harris, Esq., Chicago, Ill.,

To this there came a reply as follows:

Chicago, Ill., Oct. 27, 1873.

Messrs. B. Wagner, I. Alexander and L. E. Johnson,

Gentlemen of the Committee:

"It was understood at the time you presented the communication about pay, September 23, that I would look into the matter and see if there appeared proper grounds for increasing it. This has been done, and the conclusion is not to increase the standard of compensation. I think it will appear, all things considered, that the engineers and firemen on this road are compensated as highly as elsewhere.

Mr. Chalender is authorized to make a proper allowance, over and above the existing standard on the eastern division, for such engineers as run from Aurora to the stock yards and thence to the freight station. The division master mechanic will see that the difficulty of being called unnecessarily early before starting is remedied, if engineers will call his attention to it whenever it occurs.

Yours Truly,
(Signed) Robert Harris.

The delays, of which the committee complained, were liable to occur every day, and cost the engineers an average of three hours each trip, making an average of three hours of unpaid labor. The remark of Mr. Harris that the engineers were paid as well as elsewhere is true, if we consider the pay for the trip under favorable circumstances. The company has usually paid extreme prices on what is called the main line, and so they prevented the possibility of a united effort to correct unfavorable rates on the other parts of the system. This will be more clearly presented in the work of the committee of 1886.

The effort to set right a grievous wrong in 1873, had little effect, except to intensify a sense of injustice in the minds of the men, and also to confirm the officers of the road in their purpose to tighten their grip on their employes. Up to this time there was an apprenticeship of one year for engineers, paying $3 per day, and after one year, full pay, viz: $3.87½. But an order was issued October 1, 1876, which had something of the suddenness and the effect of a bombshell:

Chicago, Ill., Oct. 1, 1876.

"On and after October 10, 1876, apprentice firemen on switch engines, will receive for first year, $1.40

per day; second year, $1.50; third year, $1.60. Firemen on the road will receive first year, $1.50; second year, $1.75; third year, $2.00. Engineers will receive for first year $2.25; second year $2.50; third year, $2.85. Old engineers to receive $3.48."

This was a cut of ten per cent on former wages, and it included all train men. A meeting of train men was called at Galesburg in which all grades of work were well represented, and a petition was signed by one hundred and thirty employes, asking that wages be put back to the rates prior to December, 1873. The officers of the road insisted upon the necessity and the fairness of the reduction of wages, and so it remained.

CHAPTER X.

BURLINGTON POLICY DEFINED.

We now propose to ask what the necessity was which took, with one flourish of the pen, ten cents of every dollar of income from every train man on the C., B. & Q. system. Then bear in mind that a small assessment on a very large number will produce an enormous sum. For example: the Union Pacific Road, according to its president's report in 1888, employs 14,000 men. Their pay ranges from $1 to $4 per day. Let the average be, say, $2 per day, and ten per cent on all salaries would yield an income of $2,800 per day, or in a year of 315 days, $882,000. These figures show that railway managers can play a great game with small factors. Employes will not leave for trifling reasons. To take the risk of finding other work, with probable loss of time and expense of moving, and perhaps leaving a little property, is a serious matter, and the laborer will submit to extortion till endurance is no longer possible. Then the corporation defines the required labor and its conditions, and fixes the wages, and so settles at once both the buying and selling price of labor. The laborer, therefore, in beginning work for a railway of close calculations, assumes the risks of the company without being a sharer in its profits. Now the railway laborer may have to suffer a reduction of wages for either of two reasons:

One way in which he may lose, is when he is compelled to build up the position and the fortune of the chief officers of the road, personally. A few years ago, the mayor and aldermen of Toronto were investigating the affairs of the Grand Trunk of Canada. In the examination, alderman Tinning asked a witness: "Mr. Duffin, will you explain about the thirty-five per cent?"

Mr. Duffin: "It means that by whatever means the chief officers of the road reduce the working expenses of the road, they have a guarantee from the board of directors in the old country of thirty-five per cent on that account."

Alderman Bronsted: "But who gets that?"

Mr. Duffin: "The heads of departments, Messrs. Hickson, Wallace, Blackwell, Spicer, and Roberts. Probably, when they see this report, they may try to deny it, but I am prepared to prove it. Roberts denied, but Blackwell said it was true, and that he had $130 over his last quarter's salary, from savings he had effected in his department. I told Mr. Hickson and Mr. Wallis that that was a grievance last year, and that men could not see how the officers could demean themselves to try to reduce our wages in order to put thirty-five per cent in their pockets."

After all, the affairs of the Grand Trunk prove nothing concerning other trunks, but one thing is certain, if a high officer anywhere, has the faculty to annually increase the gross product of his department, and as regularly reduce its working expenses, the company would grapple him with hooks of silver, and he would be too valuable to lose. Before such a man, higher positions and finer salaries would open, and tempting offers from other roads would descend upon him like gentle rain on the tender grass.

Another way in which a railway laborer may be a loser, is when his wages must be cut down to make up for losses by mismanagement at headquarters. Every reader of these facts will remember the cut of rates in 1876, in which there was a powerful combination against New York City. It was a universal, magnificent strike. It was official striking official, road striking road. Freight was carried for less than it cost. Passengers were almost hired to ride in the sleeping cars. The old rate of fifteen dollars a ton from New York to Chicago went down to four. So wild did the rivalry of rates run, that the stockholders of the Michigan Central Railway Company, four hundred and fifty-four of them, employed the best legal talent in the land, Henry S. Bennett, 14 Wall street, New York, and served a notice on Hon. Samuel Sloan, president of that company, insisting upon it that the ruinous, suicidal policy of cutting rates must be at once abandoned. The shareholders directed their attorneys to say to President Sloan, "We ask you to restore and maintain the former rates for travel and freight, and to withdraw from any combination which has for its object any undue reduction, with a view to compete with other roads. If you refuse, or fail to comply therewith, I, and my associates, are directed by them, to employ such remedies as the courts will afford to enforce their rights, and to protect the property and interests of the company." The mismanagement and madness of the Michigan Central seemed to be epidemic among all the chief roads of the country.

JAMES L. MONOGHAN.

GRAND MASTER, S. M. A. A.

The inevitable result was the exhaustion of great surpluses, and the depletion of treasuries. There was one untried source of income,—the management could cut down the wages of laborers on the roads. What did they do ?

The New Jersey Central ordered a cut of ten per-cent to take effect August 1, 1876. At a stockhold ers' meeting on February 7, Mr. Knight, president- of the company said: "The Central R. R., of New Jersey, had declared since 1866, dividends aggregating $14,400,000. That had these been averaged at eight per cent, there would have been left in the treasury $3,413,666.13." This meeting was called to borrow, or assess the stockholders $3,000,000, the result of an effort to ruin other roads through a war of rates. This was made to appear at a meeting held at St. James Hotel, in New York City, on December 16, 1876, which was attended by the presidents of the Erie, New York Central, Pennsylvania Central, Baltimore and Ohio, and others, when an agreement was entered into to restore the rates, and terminate the discrimination against New York, as an export city. This was an acknowledgment of the cause of the financial depression of the railroad companies, whose unwise policy had caused the loss. The method of replenishing was not to assess the loss on capital, but on labor, and by their great power to compel the laborer to make their losses good, or at least to assist in doing so.

In accordance with this policy the rate of wages was reduced, not by common consent, nor by any pretense that a general financial change in the country would enable the laborer to endure it, but by a sovereign order that on such a day, "your pay will be reduced ten per cent." These orders flashed across the country in alarming rapidity. The New Jersey Central cut wages on August 1, 1876; the Chicago, Burlington & Quincy on October 10; the Cairo & St. Louis on November 1; the Grand Trunk, of Canada, on December 7. Many other roads fell in line with the same policy. The third cut on the Pennsylvania Central was made on May 27, 1877, reducing engineers to $2.70 per day, and firemen to $1.25.

Some railroad companies, whatever they had done in the war of rates, had not the excuse of poverty for cutting down salaries. For example: "The net earnings from lines operated by the Pennsylvania R. R., company during the year 1876 amounted to $12,-834,385.78, and yet retrenchment is the cry.[1]" From this statement it is evident that this road survived the war in good shape, as it shows an increase of over a million dollars over the year 1875. But it was a good time to join in effectively tying up railway labor, by the exercise of a right that comes not from justice, but from the merciless power of capital.

We have already alluded to the fact that a petition of one hundred and thirty engineers was presented to Mr. Hitchcock without result. The engineers sent their committee to Galesburg, where they met on October 10, 11, and 12. This committee consisted of S. R. Clark, of Divison 62; F. A. Chase, Division 32: F. H. Reynolds, Division 154; J. McGuire, Division 134; and G. B. Webster, Division 112, who was chosen chairman. The committee met with Mr. Chal-

1 Engineers' Journal, July, 1877.

ender, master mechanic, and Mr. Strong, division superintendent, and represented:

That the pay of engineers had been reduced.

That the plan of apprenticing engineers for six to ten years before getting full pay was oppression. That the Burlington stock yards run was reduced fifty cents per day and the hours were increased. That at Mt. Pleasant and at Chicago, switching was required for from two to eight hours without pay being allowed for it; that with overloaded trains they must double the hills, losing one to five hours; also that they shall have respectful treatment from division master mechanics.

Some of the minor complaints were adjusted, and others were referred to the general superintendent, Mr. Robert Harris. That gentleman was away from the city, and to their telegram he replied that he could not return until the midlde of the next week. The committee then reported to their respective divisions, and they voted to refer the subject to the convention to be held in October.

On December 8, 1876, the committee went again to Chicago, in company with Grand Chief Engineer, P. M. Arthur. They went to the office of the general superintendent, Mr. Robert Harris, and found him in an excited state of mind, pacing the floor, stroking his hair with one hand, and so absorbed as to forget to give any civil recognition to his visitors. Mr. Arthur respectfully told him the occasion of the call, whereupon Mr. Harris said in a petulant manner, that he did not propose to have any pope come here to interfere with him and his engineers. Mr. Arthur told him he did not come here as a pope, but as a gentleman, and he expected to meet one, and in the hope that they could together fix up the differences and have peace. Mr. Harris: "If that is the case, we will hear what you have to say," still pacing the floor.

Mr. Arthur: "Sit down then; I cannot talk to a man's back."

Mr. Arthur then went over the complaints of the men, some of which were so grossly unjustifiable that Mr. Harris said they should be remedied. The classification system was reduced from four years to three.

Mr. F. A. Chase, Division 32, was uncompromising in his censures of the company. He would yield nothing; not an iota. But for him, good terms could have been made, and the almost complete failure of the committee turned on the violence of his feelings. Said he to Mr. Arthur, "If I should go home and tell my wife that I had given in to the company, she would disown me." He was so radical as to disable the others. No satisfactory agreement could be reached. No better conditions could, in his presence, be made. The favoring moment went by. On December 20, this committeeman wrote a letter to his division, begging of them the kindest feeling they could command towards him, expressing great fear of their disrespect, and asking to be allowed to withdraw from the Order. A few words will complete his history as a committeeman: After he began his duties in the committee, he took a ride with Mr. Chalender, the master mechanic of the road, in which ride, he said afterwards, the grievance business was not mentioned. Then in the committee he was so radical as to defeat his fellow members. Immediately he withdrew from the Order, after receiving for his time and expenses $96.87. Then honors and promotions began to shower upon him from the company. Very soon he obtained an engine on a passenger train, though not entitled to it from age in service; then he was foreman of the round house at Aurora, afterward master mechanic at St. Joseph. His conversion from Brotherhood to Burlington was as sudden as St. Paul's, and like that eminent martyr, his zeal was greater in his second consecration than in his first, and all that without a scrap of the material of which martyrs are made. The company showed great skill in using means to break up the committee by discharge or otherwise, but did not often succeed. The result of this appeal to the company was not received with good grace, and it united all concerned in a determination to effect a change for the better, which resulted in a strike and suspension of business in July, 1877

CHAPTER XI.

THE STRIKE OF 1877.

A call was made for a meeting at Burlington, to which all class of train men responded, and a committee was appointed to present their requests to the Company. Then commenced the usual maneuvers of officials to intimidate by threats of discharge, etc. They had posted a notice that unless the men came to the office and signed, ready to go to work, that after such an hour they could consider themselves discharged.[1]

Wheaton and Belknap, in their famous circular of 1888, charge the engineers with bad faith, but the charge is not sustained by the documents before me, or by living witnesses who were participants. Both factions charge bad faith which was probably true of a few men. This is always the case in such trials of character. It is said that "self preservation is the first law of nature," and we find this principle actuating men in an inverse ratio to the character they possess—the less of character the more of preservation. It is not often that a bad man performs good deeds.

The side tracks were blocked with cars; the Chicago end of the line being tied up in consequence of the spread of the great Pennsylvania strike of that year. A switch having been thrown in front of a freight train running into a spur track, and the whole train going off the rails and upon the ground, the engineer, fire-

1 Living witnesses.

man, conductor and brakeman were obliged to flee for their lives. Women, children and men, of all kinds and colors, swarmed in the yards, and threw stones and all sorts of missiles at the men. They had no interest in the railroad, but had taken the fever and were ready to commit any depredations against a railroad, even to kill its employes.

The Burlington Company knew this could not last and that they must get their own troubles over in some manner, so that they would have men to do business with. The men at Creston, Iowa, had an understanding with W. P. Montgomery, the committeeman at Burlington, that no notices would be received by them unless the initials of his name were reversed to P. W. Montgomery. Mr. Potter, then superintendent of the Iowa lines, sent telegrams to Creston telling the men that all was settled, and signed Mr. Montgomery's name, but not knowing the understanding about the signature did not sign it right, and the men would not believe it was authentic.

Some of the conductors started for Burlington with a hand car and the engineers demanded an engine and way car to go and see the committee themselves, which was finally given them. Such was the condition of doubt and mistrust all along the line. July 27, the following letter was written, to wit:

Chicago, Burlington and Quincy R. R. Co.
Office Division Superintendent.

Burlington, Iowa, July 27, 1877.

I am authorized to say to you that if the engineers, firemen, and switchmen return to work without further delay, that they in common with other employes shall not be discharged for any participation in the present strike. And that any grievance, either set forth in writing, or by word of mouth, presented to the manager of the road, shall receive a respectful hearing, and action shall be taken in the matter within a reasonable time.

C. E. PERKINS,

Vice-President.

It is certain that not much respect was intended in this letter. It was evidently addressed to the committee representing the Burlington employes, but no complimentary address is either at the beginning or end, and the conductors are not mentioned at all.

Mr. Perkins is autocratic, and yielded this much because of a necessity. But this did not cure the difficulty, although it might have had a tendency to induce them to accept the promise that was made in the name of Robert Harris, general manager, in a dispatch received at Aurora, promising that if the men would go to work, as soon as the panic was over their pay should be adjusted satisfactorily, and signed—Robert Harris, general manager. The men having great confidence in Mr Harris, accepted his proposition in good faith, and sent the following dispatch to Galesburg :[1]

Aurora, July 30, 77.

Kimball & Porter, (Grievance committeemen.)

The Engineers, firemen and trainmen of

[1] Living witnesses.

Chicago Division accept Mr. Harris's communication of July 30, received at 4:27 p. m.[1]

A. S. Darling, Engineer,
Jno. White, Conductor,
Harry Calkins, Fireman,
H. Dammer, Brakeman,
F. Reed, Switchman.

Another dispatch was sent from Burlington to J. C. Porter.

"Committee from Ottumwa just arrived here. Did you receive our agreement of settlement last night? Everything settled and quiet at this point and men all at work."[1]

W. Green, Chairman.

1 Dispatch as sent.

CHAPTER XII.

INCREASING IRREGULARITIES.

Everything moved off again as though there had been no differences existing, all feeling that the promises would be fulfilled, but as time passed and business resumed its former briskness, doubt began to take the place of confidence, and the men began to inquire into the cause, and they were told by those who were in a position to know, that Mr. Harris did not make the promise, but that superintendent Strong did, using Mr. Harris's name; and that Mr. Harris, on being informed of the action taken, said he never made any promises he did not fulfill, and that the adjustment must be made.[1] In consequence of this, Mr. Harris was notified that his resignation would be accepted, and Mr. Harris resigned and went to St. Louis, Rock Island & Chicago road, and Mr. W. B. Strong was appointed in his place; Arthur A. Hobart in Mr. Strong's place.[2] This ended the promise, and the classification established by the order of October 10, 1876 still stood. The official plans were laid and carried out without regard to personal obligations, and with utter disregard for truth, but in a direct line with all their dealing with their employes.

Mr. Harris was out of the way, and a policy was inaugurated of getting rid of—in some manner—the presumed leaders of any movement for the better condition of the employe. At this time, Mr. L. E. Johnson,

1 Statement of living witnesses. 2 Firemens' Mag., Dec., 1876.

who, the reader will remember, was chairman of the grievance committee who waited on Mr. Harris in 1873, was made foreman at Ottumwa in the early part of 1878, and Mr. Chase was provided with a passenger train, and later was made foreman at Aurora; enlisting these two—who had been a thorn in their side as representatives of the Brotherhood—on the side of the company.

Mr. Johnson was expelled for non-payment of dues,[1] and Mr. Chase demanded a withdrawal card immediately after serving on the committee of 1876, and of all the official force of the Burlington, no greater demagogues were found than these two who had turned their back on the Brotherhood, and having got a place, undertook to prove to the company their sincere conversion.

After being deceived in 1877, no further united effort was attempted until 1881, when Division 112, situated at Creston, asked that a committee be appointed from each division and to try again to cure the evil conditions of pay, but they did not succeed, as only the main line proper had organizations, and some of them were disgusted at the result of the 1877 effort. The St. Louis Division, from Rock Island to St. Louis, 249 miles, was not organized. L. E. Johnson was transferred from Ottumwa as foreman, to Beardstown as master mechanic of this division, and under his management the grievances were very numerous. It was his delight to lay the men off for the most trivial offenses, whether accidental or careless, and the men were paid as best suited the local officers, without any uniform standard.[2] To illustrate: from Beardstown to

[1] Engineers' Journal. [2] Statement of employes, St. Louis Div.

Monmouth, seventy-two miles, the engineer was paid \$2.55. If it took seven hours or twenty-four hours, the pay was the same. They would start out on a through Monmouth run, and on arrival at Astoria coal mines, would be stopped and made to switch from three to five hours, without pay.

In the fall of 1881, Johnson was transferred to Aurora, and A. Forsyth was appointed to the place vacated at Beardstown, but this did not improve matters. At this time, one W. K. Hollis was appointed roundhouse foreman at Beardstown. This man Hollis had been a member of Division No. 38, at Baltimore; had served on grievance committee for that division, and in that capacity made demands on the company contrary to his instructions, and the officers found him out and discharged him. This action on his part broke up the division, which had some \$200 in its treasury, and owned its furniture, and Hollis was charged with making way with it, for which he was expelled. This man being put in an official position on this division, did not tend to allay the irritation the men felt, but rather had a tendency to increase it. Yet they had no means of redress until after the organization of Division 127, at Beardstown, in 1882. There was a few brotherhood men there, but, anticipating dismissal for any aggressive move they might make, said nothing, until in July, 1882, when a committee was appointed to wait on master mechanic Forsyth, in regard to their engines being taken to East St. Louis yard, as had been previously done by the hostler. It took from thirty minutes to one hour to do this work, and the men wanted this time for rest, but Mr. Forsyth would not grant the request, and no further effort was made. In November, 1882, the following circular was issued:

Chicago, Burlington & Quincy R. R.

Office of the General Superintendent.

Chicago, Nov. 9, 1882.

W. K. Hollis, who has been roundhouse foreman at East St. Louis, Ill., has been discharged for dishonesty, viz: in selling a car of company coal and appropriating the proceeds to his own use, also in drawing another man's pay and appropriating it.

H. B. Stone, Gen'l. Supt.

We want the reader to keep this man Hollis in mind, because he is found good enough to be re-employed under the direction of H. B. Stone.

CHAPTER XIII.

THE CONDITION OF TRAINMEN MADE WORSE.

Evils existed all along the line of the Burlington, but the organization was too weak to resist. They were of such an irritating nature that the thoughts of the men were always in the direction of securing some means by which redress could be had, and at the convention held in Louisville, in October, all the representatives from the Burlington met and adopted plans for the grievance committee of 1883, which committee met in Burlington, March 27, and elected Chas. Fisher, of Creston, Iowa, chairman. This committee, met Mr. T. J. Potter, general manager, and H. B. Stone, the general superintendent, who refused to grant any concessions, and the sitting culminated in hot words between Mr. Potter and the committeeman from Division 107. Great complaint was made on account of overwork without pay. Mr. Potter gave the men no satisfaction on this point, but after they were gone he told the officers of the Kansas City, St. Joseph & Council Bluffs railroad, that if the men made any more fuss about delayed time they could allow it, but that under no circumstances were they to tell them he said so. This Mr. Potter acknowledged to the committee of 1886, and these men worked up to that time without pay for such work. In this Mr. Potter acknowledged the justice of the claim, but capital never loosens its grip unless it comes in contact with some compelling power, and Mr. Potter knew the numerical strength of the committee's backing. The Grand Chief, P. M. Arthur, met with this committee, and advised that they go home and get all the men together, and let them know the indifference manifested by the officials, put new energy into their efforts to increase their number, and when two-thirds of the men were members, they would try again.

To head off this effort, George Calkins was ordered discharged in July, and on August 5, a committee was appointed (by Division 32, of Aurora, of which Mr. Calkins was a member) which was instructed to wait on Mr. L. E. Johnson (the same man who was chairman of the grievance committee of 1873, now master mechanic at Aurora,) and ascertain the cause of Mr. Calkins discharge. Mr. Johnson said that Mr. Calkins was discharged for being too earnest a worker for the Brotherhood of Locomotive Engineers. On Mr. Calkins being discharged, the chairman of the general grievance committee, Mr. Chas. Fisher, of Creston, addressed a letter to all divisions along the line, asking them to vote on the question of whether they would make an effort to reinstate Mr. Calkins. For this active part taken by Mr. Fisher, Mr. T. J. Potter ordered his discharge, and in the fore part of August, votes were taken to sustain these men; but the fear of dismissal and the realization of a lack of power to carry all the men with them, (only about one-half being members) the case was never brought to an issue. The convention, in October, paid to each, three months salary, and Mr. Calkins was paid until he obtained another situation. Mr. Fisher has never been employed as engineer since.

All this time the corporation screw was being tightened. Efforts were made at local points to correct local affairs, but always with the same results. Times were dull and every division officer was trying to make a better showing than his neighbour on another division. On the St. Louis division, Mr. Forsyth in 1884, concluded to do away with hostlers at Monmouth and make the engine men clean the fires and put away their own engines in the roundhouse without pay. The local committee waited on him, and as this, like most other evils, emanated from some local official, he was induced to leave the hostler.

They then increased the number of cars so that the men would have to double on the hills. Not being able to pull all the cars they would have to take part of them and go to the next station and set them on the siding, and come back and get the other part and then couple up and go on. Perhaps they would have this to do several times during the trip, and without any additional pay. This is dangerous work, as many accidents happen going down grade after these parts, and many men have been discharged in consequence. They tried to cure this, but were told that they only had the regular number of cars. The men knew that the number had been increased to get this work done for nothing, but they could not help themselves..

Every act of this kind tended to increase their power, as the men found there was no redress except in organized effort.

The men all lived at Beardstown and were run from there whenever they needed them. They would run

S. E. WILKINSON.

GRAND MASTER, B. R. B.

then to Monmouth, and unless they had twenty-five cars for Beardstown, would stop them at Bushnell and and send them back to Monmouth. This run is fifty-six miles, for which they would get $2.10, then lose a day, then make another of this kind of a trip and lose another day. Some of these men were kept away from home for ten days, and finally one of them telegraphed for a pass to go home for a change of clothes and was refused and he quit. Who will defend such management as this ? The men appointed a committee and waited on the master mechanic, and the conditions were so outrageous that he agreed to send them home after holding them three days at Monmouth. This would limit the time away from home to five days.

CHAPTER XIV.

PURSUING A SUPERINTENDENT.

No further effort of note was made until Feb. 1, 1885, when Division 32, situated at Aurora, made a call for representatives from the various divisions located along the system to meet in Burlington on March 3, 1885, which was responded to by J. C. Porter, of Aurora, Div. 32; Heimer of Galesburg, 62; O'Brien of Keokuk, 56; Kirch of Creston, 112; and Fowler of Burlington, 151. Divisions 79, 98, 107, 127, 164, 271 and 290 were not represented. They made a temporary organization, with P. O'Brien as temporary chairman, and Wm. Fowler as temporary secretary. Communications were read from nearly all the other points not represented in person.

The men along the line had evidently not forgotten what befell their predecessors for serving on committee, and one of the letters states, in the following language that "It is going to be a hard matter to send a man from here to organize or meet with a general grievance committee, for the man that goes from here will be discharged, if found out. You may think this strange, but if any engineer lays off he must get a permit from the master mechanic if he wants to leave town. I write this to show you how we are fixed since the last time the committee met in Burlington, but we will get there in some shape."[1]

Realizing the situation, judging from the precedent

[1] Letter from Div. 107 to chairman Grand Grievance Committee.

of 1883, they arrived at the natural conclusion that very little could be done without a concert of action on the part of all interested, and they concluded to refer the whole matter to the delegates to the convention to be held at New Orleans in October. Accordingly, the temporary chairman, Mr. O'Brien, of Keokuk, reported this meeting, with all the correspondence, to the convention at New Orleans, and this action resulted in a call, at that convention, for a meeting of the delegates of the C., B. & Q. R. R. which was held in room 282, of the St. Charles hotel, Oct. 24, 1885, and resulted in the formation of the committee of 1886, with J. C. Porter, of Aurora, as chairman, and L. E. Hinckley, of Galesburg, as secretary.

On Jan. 25, 1887, a call was made by the chairman for the committee to convene at Burlington on the 22nd day of February, 1886, for the transaction of such business as might properly come before it. On the assembling of the committee, it was found that nearly all had extensive reports of local affairs, consisting of delayed time, which they were obliged to perform without reremuneration, men laid off without cause, others discharged, and many otherwise annoyed, none of which they had been unable to correct with their local officers. There were volumes of this, especially from the representatives of the Burlington & Missouri, but it was decided that they did not properly come before this committee, and it was advised to try and secure some rules, and have them signed by the general manager or president, that would take the power out of the hands of the local officers to manipulate conditions to suit their own fancy.

The men contended for the principles enunciated in a circular issued in 1888 to the officers of the Pennsylvania R. R. Company which says: "The employes of the Pennsylvania lines are compensated sufficiently to make them self-respecting and reliable, and are disciplined to the highest standard. A powerful preventive of discord is that men filling the highest offices are expected to consider themselves employes as well as the humblest subordinates, are instructed to follow their orders to the letter, and pay due respect to their superiors; and at the same time superior officers are required to be considerate and just in intercourse with subordinates."[1] Unfortunately both for the financial interest, as well as for the employes, of the Burlington, there were no rules that required the officers to be considerate and just. But an appointment to office, in the mind of the appointee, carried with it unlimited individual rights, to have and to do as seemed best suited to the individual interests and disposition of the individual so appointed.

Those who have not given this subject thought, little realize the contentions that emanate from the unlimited exercise of personal prerogative, through the 999 grades of necessary officials of a great railroad corporation. A section foreman as an officer in command of his squad, hires and discharges men. He can be as autocratic as a king, and there is no redress, except to leave the service, or to appeal to higher authority.

A foreman of a roundhouse may suspend engineers and firemen. He may take away any rights earned by years in the service and give to another. He is gen-

[1] Railway Service Gazette.

erally governed by his likes and dislikes, regardless of the good of the service, and an appeal to a higher authority becomes necessary.

A division master mechanic may discharge, suspend, or assess for damage, for any infraction of rules, and be governed, not by principle, but by personality or by a grudge; not as a direct beneficiary, but to decrease the expense of his division; to make a more favorable showing than other master mechanics of the same system, in order to make sure his own place or a better one.

Train masters and superintendents scattered along the 6000 miles of the Burlington, each trying to outdo the other in cheapening transportation, lessening the cost of material by assessing the employ for damages to rolling stock, or for stock killed; increasing the number of cars in the train until they cannot be handled by the men without doubling the hills, necessitating additional work and danger without additional pay. The list of encroachments and unwarranted exactions might be strung out almost indefinitely, but so long as they increased the dividends they were always sanctioned by the management; and they invariably refused to cure them unless confronted with some combined effort.

"The acquiring of gain by means of enforced levies upon the meager earnings of employes, for petty infractions of arbitrary rules, will hardly be accepted as a legitimate feature of any business. And the taking of the small sums from the many who have little, in order to inspire in them greater zeal in the service of their despoilers, may enforce discipline, but cannot promote concord nor content. Attention is drawn to this practice in order to indicate one of the methods by which discontent and resentment may readily be engendered among a large number of employes.

They see their extremities taken advantage of, and submit to it because their necessities do not permit them the luxury of revolt, but they can hardly be expected to like it, or to congratulate themselves upon a commercial prosperity reared, in a measure, upon their own adversities."[1]

The committee composed of J. C. Porter, of Aurora, Ill., chairman; L. E. Hinckley, of Galesburg, Ill., secretary; John A. Beaureisen, of Aurora, Ill.; Charles Dean, of the C. & I., Aurora, Ill.; John Cuykendall, of Burlington, Iowa; John Stockdale, of Creston, Iowa; H. M. Martin, of Keokuk, Iowa; Phil. Seidenstriker, of Plattsmouth, Neb.; George Wheatly, of Beardstown, Ill.; C. H. Salmons; of Brookfield, Mo.; Charles Thomas, of St. Joseph, Mo.; O. W. Hutchinson, of Wymore, Neb.; S. E. Hoge, of McCook, Neb.; and W. T. Odell, of Chicago, Ill. As this committee was general in its nature, their efforts were directed towards formulating rules that would apply to the whole system. They had provided themselves with the schedules and fixed conditions of all the roads centering at Chicago, and from them was made—devoting a whole week of earnest deliberation to the subject, voting upon each proposition—the schedule as presented to the general manager. The committee adjourned on Saturday to meet in Chicago on Monday, March 1, at 10:30 A. M., at the Grand Pacific Hotel. A dispatch was sent to Mr. H. B. Stone, then general

[1] Bureau of Labor Statistics, Ill., 1886, pg. 15.

superintendent, requesting an appointment, and the communication was answered by the chief clerk, stating that Mr. Stone was out of town. and he was requested to forward the dispatch and obtain an answer if possible. An answer was received Tuesday morning, appointing 3:00 P. M., March 3, for the conference. The committee was admitted at the appointed time, and a two hour's sitting was had, in which Mr. Stone said he could not consider the Hannibal & St. Joseph; the Kansas City, St. Joseph & Council Bluffs; or the Burlington & Missouri, and wanted the committee to cut these lines out of the consideration, which they properly refused to do. The conditions most complained of were placed on these lines by the Burlington's authority, but Mr. Stone denied having the power to take them away. The committee then retired to their quarters at the Grand Pacific Hotel and sent a request to General Manager T. J. Potter, stating that they had had an audience with Mr. Stone, and that he had declared the leased lines out of his jurisdiction, and asked an audience with him at his earliest convenience. As soon as the committee made its appearance at headquarters, Mr. Potter arranged to leave the city, Mr. Stone stating that he would probably be away for a fortnight.

This the committee took for a part of an understanding between the two to discourage them. But they were not in a temper to be discouraged. Mr. Potter went to St. Louis and started from there on a tour of inspection of the whole line of the Burlington, for the evident purpose of evading a meeting with this committee, and to find out the numerical strength of the men represented by this committee. The telegram from the committee to Mr. Potter was handed to him on his way from St. Louis to Burlington. He answered, saying he was on his way to Colorado, on a business trip, and that it would not be convenient to meet them. Mr. Potter was then asked to delay his departure for one day, that there were fourteen of the committee and they had come to see the officers. Mr. Potter answered on the morning of March 5, stating that business engagments would make it necessary for him to go to Colorado, and he would appoint March 20, for a meeting in Chicago, and asked the committee to see Superintendent Stone and he would furnish transportation to their respective homes and return on the above date. But this committee had not forgotten the fate of the committee of 1883,[1] and did not propose to go home and have part, or the whole of the committee, discharged to break it up, as was then done, and Mr. Potter was answered that the committee had come to stay until its business was transacted, and they would await his return. This brought another telegram from Mr. Potter, saying that business of great importance and of previous engagements would prevent his meeting them until the day appointed. The committee saw behind this a ruse to keep out of the way, and it was learned that he was in Burlington long enough to have complied with the request, if he so desired. The action of the general manager made it necessary for the committee to remain in Chicago fifteen days.

On Sunday, March 7, the local officers were congregated in Burlington discussing the situation and preparing an answer to the conductor's committee,

[1] Grievance Committee.

who had been asking an increase of pay, and the committee was informed that the officers decided to make a reduction of the engineer's pay, and add it to that of the conductor's, but Mr. Potter was reported as saying, "We will have to advance wages 10 per cent." On March 10, one of the committee was in Aurora and on his return reported that the officials were congregating at Aurora, and it was evident that the committee of fourteen had to contend with the combined official talent of the Burlington system. On the 6th a letter was sent the Grand Chief Engineer of the Brotherhood of Engineers, P. M. Arthur, which was answered on the 8th, saying to the committee: "Have the men vote on the whole system, whether they will sustain you in whatever action you deem advisable. Avoid all outside discussion of your grievances. Keep your own council, and when you have exhausted all your efforts, and want my services, wire me and I will come at once."[1] P. M. Arthur, Grand Chief Engineer.

The grievance committee, in their preparation to meet the Burlington officers, appointed sub-committees and sent them to each railroad centering in Chicago, to obtain a schedule of wages paid on road and in yard service, for comparison with the Burlington. The methods of the committee were so quiet that the reporters did not know they were in Chicago until about ten days after their arrival. Correspondence was kept up with the Grand Chief Engineer, and he advised in his letter bearing date Cleveland, March 12, 1886. "Your very interesting letter received and read with care. The time appointed to meet Mr.

[1] MS. of P. M. Arthur.

Potter is rapidly approaching, and the best advice I can give at this stage of the proceedings is to meet him in a spirit of fairness. If he does the same you will effect a settlement honorable to both sides. If he is stubborn and will not make any concessions, go at once to the president. If he refuses to do anything, send for me, and I will see what I can do. If you cannot obtain all you ask for in the schedule drawn up, then compromise on something near it. It is far better to do that than to resort to coercion. I have sufficient confidence in your committee, that they will do what is fair and just between the company and the men. Let us hope for the best, and rely upon our manhood and providence for our success. I have declined to go to Corsicana, Texas, until your case is settled. With kind regards to all, I remain,

Yours Fraternally,

P. M. ARTHUR, G. C. E."

General Manager Potter went over the whole system to Denver, and on the way questioned the local officials as to the numerical strength of the brotherhoods, and their sentiment, and upon his arrival in Chicago, on March 19, knew what he had to contend with. But he was as well prepared as one could be, for defense of his side of the question.

1 MS. of P. M. Arthur.

CHAPTER XV.

THE COUNCIL OF WAR.

At the appointed time, March 20, the committee were invited to Mr. Potter's office, and after the usual introductions and recognitions of old acquaintances, we entered upon the subject of the meeting. Mr. Potter, like Mr. Stone, took the ground of supply and demand, and asked why they did not go to some other railroad if the pay was not satisfactory.[1] The principle of supply and demand in an open market is deemed a commercial balance. But labor employed by a large corporation is subject to the will of the money power, the same as the poor are affected by a corner on wheat. The scope of the control is such that there is virtually but one market, and if labor withdraws from the service of a railroad corporation six thousand miles long, it must go perhaps hundreds of miles to find a new market.

Section men's pay is reduced to 95 cents per day by the order of a general manager of the Burlington, when common labor is worth $1.25 on the market. The section man having no power of redress, and being ignorant of other business, has no alternative but to submit. The Jute Trust increased the price of manufactured jute 50 per cent, while the labor which produced it was at the pauper point, and received no benefit from the advance. The consumer looked for another market but found nothing but Jute trust Jute,

1 Minutes of General Grievance Committee.

and resorted to substitutes, and state legislatures. But where is labor's substitute, or legislative influence ? It has neither, and must submit to the inevitable result of combined capital.

Mr Potter was manager of the Burlington system, and all its leased lines, yet he, as Mr. Stone had done, denied having authority to fix the pay and change the conditions complained of. But he would make things pleasant east of the Mississippi if the committee would drop the Burlington & Missouri and the other leased lines, which the committee again refused to do. Mr. Potter was asked if there was any official higher than he was that could settle with the whole system,[1] and he answered that he had as much authority as any one. He denied the right of the Chicago & Iowa railroad to be represented, but he was obliged to acknowledge that he was vice-president of that road. He argued that it was not fair of the men to ask a uniform pay, as the conditions and expense of living varied; that, for example, a man ought to have better pay in Nebraska and Colorado than in Illinois, because it costs more to live there. Mr. Hoge, of McCook, asked why the company refused to pay as much in Nebraska as they do in Illinois, and Mr. Potter had to acknowledge a strong point made against him. He was not practicing what he preached. The committee had the schedule with them which they had consumed so much time in preparing, but they thought best not to present it unless Mr. Potter would consent to treat with all concerned. Mr. Potter asked if the plan of schedule which we had made out, contemplated the abolition of classification, and he was aswered by the chairman,

1 Minutes of General Grievance Committee.

Mr. Porter, that it did. Mr. Potter called it apprentice pay.

It will be remembered that the committee of 1876 asked that apprentice pay be restored, and classification done away with. Apprenticeship, as practiced by all trades, has in it the principle of equity, the conditions being fixed by common consent, while classification represents the power to fix conditions without regard to equity.[1] The committee told Mr. Potter of many of the evils of classification and its abuses by local officers, and Mr. Potter said: "Officers, a good many times, make mistakes and do things they had not ought to do." Yet he could not make that change, and said: "Fancy pay is the cause of so many roads going into the hands of a receiver." The Burlington company had been selling rebate tickets, from Kansas City to Chicago, which, after the rebate was paid, left the company 50 cents each. The committee asked Mr. Potter whether this did not conduce to more receivers than any kind of pay.[2] Mr. Potter said: "Officials get mad as well as any body, and do foolish things, which to us, is only a strike of one capital against another. They do not think that they get their proportion of the pool." Where then, was Mr. Potter's principle of supply and demand? The meeting closed at noon to convene at 2:30 P. M. Mr. Potter said he did not think he could consider classification on the leased lines, and closed by asking: "Now your demands are, an equalization of pay, and doing away with classification."

1 Order of Oct. 10, 1876. 2 Quotation of a member of Committee.

CHAPTER XVI.

SKIRMISHING FOR POSITION.

Promptly at 2:30 P. M., all parties being present, the discussion was continued, Mr. Potter taking positive ground upon the two points of his last question at the adjournment of the previous meeting—equalization of pay, and classification. He did not try to defend the justice of the position, but knew the financial advantages and considered them of great importance. The committee contended for the justice of their position with pertinacity, and knowing all the evils of the law and the abuses by the local officers in its application, had Mr. Potter in deep water as far as argument went.[1] He asked whether the committee had come with a positive ultimatum. The chairman answered: "We only ask justice, and where injustice can be shown in our proposition, concessions will be readily made."

After a silence of considerable length Mr. Potter asked if the committee expected to have uniform pay if the Company abandons classification, and he was answered, "Yes." Mr. Potter said, "I only asked the question to see how far apart we are." He contended that the financial condition of the Company would not admit of such changes, and consequent increase in expenses. One of the Committee produced the annual financial statement of the Company, showing they had collected "$26,172,819.54, and had a net income over operating expenses of $12,845,786.43."[2] Mr.

1 See chapter on classification. 2 Railroad and Warehouse Commissioners, Ill.

Potter knew that the Burlington was one of the best dividend-paying roads in the country.

The Committee had been away from their homes thirty days, and were anxious to come to some kind of an understanding. They had discussed the matter and concluded to divide the difference on classification; the men to give one year and the company one year, the one year based on second year pay. Mr. Potter was not inclined to compromise. The pay of the firemen was discussed, and Mr. Potter asked what they wanted. The Committee told him, 55 per cent of the engineer's pay, and only one year of apprentice pay. Mr. Potter finally concluded to take the whole matter home and deliberate on its merits. The schedule had not been given to him because he had positively refused to consider the Burlington & Missouri, and other leased lines. But his expressed willingness to take up the whole subject was what the committee wanted, and he was then presented with the schedule. When this was given him he observed that he had expected the papers to be presented before, but he concluded he would not ask for them. He then proposed they adjourn until 10:30 A. M. Sunday, which was agreed to.

At the appointed time, Mr. Potter opened the discussion by saying that he did not want to abolish classification, or establish a uniform rate of pay, and he made this proposition: To call all the local officers in and go over the grounds of complaint. To which the chairman of the committee replied: "That might benefit a few, but would give us no rules to control the future. Local officers could change the conditions again to suit themselves, and we should be left just where we started." Mr. Potter said: "You are the judge on one side, and I am the judge on the other. I cannot concede the two main points, as it is against my principles, which are based on the laws of supply and demand."

The Committee having conceded all that was consistent with their instruction from the men they represented, told Mr. Potter they would have to send for their Grand Chief Engineer, P. M. Arthur, the chairman stating that though Mr. Potter conceded one year of classification, we are no nearer a settlement. Your whole line is closed against employment for engineers, in consequence of this law.[1] It was evident Mr. Potter did not want a strike on his hands—he had too much business sagacity for that—yet he did not propose to give anything he was not compelled to give to prevent it. He said he did not like the idea of signing any agreement; "That is too much like giving the road over to the men to run." He objected to having Mr. Arthur, but finally consented to meet him. Then the committee retired and sent for Mr. Arthur, and he arrived on Monday morning.

1 Minutes of General Grievance Committee.

A. R. CAVNER, S. G. A. E.

CHAIRMAN COMMITTEE OF NINE.

CHAPTER XVII.

THE TREATY OF PEACE OF 1886.

After meeting with the committee and advising moderation, Mr. Arthur and the chairman went to Mr. Potter's office, to arrange for a meeting, which was appointed for 2:30 P. M. On the arrival of the committee at the Burlington offices, Mr. Arthur and the chairman again went into Mr. Potter's office. Whether Mr. Potter had changed his mind, or had adopted a new role was not known, but he had concluded not to see the committee, saying it would do no good. However, he finally consented when the schedule was presented by Mr. Arthur, with the classification left out by the advice of the Grand Chief Engineer. This left only a uniform schedule of pay, and laws to govern subordinate officers. Still, with all the concessions that had been made by the committee, they seemed no nearer a settlement than at the first meeting. Mr. Potter said he would not adopt a uniform schedule, when Mr. Arthur said: "As you will do nothing, it is left with the men to say what they will do. As grand chief, I cannot make them strike, but when my consent is given, it carries with it the consent of the Brotherhood of Locomotive Engineers of the whole United States, Canada and Mexico." Mr. Potter said: "Then they will strike if you give your consent?" Mr. Arthur answered: "Mr. Potter, you have had your own way so long, you think you must have it always. Now I will sanction a strike, and if you can hire men to run your engines you can do so, but the Brotherhood of Locomotive Engineers can pay as much to hire them not to run them." Mr. Potter evidently did not like this picture, and said he would submit a proposition, but he would want ten days. Mr. Arthur asked each one of the committee if he would grant the time, and each answered "No." It was evident to the committee that negotiations had come to an end, and all, including Mr. Potter, arose, taking their hats, when Mr. Potter said: "I have talked with the stockholders, and they say we cannot accept your schedule, because it would allow labor to dictate to capital." Then said Mr. Arthur, "I will give you forty-eight hours to make a proposition to us, and if reasonable we will accept it. That will give you a ladder on which you can come down from your autocratic position." Mr. Potter said he could not do it in that time. He would have to call in all the officers, as he did not know enough about each run to make a schedule himself. Mr. Arthur said: "If you had any proposition to make you could have made it long ago. You have kept these men waiting around here for twenty days, without any good reason, but to be fair with you we will give you until Friday." Mr. Potter said he could be ready on Thursday, at 2:30 P.M. He had made his point of not accepting any proposed change as dictated by labor, but to prevent financial disasters, which he knew would be the inevitable result of a strike, he had allowed his autocratic position to become badly undermined and had consented to have changes made in both rules and pay, and had signed them. Immediately after the close of this meeting, orders were sent in every direction for the superintendents and the master mechanics of all divisions, to come to Chicago for this conference. On their arrival, Mr. Potter set them at work, fixing up a proposition to present to the committee of engineers.

At the appointed time, on Thursday, March 25, the committee was notified that Mr. Potter was ready to see them. The committeemen again wended their way to the manager's office, with patience and a strong determination to follow the usual conservative course of the Brotherhood. Yet they were resolved, if possible, to secure some kind of an agreement signed by the general manager, as it would carry with it a recognition of the right of the laborer to be a voluntary party to any contract for work. Such an agreement would also be an official recognition of the Brotherhood.

On arriving at the Burlington offices, the committee was invited into Mr. Potter's private office on the ground floor, and presented with the result of the local official deliberation. It had nothing in it to commend itself to the committee, and it was promptly rejected by them. In Mr. Potter's trip over the system, he found that 95 per cent of the enginemen belonged to the two Orders, and he was anxious to prevent an issue with them. In pursuit of this policy, he asked if they would meet the local officers of their respective divisions, and take up each run and condition and see if they could not arrive at some conclusion. Mr. Potter said he was astonished at the lack of ability of some of his local officers, and was satisfied they could not make a schedule. The committee consented to this and adjourned to meet them the next morning.

On Friday, March 26, the committee took the elevator at the Burlington headquarters and landed at the room which had been previously used as a meeting room, and met their respective officials. After the usual recognitions they proceeded to business. There were two officers to each grievance committeeman, and they divided off in squads of three, and took up the home work. They went over each run, and increased the pay very materially on many of the runs for both engineers and firemen, discussing delays and other evil conditions. The consent of the local officials was given very reluctantly to these changes, and they should not, by any means, be credited to their liberality. Mr. Potter knew it was concessions or a strike, and the officials were brought in for the purpose of making them. The chief men delegated to their inferiors the work of making the changes, but reserved the credit of being magnanimous. The committee work not being done at noon, the meeting adjourned until 2:30 P. M., when time would suffice for all the runs to be considered. The rules were taken up and an agreement was finally reached. The meeting adjourned until Saturday at 11 o'clock, to receive the schedules and rules which were being prepared by the Company, and which would then be signed by its officers. We append here a note from Mr. Potter, accompanying the revised rules, to which were added signatures of the highest authority. The committeemen who had been away from their homes over forty days, made their preparations to return with pleasant anticipations.

Chicago, March 25th, 1886.

J. C. PORTER, Esq.,

Chairman Committee of Engineers,

Chicago.

DEAR SIR:

I hand you herewith changes in rate schedule and rules governing the pay of engineers and firemen, on the Chicago, Burlington & Quincy; Burlington & Missouri, in Neb.; Hannibal & St. Joseph; Kansas City, St. Joseph & Council Bluffs; Chicago & Iowa; St. Louis, Kansas & North-West; and Council Bluffs & Kansas City roads.

The officers of these roads have gone over the rates of pay, and recommend that these changes be made, and I approve of their recommendation.

Yours Truly,

(Signed,) T. J. POTTER.

CHANGE IN RATE SCHEDULE AND RULES GOVERNING THE PAY OF ENGINEERS AND FIREMEN, TAKING EFFECT APRIL 1, 1886.

ARTICLE I.

No engineer will be dismissed or suspended from the service of this Company without just cause.

Every engineer will be entitled to a full and impartial hearing and investigation by the Superintendent and Master Mechanic.

It is understood that in ordinary cases superintendents and master mechanics will not suspend engineers until such cases have had full investigation.

ARTICLE II.

Engineers delayed two (2) hou. or over, in starting from or arriving at terminals, will be paid at work train rates per hour, for the full delay less one hour.

The same rule will apply in case engineers have been called, and afterward, on account of wreck, are notified they are not wanted.

When delays of over two (2) hours occur at any one point during a trip, on account of no orders to go on, engineers will be paid at work train rates per hour for the full delay, less one hour; but if the delay is occasioned by a wreck, washout, or other physical cause, then engineers will be paid at one-half (½) work train rates per hour for the full delay, less one hour.

ARTICLE III.

Should engineers be obliged to double hills on account of having more than established rates, they will receive pay for one hour's time, at work train rates.

ARTICLE IV.

If one or more engines are coupled in with snow plow engines for bucking snow, the engineer of each engine will be paid at one and one-half work train rates; but in no case will the amount paid be less than regular freight rates for the distance run.

In case an engineer called to buck snow is held under orders, such engineer will receive pay at work train rates for all time he is so held.

ARTICLE V.

Engineers will be called a reasonable time before

leaving time. The caller will have a book in which engineers must register their names and hour when called.

ARTICLE VI.

Right to regular runs when merit and ability are equal will be governed by seniority. Engineers having had regular runs prior to the date of this circular will not be affected by this article.

ARTICLE VII.

No more extra engineers will be assigned than is necessary to move the traffic with promptness and dispatch, and should any engineer feel himself aggrieved by the assignment of extra engineers he can proceed as in Article 1, but will receive no pay for loss of time.

ARTICLE VIII.

Engineers dead-heading on Company business, will be paid at the same rate as on passenger runs.

ARTICLE IX.

No fines will be assessed against engineers.

ARTICLE X.

Fireman's pay will be adjusted in proportion to the engineers.

ARTICLE XI.

All officers will be provided with copies of this circular, which will be kept posted in the several engine houses.

HENRY B. STONE, General Manager.

G. W. RHODES, Supt. Motive Power.

J. D. BESLER, General Superintendent.

When the committee went from Burlington to Chicago, they paid their fare and took receipts from the conductor. Mr. Potter, of his own motion, paid the money back on presentation of the receipts and gave the men passes home. He then told the members of the committee that they had exceeded their leave of absence and that they should not repeat this. The company wanted to know where their men were, and when they wanted to come again they must notify their respective officers where they were going. Mr. Potter was asked to make some provisions, whereby the men could help railroad men over the road, who were out of work; men whom they knew to belong to either of the Brotherhood of Locomotive Engineers, or Locomotive Firemen, but he said he could not do that until he had consulted with the general managers, Holdridge, of the Burlington & Missouri; and Merrill, of the Kansas City, St. Joseph & Council Bluffs railroad. All parties separated pleasantly, and the men thought they had accomplished very much, in getting what they supposed were rules under which the local officers would be governed. How much we were disappointed will be seen in the following chapters.

Securing recognition of the Brotherhood from the Burlington system, which always refused to recognize its labor as having any rights not voluntarily granted by the Burlington officials, was considered a victory. The Grand Chief, P. M. Arthur, in acknowledging the receipt of a group picture of the grievance committee, wrote: "I prize the picture highly, and I will preserve it as a memento of one of the greatest victories achieved by the Brotherhood. Please accept my heartfelt thanks."

(Signed,) P. M. ARTHUR, G. C. E.

The men all felt that to secure written laws, to insure just treatment—the first of its kind in existence on the Burlington—was a victory for just principles. "Unfortunately, injustice will always prevail this side of heaven, and it is the part of wise men to reduce that to the smallest amount possible, and the surest rule for its rapid diminution is, that each man should himself act justly toward all others. The unjust act of a corporation is made up of unjust acts of the members, or directors, or managers of that corporation, and it is absurd for any man to feel that he can use corporate power unjustly, and shirk off from the responsibility of such a sin."[1] Yet this is done with perfect impunity; and officers are kept by corporations, who are known as aggressive violators of all laws not in the interest of the corporation they represent, and the Burlington was no exception.

[1] Elliott F. Shepard.

CHAPTER XVIII.

THE NEW TREATY—A ROPE OF SAND.

The members of the committee returned to their respective divisions and met with the local officers, anxious to know whether the new laws were understood and how they were liked. The men were satisfied and everything moved off pleasantly. The officials however, smarting under the restraint of the new rules, and no doubt remembering the undignified position they had been placed in at the Chicago meeting, commenced immediately devising means of evading the rules and construing them to the greatest disadvantage of the men. Before the month of April was out letters began to come to the chairman, Mr. Porter, entering complaints of the violation of article II. Mr. Wheatly, of Beardstown, wrote April 30, that "master mechanic Forsyth said if we arrive two hours or more late we get nothing for it, and that the men have to be held two hours or over after arrival in yard before we get anything for it."[1] Article II was understood to mean two hours over schedule time by both the committee and most of the officers. They thoroughly discussed this item and the two clauses, viz: Two hours before starting, and the two hours or more waiting. This was contended for by the committee to prevent loss of time by unnecessary delay. At Council Bluffs, the engineer was obliged to take his train from two to three hours before leaving time, and

[1] Letter of G. W. Wheatly.

go to the union depot, a mile away, and wait there until leaving time, without pay. Other roads have a man to do that work, and the men wanted pay for it, or have some one else do the work. There was another reason for the needless loss of time; it was branch runs that went part way on the main line and then on the branch road, and the trains would often be held two or three hours waiting for orders, at the junction point; and they wished to effect a cure, as this delay was unnecessary. The following letter from McCook will show what the men had to do for nothing before the adoption of this rule: "We wait in Denver, for Denver and Rio Grande trains, from one to eight hours. We have to take the train to the depot ready to leave on time. Now we put in the full delay, and the time-keeper deducts one hour. I waited six hours and forty-five minutes for No. 2, put in claim for seven, and got allowed six hours. There has been no complaint here and all seem satisfied.

S. E. Hoge, of the committee.

The officers of the Hannibal & St. Joseph Railroad so understood it, and on completing the arrangements, the time of an extra train was limited to the average of all freight trains on the division, and the engine crew was entitled to pay for all time over that schedule, less one hour, which was always given the company. But the Hannibal & St. Joseph and the McCook officials were exceptions, and if all had been like them, it is reasonable to suppose that the strike of 1888 would not have occured.

It will be remembered that the committee made a

request upon Vice-President Potter to arrange some plan whereby the men could render assistance to engineers out of work, by getting them passed over the road, and in answer to this request the following letter was received:

Chicago, May 10, 1886.

J. C. PORTER, Esq., Engineer,
Aurora, Ill.,

DEAR SIR:

I have taken considerable pains to talk with our managers and superintendent, and also the managers of the Rock Island, North-Western, and Alton roads, with reference to passing engineers, and it is the unanimous opinion that we cannot adopt any wholesale plan for passing one class of our employes unless we do the same for the others. What we aim to do is to treat everybody as near alike, and as fair as we possibly can. My notion is, while I do not say that it will be carried out, if an engineer in good standing makes a request on his superintendent for passes for a brother engineer, the chances are that they will be granted.

I am sorry to have delayed answering the committee so long, but I have been busy and have just been able to get reply from the Chicago & Alton, dated the 8th inst.

Yours Truly,
(Signed,) T. J. POTTER.

The hint contained in this letter was not complied with to any extent, and finally was denied altogether, and they would not grant a pass unless it was requested by a superintendent, under whom the beneficiary worked; so that an engineer out of work could not be passed. These courtesies between engineers are shown on nearly all roads, and the Burlington men on many divisions, were soon retaliated upon and badly scored by engineers employed on other roads, for this lack of courtesy; they were glad, when away from home, to be courteously carried themselves, but could not return the compliment. It was not permitted.

The officials, in order to understand how each one was doing in relation to this matter, held a meeting at Burlington. The superintendent of one of the divisions told me [1] that at one of these meetings all the officials said they were giving no passes for this purpose. But he [2] did give some, and gave me one at that time, but very reluctantly. Another object of the meeting was to discuss the best means of defeating the intent and purpose of the recently enacted rules, and they succeeded remarkably, both in that, and in creating a deep feeling of animosity between local officials and the men.

On May 19, 1886, the second letter was received from Beardstown, stating that Mr. Forsyth, the master mechanic, claims that unless the men are held two hours on their engines after arriving at a terminal point, they are not entitled to any delayed time, and the chairman is requested to come to Beardstown and have him understand it as we all do. On the 25th of May another letter was received which said: "I was kept on the road three hours and twenty minutes more than schedule time and Mr. Forsyth says I am not entitled to any delayed time. How is this? C. H. B." It was understood at the meeting that if you were de-

[1] The compiler. [2] The name can be given to any whom it may concern.

layed two or more hours in starting, the company got the first hour without pay, and the men were to be paid after the first hour. If the train left on time and arrived two or more hours late, the company got the first hour and the men were paid for the balance, the company always getting an hour's work for nothing.

On May 29, the chairman, J. C. Porter, received the following letter from the superintendent of motive power:

J. C. Porter:

I have not yet sent you any understanding in regard to Article II, which we talked over the other day. In discussing the matter with some of our master mechanics, I am not sure but that we may both be mistaken in regard to Mr. Stone's construction of this rule; I therefore will get Mr. Besler's approval before I submit you anything.

G. W. Rhodes.

After Mr. Rhodes obtained the manager's understanding of Article II, the following letter was written and sent to Chairman Porter, at Aurora, and A. Forsyth, master mechanic at Beardstown, Ill.:

Chicago, Burlington & Quincy R. R. Co.

Office Supt. Locomotive and Car Dept.

Aurora, Ill., June 9, 1886.

A. Forsyth, Master Mechanic,

Beardstown.

Dear Sir:

Replying to yours of the 4th inst., in regard to the meaning of Article II, of rules governing the pay of engineers and firemen. The easiest way to understand this rule is to interpret it as meaning just exactly what it says, i. e., in clause 1, engineers delayed over two hours in starting from a terminal, will be paid for the full delay, less one hour. This is perfectly plain. It does not say anything about what should be done in case a quick run was made afterwards, so that there was really no delay at all; the fact remains the same that there was a delay at starting, and therefore it is to be paid for. The same in regard to after arriving at a terminal. Supposing a train arrives six hours late at a terminal, and is taken care of. There is no delay in this case after arriving, and there will be no pay allowed for it. It does not matter whether a train arrives ahead of time or late; if there is over two hours delay after arriving, engineers and firemen will be paid for the full delay, less one hour.

The second paragraph needs no comment. The third paragraph is also plain in view of what has preceded. Under this paragraph, delays are paid which produce delays arriving at terminals, or have any connection with those after arriving.

(Signed) G. W. Rhodes,
Supt. Motive Power.

It will be seen by this construction that no delays were paid for, unless they were held two hours or more in one place. It is no uncommon occurrence, for what is termed a local freight, to start out on time, when the business of the company would require thirty minutes to an hour and a half at each station, with probably twenty stations on the run, and they arrive eight or ten hours late, they get nothing for the over time. It should be remembered, in this discussion of pay, that the engineers—though they must hold themselves in readiness at all times, to be called when wanted;—receive nothing only for actual work performed; you must not absent yourself without permission, though you may not be called for a week or a month, and you will get nothing for the month in which you waited. The number of engine men on the rolls of a company, makes no difference with the company's expenses. To make this plain I here quote from the Burlington book of rules:

RULE 185.

"Every person employed by the Company must devote himself exclusively to its service, and must not connect himself directly or indirectly with any other trade or business, without permission from the General Manager."

RULE 188.

Every employe will be liable to suspension from duty, and dismissal for disobedience of orders, negligence, misconduct, or incompetency, and to immediate dismissal without cause assigned. The pay of every employe suspended from duty will be stopped during such suspension.

RULE 189.

No employe is allowed under any circumstances, to absent himself from duty without permission from the officer at the head of his department. In case of

GEO. WATT.

KILLED AT BROOKFIELD, MO., MARCH 3, 1888.

sickness, immediate notice must be given to his superior officer. The pay of employes, absent on account of sickness, or with permission, will be stopped during the period of such absence, unless otherwise directed by competent authority.

The report of labor statistics of Michigan, 1886, says: "Of 1858 men employed on twenty-four railroads, agents average $47.10 per month; brakemen $47.64; conductors $74.97; engineers $85; firemen $45; and laborers $32.52. After the trip is performed, which is paid for, the engineer is expected to go to the round-house, and thoroughly inspect and take care of his engine, wedges, and rods, and do packing etc.; and the firemen has to go and clean his engine, which is no trifle, and this without remuneration. It is reasonable that when the company assigns men to duty, they ought to be willing to pay for what time is consumed in work ordered to be done."

On the other hand, the management has the skill to keep men waiting for work, and if the business runs low, the loss is assessed more on labor, in proportion, than on capital. This need not be so, and it ought not to be; but it has to be so according to the Burlington system of economy. For example: In a time of dull business, a man will be out on a trip. He is paid for going, and when he comes back he will be paid for the return trip also. But he may be obliged to wait at the other end of the road three days, for a train to return with, and all that time without pay and on expense, taking five days to make two, and all this time subject to call and liable to dismissal if not found when wanted. Then again the men are sometimes worked beyond endurance, at so much per trip, which brings large salaries, and these are always quoted by the officials, yet the average is not large.

But the screws of capital were always tightened, never loosened, and the officials of the Burlington, seemingly forgetful of the obligation implied in the signature of Vice-President and General Manager, T. J. Potter, studied not to live up to the intent and purpose of the settlement, but entered into a strife among themselves to see who could outdo the other, in violating the most, and paying the least for delayed time, and most intercept other benefits to the men provided for in the rules. Master Mechanic West, of Burlington, would not allow the delay unless it was over two hours, and would not take the engineer's statement, but would ask the station agent where the delay occurred. The conductor, after the train is stopped, usually does what work there is to be done first, before he goes to the office, perhaps fifteen or twenty minutes after arrival. He then goes to the office, and failing to get orders to proceed, waits one hour and fifty minutes, making two hours and ten minutes. But Mr. West would not allow it, because the conductor's report did not show it, doing both an injustice in not allowing the time, according to the construction of the rule, and casting a reflection upon the honesty of the engineer.

A wreck occured at Riverside, twelve miles out of Chicago, and Geo. Minot, an engineer, left Aurora with a passenger train for Chicago. At Hinsdale, twenty miles out, he was stopped for one hour and fifty-five minutes. He then received orders to run to Stone Avenue, and there he waited for orders one hour and fifty minutes, and then he was ordered to run to Riverside, where the wreck occurred, and waited there for the track to be cleared one hour and ten minutes, making four hours and fifteen minutes delay. Mr. Minot made the claim for this time which was returned to him as not allowed. On meeting Mr. Johnson, the master mechanic, he said: "We were a little too smart for you, weren't we? We have instructed the dispatchers so that there will be no delayed time." Mr. N. J. Paradise, master mechanic of the Hannibal & St. Joseph R. R. was present and Mr. Minot stated the case to him, and he said: "Yes, you are surely entitled to all the time, less one hour." Mr. Johnson did not agree with Mr. Paradise and said, "It would not be allowed, and did not want any more such reports put in." This is the same Mr. Johnson who served on the grievance committee in 1873, as a member of the Brotherhood of Locomotive Engineers, and is said to have stated to Mr. Harris he would never trouble him again with any grievance.

There is a long yard at Creston, Iowa, and to defeat the object of the delayed time rule, the officers cut the yard in two, making it East and West Creston, and if the yard was blocked so the enginemen could not get out of the yard, or get their engines to the roundhouse, the officials would move them from one end of the yard to the other, and then claim they were not entitled to delayed time because they were not in one place two hours or more. It was not so much the money the men cared about, as there is nothing so aggravating to a railroad man as delays, and they wanted them cured. How were these things to be met? To denounce them would not alter their condition. Denunciations never accomplish much, and in the present case they would amount to nothing. Each officer falls back behind his superior, when cornered, and says "It is not I," and no one individual can find the responsible party. A union of action became necessary. A power that dared to measure swords, even with a railroad corporation, was a necessity. The laws violated as they were did not effect any cure and the officials' conduct incensed the men greatly. The good feeling caused by the settlement was fast disappearing, and animosity toward a company that would allow such practices by its officials, took its place

CHAPTER XIX.

CLASSIFICATION.

The animosity against the Burlington management was not confined to the Burlington employes entirely. It will be remembered that this road was classified by the order of Oct. 10, 1876,[1] and the gates of employment were, from that time on, gradually closed until 1886. No engineers were hired if it could possibly be helped. Six thousand miles of road were locked against all comers seeking that kind of work, and the firemen's places held for these men only who were of age, and not over 26. The Burlington was not alone in working into this channel of creating a supply and diminishing the demand. The enginemen throughout the continent saw in this classification the formation of a trust, or combine, that forshadowed a future which had in it the learning of a new business, or no occupation and poverty.

The Burlington is the best illustration of the evils of the classification system, which is practiced more or less throughout the country, it being the longest line with its doors absolutely closed to applying engineers. Such an immense road, traversing the states of Illinois, Iowa, Missouri, Kansas, Nebraska, and Colorado, and still stretching its long arms out to grasp more territory; and along the whole vast distance, "No engineer need apply!"

The men who supply this department are first hired

[1] See page 36.

as wipers in roundhouses, and helpers, and are eventually put to firing a switch engine, at $1.40 per day, then to work on a road engine as third-class firemen at $1.65. When they have worked a year at this, their pay is advanced to $1.85 per day. Some of the Burlington officials made the year to include 365 days of actual work, if it took a year and a half to do it.

When they have worked out the second year they are advanced to $2.10 per day, full first-class pay. They will average at least two years at this, and then, if found qualified, are promoted to be third-class engineers on switch engines, at $2.25 per day. If kept on switch engine second year, $2.50; third year, $2.75; on road engine, first year, $2.50; second year, $3.05; third year, $3.60; requiring from seven to nine years to become first-class engineers. They are held to a strict account for any violation of rules, the rules to be defined by the superintendent, master mechanic, foreman or train dispatcher. Any one of these can, by complaint, exercise an influence that would make holding one's position almost impossible.

None are infallible, and the best of men are liable to be discharged. If you should be so unfortunate as to have to seek work elsewhere, you start out, not for the Burlington, for they do not hire any. You will make application at many places, where you will receive the same answer: "We do not hire any men; we make them." If you should meet a master mechanic who does want a man, you will probably be confronted with a blank form of application which you are to fill out and return to him for inspection, of which the following is a copy:

PERSONAL RECORD.

The Superintendent will require all persons, before entering the service of this Company, to answer the following interrogatories in their own handwriting. This blank, when filled up and signed, must be forwarded to the Superintendent, with any letters of recommendation such applicant may have, of which a record will be made, and returned.

The applicant should fill and sign this blank in duplicate, and keep one copy for future reference.

—————— General Manager.

To..................................

Division Supt....................Division.

1. Age............ ....Married or Single ....
2. Birthplace...........................State..................
3. Name of Parents, if living ?..................................
   Residence........................ State..................
4. Name and degree of nearest relative, if parents are dead?..........
   Residence........................ State..... ....
5. How many years' experience in Railroad service ?................
6. Ever injured; if so, on what road, and to what extent ?...........
   ....
7. In what business before entering Railroad business ?.............
   At what place............... ....State................
8. Name ALL roads on which you have been employed·

Railroad.	At what Sta. or Div.	In what Capacity.	In what Year.

9. If you have been employed before on any Division of this Road, or Branches, state which one, when and in what capacity ?.........
10. On what Road last employed ?................................
    Cause of leaving ?......................................
11. Number of letters of recommendation enclosed...............
12. How have you been occupied since your last employment terminated?
    ....

This application made by............ ....
(Sign your name in full, no initials.)

Located at..........................

WITNESS: Date................18....

....

NO..................

Northern Pacific Railroad.

PERSONAL RECORD.

Name...

Occupation...

Date of Application..............................18....

Date Employed.....................................18....

Division..

☞ Above to be filled by Division Superintendent.

Description of Person Named Within.

1. Height..
2. Form..
3. Weight..
4. Complexion.......................................
5. Color of Hair.....................................
6. Color of Eyes.....................................
7. If Beard is worn, what color, and in what manner...................................

☞ Above to be filled by Applicant.

Certified to as correct:

....................................Employer.

After the master mechanic has found out by this record whom you worked for last, he will likely tell you to call again and he will give you an answer. In the mean time, he writes or sends a telegram to the officer who discharged you. If he has no objection, you will probably be hired when you return, if you can pass the examination. But if this officer written to, holds any grudge against you, or from any other cause makes an objection, the master mechanic will conclude he does not want any one. The Burlington's rule, No. 182 says: "An employe discharged from any department shall not be employed in any other department without the consent of the head of the department from which he was discharged." This rule has been adopted by different systems, each one of which says: I will not hire a man unless he comes recommended by the officer who discharged him. If you go to the Atchison, Topeka & Santa Fe, with its 7000 miles of road, you can only work there by the consent of the officer on the

Burlington, if you worked for the Burlington last. If you go to the Northern Pacific, with its great stretch of roads, you must meet the same obstacles. On these three systems, owning not less than eighteen thousand miles, the engineer who is unfortunate enough to have been discharged, must submit his future and that of his family, to the good will, or the ill will of one man, viz: the officer who discharged him. If the officer to whom you apply persists in saying "No," what are you going to do about it? The liberties of laboring men are in a sad condition when the officials of a corporation can hold within their grasp the future of the 45,000 people employed by them.

When these 45,000 people undertake to cure this injustice, all the Pinkerton detectives, deputy sheriffs and state militia, are called into requisition to suppress them, as violators of the law. If the rights of labor were as much looked after and catered to, as are the rights of capital, the oppressions of corporations could not exist. The engineer expects to be rigidly examined and give references, but when his recommendation must come from one who has discharged him, his chances are decidedly poor. What object can these companies have in entering into such an agreement between each other, to so abridge individual liberty? What do they want with this personal record? This death warrant, the men call it. It would do credit to the genius of a detective agency. It makes every honest laboring man who fills one out, feel as though there was something degrading in it, and as though he was to be watched like a criminal. I can see but two reasons—the most potent is, desire for cheap labor; the other is to keep a supply in excess of the demand. When they cease hiring, they do not cease discharging, and the natural consequence is an excess of idle engineers.

The companies assert that when they promote a man to be an engineer, they are taking a risk, that the man's ability has not been tested. This principle must be conceded as right, and the engineers have always been willing to allow this test for six months or one year at reduced pay. The men promoted have been on an engine an average of four years before they are tried with full responsibility. In other trades a term of three years is considered time enough for the average man to learn a trade, but the company want him to work seven years. It will be remembered that the 1876 committee requested the company to annul classification and return to apprenticeship, which paid $3 for first year and then full pay.[1] Mr. Potter was asked, "If you are obliged to assume a risk in promoting a new man, why is it you will not hire a man of undoubted ability and unquestionable reference?" Mr. Potter replied: "We have found we had better luck in making engineers than in hiring them." He also denied any knowledge of any intended effort to interfere with the engineer's future. But this is hardly plausible. Local officials are usually allowed some privileges in selecting their employes, and if there was not a set principle involved, why should they be denied the privilege of hiring their best friend in this department? Why do they not practice the same rule with conductors?

It is evident there is an antagonism existing against the engineers' organization because it has power to

[1] See page 43.

demand fixed and equitable conditions. In the classification system there are two motives—one to secure cheap engineers and firemen through the long years of preparatory work; the other to create a surplus of men by not hiring, so that these unemployed men could be used to break down that power. It became the definite object of the engineers throughout the country to change this odious classification system, and at the convention held in October, at New York City, laws were enacted to govern their future action in trying to do away with this evil. The grand chief, P. M. Arthur, when asked his opinion, said: "Apprenticeship is a right principle, but when a law is so badly abused as this, I know of no way only to do away with it." Engineers have traveled thousands of miles, and wasted the savings of years hunting work, and at each place would hear the same old story, "I make all my engineers." The reader can better imagine than I can describe, the feelings of a man who has spent twelve or fifteen years of the best part of his life in learning a business, —with family responsibilities upon him, too old to begin learning a new business, unable to support his family while he tried, and not allowed to work even as fireman, if past the age of twenty-six; his whole future blasted by the system of classification.

As theBurlington has had the reputation of having the most unyielding and illiberal management in the country, and being the leader in the aggressive work against organized labor, it naturally called forth like opposition from its men, and the strike of 1888 was not in its true sense, a local strike. The Brotherhood, from Maine to California, felt that an aggressive step was necessary to put a stop to further encroachments upon their individual and collective interests.

In the year 1877, the Philadelphia & Reading railroad issued a circular letter to their engineers, demanding their withdrawal from the Brotherhood, and the engineers on that road replied: "We would do violence and dishonor to an intelligent manhood, were we to accept any thing less than the withdrawal of said circular." The company failing to withdraw it, the men stopped work in a body.

On the 30th of July, 1888, eleven years after, Jacob G. Freas went to the Reading officials and obtained a letter recommending both his ability and character, but containing this: "He was in the strike on our lines in '77." He had, like his forefathers, rebelled against encroachments upon his individual liberties. He traveled the country over, but found none who would employ him because the Reading officials had implied their objections. His manhood was preserved; his reward for its preservation—poverty; because of this unjust alliance of corporate officials.

CHAPTER XX.

CONSERVATISM.

The conduct of the engineers had been extremely conservative. They had worked faithfully forty days, and spent $2,906 in an effort to secure these laws; had waited patiently for fifteen days for Mr. Potter to go over the system and find out that 95 per cent of the men belonged to the Brotherhood. They were conservative both in their actions and teachings. A union meeting was held at Kansas City, on July 11. The *Kansas City Journal*, a leading daily paper which had fought and defeated the Typographical Union, and was considered an enemy to organized labor, printed the address and commented as follows:

CHIEF ARTHUR'S ADDRESS.

"This morning we publish in full the address of Mr. P. M. Arthur, chief of the Brotherhood of Locomotive Engineers of North America, delivered at the Coates opera house yesterday afternoon."

"We thought the address would be good, and we are not disappointed. We have no hesitation in saying that we have never seen a clearer and more dignified statement of the relations of labor to capital than is contained in this address. It is an honest, manly statement, in which the rights of honorable labor are asserted and the obligations of capital to labor, and labor to capital, fairly and honorably defined."

"If the doctrines taught by Chief Arthur are observed by the organization he represents, the standard of railroad management, in its relations to its engineers, will soon be lifted above the low plane of suspicion and contention, and in one respect at least the equitable relations of capital and labor will be maintained. With the inauguration of the sound sentiments expressed by Mr. Arthur, we can justly commend organized labor."

"The essence of the whole question lies in the admirable motto taken by the Order of Locomotive Engineers at its organization: "Sobriety, truth, justice and morality," for their rule: "Do unto others as you would have others do unto you, and so fulfill the law." These are indeed rules for action which are calculated to soften asperities in the relations of man to man."

"Standing for the principles of justice and right, offering equity for equity, asking forbearance and granting forbearance, demanding facts and presenting facts; these are the forces which, backed by intelligence, public opinion and justifiable firmness, will win victories for labor and compel concessions from capital."

"Following an insane attempt to cripple capital, to defy law and harass society, this calm enunciation of a safer and better doctrine is indeed encouraging."

"'He must be a man of good moral character, temperate habits, be able to read and write, and have one year's experience as a locomotive engineer. And then he must behave himself after he gets in, or we will put him out.'"

"Such are the simple conditions of admission to this body of organized laborers. There is no oath that conflicts with the laws of state or nation. There is no obligation that forces enmity of man to man. No rules for the starvation of fellowmen."

"No wiser words were ever uttered in the labor world than the following:"

"'We claim the right, after exhausting every honorable effort, to effect a settlement. If they ignore us, and will not grant us a hearing, we claim the right to quit if we want to quit, and do quit in a body. But having quit, my friends, we do not claim the right to take another man by the throat and say: "Thou shalt not" or, "Thou shalt." That's the great difficulty and the great mistake with labor organizations, and I care not by what name they go. When you attempt to use force and intimidation; when you attempt by force to prevent another man from earning a livelihood for himself and family, you violate every law of equity and justice, and should be punished.'"

"No labor organization can live that does not recognize and sustain these plain demands of justice and freedom."

"We cannot at this time allude to the many admirable points in this labor organization as detailed by Mr. Arthur, but we commend the address to the laborer and capitalist alike."

When enemies of organized labor find nothing to condemn and much to commend in the Brotherhood, it has a right to assume that its principles are just and equitable. It is beyond question that a great majority of the members of the Brotherhood of Locomotive Engineers are in hearty accord with the principles enunciated by Grand Chief Arthur, and are obedient to the rules of their institution. That there will be found some unworthy and irresponsible men in every institution is to be expected. But that the enginemen have been extremely free from such characters is evidenced by the diversity of commendation from men of high standing, both in and out of the railroad service. We add this, first because we think the enginemen deserve credit for conservative action; and further it is meant as a timely caution to men of labor organizations not to be moved by the treachery of bad men from within, nor by the craft of enemies from without.

These are broad principles, and indicate strongly a disposition to meet on common ground, and to deal out justice while demanding it. The convention at Chicago modified the classification law, so that the changes in this direction should be voted upon, and the committee was to be governed by the voice of all the men they represented. The Brotherhood has been accused of being a one-man power, but a little light upon their principles is convincing that each member is a free moral agent outside of the well-defined rules for his moral conduct. It is true everywhere, that when men have reached positions of responsibility and of influence, by their own individual merit, and have conducted themselves consistently with their rank and station, that they acquire a powerful personal influence. This was eminently true of George Washington and of Abraham Lincoln, and, in the measure of ability and of opportunity, it is true in every variety of life. It is the very essence of the Brotherhood organization to guard with jealous care the members' individual rights, and those of their associate workmen. No

HERBERT B. NEWELL.

KILLED AT GALESBURG, ILL., APRIL 28, 1888.

Samson will ever be born within their walls, or without, who shall be able to carry away the gates of their strength, while these principles prevail.

In October, 1886, at the New York convention, Chauncey M. Depew, president of the New York Central railroad, among other things said: "Your organization arose when I first went into railroad work, twenty-three years ago, and I have watched it carefully ever since, and one thing that impresses me forcibly is the change in the character of your members that has taken place. The old method called for blasphemy without stint from the engineers as a necessary accompaniment of every duty, no matter how trifling. That type of engineer is now either dead or converted. The proper thing to brace up the nerves for a trip was whiskey, and plenty of it. Now, your Order prohibits spirituous liquors, and if one of your members is discharged for drunkenness, no committee of yours asks for his reinstatement."

Gov. Leon Abbott, of New Jersey, in an address at the same time and place said: "You do not rush into unnecessary strikes if a corporation will show some disposition to listen to your grievances. You believe in arbitration, and that there are two sides to every question, and that both employe and employer should be heard in every instance. I read the four mottoes of your organization: "Sobriety and truth, justice and morality; defense, not defiance,"[1] and I say that so long as you are guided by these mottos, so long will your order receive, as it does to-day, the approval and hospitality of this mighty city."

These leading men are quoted because they have

1 "Defense, not Defiance." Added at New York City, 1886.

direct dealing with the Brotherhoods, both of engineers and of firemen, and their opinion ought to have some weight in fixing in the mind of the reader the character of the enginemen who are members of the Brotherhoods.

The Grand Chief in his address, said: "We have no sympathy for, nor co-operation with, any class or set of men who base their claims upon the principle that might makes right, and the rich owe the poor a living. No man has a right to anything which does not come to him through the channel of honest acquirement."

CHAPTER XXI.

MEETING OF GRIEVANCE COMMITTEE.

The General Grievance Committee was called together at Aurora, Feb. 14, 1887. On assembling it was found that nearly all the committeemen were in an aggressive mood. Many of the officers on the various divisions of the system instead of being just and equitable, having stooped to absolute meanness, in order to give vent to their spleen and at the same time put more money into the treasury of the company, and so curry favor with it for themselves. The committee after some deliberation, sent its chairman, Mr. Porter, and secretary, J. A. Cuykendall, to Chicago, to wait on Mr. Potter, and see if he would not do something to compel the local officers to live up to the contract as made. The committee then adjourned to meet at Creston and receive the report. The committee anticipated much from this interview, because Mr. Potter told them when the settlement was made that "The officer who conducts himself in such a manner as to bring the grievance committee to him again, must be ready with good reasons."

The chairman presented to Mr. Potter the numerours branches of the agreement, and the assumption of authority, to make changes, and exercise a prerogative the laws were specially made to cure. He promised to more fully define their duties, which he did in the following letters:

Chicago, March 1, 1887.

J. C. PORTER, Esq., Engineer,
Aurora, Ill.

DEAR SIR:

I hand you herewith copy of letter that I have written all our general managers, in regard to the construction of rule No. 2.

I have also called their attention to the complaints that have been made of the violation of the agreement entered into last April, and said to them all that the agreement made at that time must be adhered to by all.

Yours Truly,
(Signed) T. J. Potter.

Chicago, March 1, 1887.

DEAR SIR:

I have had some talk with a committee of engineers with reference to the way rule 2 has been interpreted. I want it construed from March 1, 1887, to mean, that if an engineer is delayed two hours or more that he will be paid for the full delay less one hour, that is to say, if he is delayed two hours he will be paid for one hour at the rates prescribed by article 2.

Yours Truly,
(Signed) T. J. Potter.

Mr. Potter was contemplating leaving the Burlington for the Union Pacific, and did not give it the attention he undoubtedly would, had he intended to stay. The Creston yard difficulty remained until in May, 1887, when the chairman of the Grievance Committee was called there to see if he could not effect a cure. General Superintedent Brown, of the Iowa lines, as well as Division Superintendent Duggan, denied having the authority, claiming that it was done by their superiors in office, and the chairman went to Mr. Besler, general superintendent of the Burlington, and he ordered the two yards to be put back into one. When we consider that these officers had no financial interest involved, other than their salary, and that they were themselves employes, it is a queer commentary upon human kindness and the integrity of man, to record such violations of both these qualities.

General Manager Potter was a self-made man, coming from the foot of the ladder. He was not in the least austere or position-proud in his deportment. With a remarkable memory for names and faces, and with unusual readiness saying something pleasant to every one, he was esteemed by all classes. It is reasonable to believe that if left to his own inclination, he would have done more to protect the laborer from the evil conditions imposed by local officers. Whether the order to discharge Chairman Fisher and Committeeman Calkins of the 1883 committee, emanated from Mr. Potter, or from the president of the company is not known.[1] Superintendent Thompson, of the Burlington & Missouri division, undertook to prevent the organization of a brakeman's lodge, and to accomplish it, he commenced the wholesale discharge of the men. Mr. Wilkinson, Grand Master of the Brotherhood of Railroad Brakemen, went to Mr. Potter and asked his intercession, which Mr. Potter readily responded to, and gave Mr. Thompson to understand that he must stop such petty tyrany, and not discriminate against Brotherhood men. After that time they

[1] See page 55.

were not annoyed by him, but a part of the settlement was that there should not be anything said about it. This does not look as though he was at all times managing in accordance with his own inclinations. Yet it is highly commendable in Mr. Potter, as it shows the right disposition. But it contains proof that he was not, in all things, a free agent in the management of the Burlington, but was controlled in his administration by the men of the Boston idea—that labor has no rights not granted by the free will of the employer. I have been told that in a social conversation, Mr. Potter said the Burlington stockholders were dissatisfied with his action in signing a contract and recognizing the Brotherhood of Locomotive Engineers in 1886, and his position had become unpleasant in consequence, and that the Burlington was seeing its best days. He evidently knew the relentless disposition of some one in authority, and knowing it, could see the inevitable result. Mr. Potter appreciated the employes as they did him, and on May 10, 1887, he wrote a letter to J. C. Porter, chairman of the grievance committee representing the enginemen. I do not think I betray any confidence now, since Mr. Potter's death, to give it to the public. It was only intended for the eye of the engineers and firemen when written. The letter is as follows:

Chicago, May 10, 1887.

J. C. Porter, Esq.,

Aurora, Ill.,

My Dear Sir:

You were chairman of the committee of engineers that met me a year ago, and took up some questions of difference between the engineers and firemen on the one side, and the railroad company on the other. My reason for addressing you this letter, is on account of my leaving the service of the C., B. & Q road at an early day. I desire to express through you, my thanks to all the engineers and firemen on the C., B. & Q. and its system of roads, for their honest co-operation in carrying out all the agreements made at that time. I wish further to say that it is with regret that I part company with so many good men as there are on the C., B. & Q. and its system of roads. I want you and the engineers and firemen on the C., B. & Q.and its system to know that I had a good opinion of their ability and integrity, and of the interest they have taken in the company's service.

Very Truly Yours,

(Signed) T. J. Potter.

Mr. Potter carried with him the regrets of the employes of all ranks. He was rightly disposed and was too sagacious a manager to allow a strike if it could be avoided, although he defended the capitalists he represented, and contested for every inch of ground occupied. The committee of 1886 had listened to Mr. H. B. Stone's cold, deliberate, calculating debates on supply and demand, saying, "If I wanted boiler iron I would go out on the market and buy it where I could get it the cheapest, and if I wanted to employ men I would do the same." With Mr. Potter gone, the employes realized that all liberality went with him. There was one honorary member of the Brotherhood as master mechanic at Brookfield, but he left about the time

Mr. Potter did, and the ground was clear of official good feeling between the enginemen and the mechanical department. The master mechanics were outranked by the division superindents so that the employes were subject to conditions imposed by both; neither being very friendly because the Brotherhood had made an effort to compel them to obey the rule, "Do unto others as you would they should do unto you."

At the time of the strike of the Knights of Labor on the Gould system, a notice was put up by the Burlington Company, notifying all members of the Knights of Labor who were in their employ, to go to the heads of their respective departments and get their time checks, or withdraw from the Knights of Labor, and a great many complied with this in order to hold their places. With Mr. Potter gone, there did not seem to be any room for organized labor.

CHAPTER XXII.

COMMITTEE AT CRESTON.—ENGINEERS AT CHICAGO.

On the receipt of Mr. Potter's letter the committee was convened at Creston to hear the report of the chairman and secretary, and it was disappointing to them. They had expected Mr. Potter would define more fully the official duties of the local officers and make a special effort to define conditions that would insure peace. A copy of Mr. Potter's letter was sent to the Grand Chief, P. M. Arthur, which was answered in the following letter:

Cleveland, March 9, 1887.

Brothers Porter and Cuykendall:

Your letter of the 2nd is at hand and contents carefully perused. Article 11 is before me and have just read it. The clause Mr. Potter bases his order on conflicts with the first clause, but I do not think it would be advisable to make an issue with him on it as we cannot make an agreement that includes classification, and it would be folly to attempt to abolish this without the co-operation of the roads centering in Chicago. I was in hopes that the brothers on these roads would unite on some plan to abolish classification. Until they do I would advise the brothers to accept Mr. Potter's offer. Give it a fair trial, and if it does not work satisfactorily the chairman can again call on Mr. Potter and explain the injustice of the article. He will doubtless modify it, as I believe he is inclined to be just. The law relative to classification is working detrimentally to the best interests of our Order. It virtually ties the hands of the committee, and the grand chief. We have had two cases where the company offered to abolish all but one year, reducing from four classes to one, and we could not accept it, in consequence of the law. The law is too autocratic, and the brothers are beginning to realize it. Now, my brothers, you understand the situation; do what you think is for the best interest of all concerned.

Fraternally Yours,

P. M. ARTHUR, G. C. E.

The committee was not pleased with the situation, but the majority were conservative, desiring peace, and were willing to follow the advice of Mr. Arthur, and wait and see what the result of Mr. Potter's letter would be. The firemen were also dissatisfied, and had just organized what is called the adjusting committee, which is governed by similar rules, and has the same objects as the grievance committee of the Brotherhood of Locomotive Engineers. The engineers' committee met with the chairman and secretary of the firemen's committee, and arranged that that committee's work should be suspended until after the engineers' convention, which was to be held in Chicago in October, 1887, when they expected a modification of the law on classification, and if they then felt the necessity of waiting upon the officials, they would go in a body, engineers and firemen, and make a united effort to cure the evils that were complained of by both orders. Had they followed out this plan, and met the Burlington officials immediately after the convention, as was then understood, it would have brought the meeting about Dec 2, in the face of one of our coldest winters, and success must have attended them. But they let the golden opportunity pass. After a protracted discussion of the situation, classification receiving the greatest attention, the committee adjourned, and this ended the committee work until 1887. Votes were taken on the various roads centering in Chicago, and all voted, almost unanimously, that it was such a menace to their future that it should be done away with, or something done to mitigate its evils.

The engineers' convention met in Chicago in October, and at the opening an address was delivered by E. T. Jeffery, General Manager of the Illinois Central Railroad. Mr. Jeffery is a self-made man, coming up by force of character from the foot of the ladder to be general manager of one of the strongest and best managed corporations in this country. He has a thorough knowledge of railroad life, and possesses the confidence of all who serve under him. He sketched the relations of officers and of engineers, to each other and to the company, and in turn the relations of the company to them. The following is the address as given in Central Music Hall, Chicago, October 19, 1887.

MR. CHAIRMAN, BROTHERHOOD AND FRIENDS: "We are assembled here as co-laborers, with a common interest and a common object in view. We have a like purpose and a like aim in life. Our responsibilities, duties and anxieties are identical in kind, and differ only in degree. We stand before our employers charged with a great trust, and before the public with the gravest duties ever committed to human hands. The lives of the public and the property of our employers are committed to our care. The first is a trust of pre-eminent character and importance. How can we fit ourselves to perform these duties, execute these trusts, carry these responsibilities, and satisfy in full the public and corporate claims upon us?"

"The first great requisite is the high standard of manhood which your organization has set itself to mold and establish. Without this all else is futile. Without manly dignities and manly virtues we lose the confidence of the public, the confidence of our corporate employers, and confidence in and respect for one another."

"There are many hundred thousand persons scattered throughout the civilized world whose money is invested in railway properties. These are they whom we serve. These are they whose property is intrusted to our care. Unknown to us individually, and we to them, these people confide in us, trust us, look to us to faithfully administer their shares, be they large or small, of the railways of the land. Supreme over this is the abiding confidence of the people in our skill, our watchfulness, our sobriety, our intelligence, our manhood."

"And this leads me to the thought that there must be mutual confidence between the railway corporations and their engineers. Distrust by either of the other is the seed of discord, and discord is the growing plant upon which danger blossoms—danger to yourselves, to the millions whom you move, and to the great commercial interests of this free and progressive land in which we live."

"I speak whereof I know, when I affirm that the managing officers of the great railway corporations spare no effort consistent with good discipline to create and foster a family feeling, a feeling of close relationship between the corporation and the men. When formed, such a bond of union is a strong one, and is transmitted from father to son. To me there is no pleasanter sight than to see father and son working upon the same road; to see boys growing up trained to usefulness and manliness by the corporation which the father has served long and faithfully. It begets a community of interest which manifests itself in such loyal expressions as "My engine," "My station," "Our road," "Our company." Said an old engineer to me some years ago: "My love is divided between my engine and my wife." I hope you ladies will forgive me for naming his engine first."

"Be manly, frank and just in your relations with the officers of the railroads which you serve. Nearly all these men have risen from the ranks and appreciate the value of human labor, be it of the muscle or of the brain. The little autocrats of narrow views and brief authority grow fewer in number year by year, and so do the captious, dissatisfied, fault-finding engineers."

"For my part, after laboring in various capacities from boyhood, I am convinced that it is as unwise for the engineer to serve a corporation in which he lacks confidence, as it is for a corporation to retain in its employ an engineer whom it cannot trust. The faith must be mutual, the respect be well grounded upon both sides. The confidence must be absolute and unqualified; and right dealing, truthfulness, honesty of purpose, consideration by each for the rights of the other, form the pedestal upon which this confidence must rest."

"Success in your vocation makes faith in mankind a necessity. You must have faith in the men who make the steel and iron from which the boilers, wheels, axles and other parts of your engines are constructed; faith in the man who designs the engines; faith in the men who build them; faith in the men who repair them; faith in the men who make the rails they run on; faith in the trackmen; faith in the bridgemen; the switch tenders, the signal men, the conductors and brakemen; faith in your brother engineers who meet and pass and follow you on the road; faith in the manager and his lieutenants, and, above all, faith in the matchless love of the tender wife whose lonely hours are full of anxiety, but whose face lightens with joy each time you return safely from a trip over the line."

"Your labor has a market value. Your labor can be bought and sold; but loyalty! loyalty is priceless. It is founded on respect, on mutual trust and confidence, and its mainspring is duty. Duty! The watchword of the engineer."

"A man plows with his engine through snowstorms, moves slow, heavy freight trains, performs work at every station, operates his engine by day or by night. That is labor, and is paid for. His work is sold at the market price."

"A man stands for thirty seconds with his nerves like steel; one hand on the throttle, the other on the reverse lever; the brake set; the engine reversed; the sand running to make the brakes hold; a train of human beings behind him; he stands for them between life and death! He saves them! That is duty! The wages of a lifetime would not buy that thirty seconds of nerve and strain."

"Loyalty and duty are not for sale. Money can not purchase them. Wealth, position, power and other considerations bribe ambitious men into the semblance of loyalty and the semblance of unselfish devotion to duty; but tear aside the veil that hides the inner man, and it is seen that the motives are ignoble and the apparent loyalty and duty are hollow shams."

"Your labor and your skill, not your moral qualities, are what you sell. Your labor and your skill are made more valuable by your moral qualities. Sobriety, truth, justice, morality, loyalty, duty, thrift, industry and intelligence may not add materially to your physical powers, to the skill of your hand, to the quickness of your eye, or to your bodily activity; but they make you noble men, worthy citizens of a great nation, and respected and reliable representatives of the greatest instrument of commerce which the civilized world has produced."

"In his address one year ago, your Grand Chief used these words: "We have taken, upon the adoption of our motto, Sobriety, Truth, Justice and Morality, a strong stand for right. Right alone for itself, and in itself considered, stands upon a broad basis, and is the only lasting foundation upon which a man can build.' "

"No truer words were ever spoken by mortal tongue, and with them for your guide, the legitimate objects of your organization must be attained. And these objects are worthy ones: Greater intelligence; a higher moral and intellectual standard; greater mechanical knowledge and increased skill in your work; closer relations with your employers; a sturdy loyalty to the corporations you work for; freedom from alliances with questionable organizations. But you know these better than I do, and I will not name them all. They are objects which must call forth your most earnest efforts as men and as locomotive engineers. The great principle which glorifies your labor is the elevation of yourselves and your associates in the scale of true manhood. Your aspirations give greater dignity to honest toil and illustrate the identity in interest of employer and employe who rise and fall upon the same tide."

"The mind of the world is broadening. Our mental vision widens; the heart of the world throbs stronger; our lives are more closely interwoven. The ignorance and prejudice of yesterday pale in the light of the education and intelligence of to-day. Here and now work is honorable and idleness a disgrace. We all know, as we know the alphabet or the multiplication table, that the value of all that there is on this great, round earth is the result of labor of brain and muscle. This building wherein we are assembled, this city of matchless enterprise, derive value only from human labor. The stone, brick, iron, wood and land, in their virgin states, were of no value whatever. And so, too,

COLLISION, FEBRUARY 27, 1888, CHICAGO, MILWAUKEE & ST. PAUL CROSSING.—W. H. PIERCE, ENGINEER OF TESTS, AT THE THROTTLE.

of the rights and liberties which we as citizens of this great Republic enjoy. Human labor has carved them out. Human muscle and brains have achieved them for us. Human hands made the weapons to fight, and the pens to write, for human liberty."

CHAPTER XXIII.

CONCENTRATION OF FORCES.

Mr. Potter was gone. The official force of the Burlington was so changed as to leave none that felt in any way lenient towards the men of strength and daring, whose toil brings the money to the treasury. The men in office in 1888 were vain of their good standing with the company. The ambition of each one was to stand first in the esteem of the directors as making the least outlay for repairs and for wages, and as bringing in the largest returns for work. Egotists in their line, self-applauding, lordly men they were; their hearts without a window open towards labor, the general manager was—Stone. Superintendent Thompson, as we have seen, tried to prevent the brakemen from organizing; officers and conductors combined to defeat the switchmen at St. Louis, in 1886; and in the same year Mr. Stone had shown himself relentless in his methods in the freight handlers' strike in Chicago. The officials seemed eager for the fray. Preparations were made for a contest with any labor movement that should present itself. The shops were enclosed with high, tight board fences, made to be easily guarded. Advertisements were published in the newspapers of England in November, 1887, calling for railway men as if the officials, like the Arabian charger, smelled the battle afar off. George Cuff, an engineer of Paddington, London, stated that the advertisemen.

called for from 500 to 1000 first-class engineers for the service of the Chicago, Burlington & Quincy company. They were wanted to open a new road 1200 miles long, and special inducements accompanied this notice.[1] Taking all official conduct into account, we can arrive at only one conclusion—that the Burlington officials, Messrs. Perkins and Stone, backed by the Boston stockholders, were courting a fight with their employes, and so managed that a contest became inevitable.

Local officers were quick to take the cue. A correspondent at Lincoln, Nebraska, in a letter said: I am directed to inform all the divisions on the Burlington system, that we are in a worse situation here in regard to grievances, than we were before the settlement. Men are being laid off for little offenses of no importance whatever. Master Mechanic Hawksworth of Plattsmouth, on November 11, 1887, ordered Engineer Bosley laid off for ten days for refusing to go on an extra train without his breakfast. This engineer had waited for this train four hours without pay. Breakfast was ready as the train arrived and the engineer says he consumed fifteen minutes eating, and was laid off ten days because he did not go hungry. The train not showing any delay, Master Mechanic West, of Burlington, told Committeeman J. A. Cuykendall that there was no delayed time to be allowed on local runs. This is where the most work is done for nothing.

In February, Engineer W. H. Wilder went to Mr. West to get errors in his time corrected, he not being paid according to his age as an engineer, and during

[1] Statement of English Engineer, Denver Republican, July 17, 1888.

his stay was roundly cursed, the oaths being repeated several times. The men at Burlington had waited on the superintendent and entered complaint of the treatment by the master mechanic, and had received assurance that it should be stopped. When this occurred they were much incensed, and asked the grievance committee to try and have Mr. West removed, or secure an assurance that they should have respectful treatment in the future. Serious complaint was made by the men on the St. Louis division, against the master mechanic and the roundhouse foreman, for violation of the rules which were made in 1886. We call attention to a few of these complaints to show the necessity of laws to govern and hold in subjection, officials assuming authority that did not belong to their position

The companies have an unquestionable right to fix conditions and to manage their own affairs; to appoint agents and to delegate to them authority to hire and discharge and transact the business of the company. But their duty does not stop here. These companies have reached such magnitude that they control the labor market, and the laboring man has virtually no option but to accept the conditions so fixed by the powerful corporations. It is simple justice to say that they are under moral obligations to form and to execute equitable rules for the guidance of the employe of whatever grade, whether officer or laborer.

It is the usual policy of railway administration to give individual privileges to hundreds of middle men, local officers, to do what they please; to fix evil conditions, to suspend or discharge according to his whims or animosities. This is the grossest injustice. Labor has the right to protect itself just the same as capital has and it has a right to employ the same methods, i. e. to concentrate its force,—moral, social or political—and to express it through its own chosen representatives. Moreover, the rules made in 1886, after so much effort by the engineers, having been practically annulled by the local officers, the men who felt themselves aggrieved and injured, resolved to seek redress by all legal and honorable means. Naturally, the grievances accumulated in the hands of the grievance committee, and the necessity grew upon them of holding a meeting and devising some definite remedial measures. That meeting and its measures shall receive our attention next.

CHAPTER XXIV.

COMMITTEE OF 1888 AND ITS WORK.

The chairman of the grievance committee, Mr. J. C. Porter, at the earnest solicitation of men all along the line, convened the committee at Burlington on January 23, 1888. In the meantime Mr. Porter had written the Grand Chief, P. M. Arthur, that he contemplated resigning from the committee, and he received the following letter, which was read to the committee:

Cleveland, Ohio, January 24, 1888.

Dear Brother Porter:

Your letter received and noted. If the brothers are united upon the system and ready to sacrifice their situations if necessary to accomplish what they want, I think they will succeed. On the contrary, if they are actuated by a spirit of selfishness and jealousy, no good will come from their meeting. I do not blame you for wanting to resign as chairman, yet I do not think it would be wise to do so unless the committee require it, as we want conservative men in such positions. If the committee claim the company has violated the agreement they must be prepared to prove it. Do not make assertions unless you can substantiate them by positive proof. Please keep me informed of your progress.

Yours Fraternally,

(Signed,) P. M. ARTHUR, G. C. E.

It would appear that the men had abiding faith in the justice of their position. Mr. Arthur pictures the possible results, advises conservative action, and ends by saying, "You must make no assertion you cannot positively prove;" and yet after this dismal picture purposely giving the dark side, the work is continued. Mr. Porter tendered his resignation as he had intended to do and was presented with a fine meerschaum pipe by the committee, and S. E. Hoge, of McCook, Nebraska, was elected to fill the place of chairman. It will be remembered that the firemen, feeling the same necessity for decided action, had organized their adjusting committee and had, like the engineers, formulated grievances and desired rules enacted to govern their affairs as well. The firemen recognized that whatever was injurious to them, or to the engineers, would be detrimental to the future of the firemen as they naturally expected to become engineers. Their committee was called at the same time and place, but they met in separate bodies. Each of these bodies deliberated Monday and Tuesday, discussing the various questions, and on Wednesday January 25, both of these committees met together as a joint committee. This committee was composed of fourteen engineers and fourteen firemen.

COMMITTEE OF ENGINEERS.

J. A. Bauereisen,
Aurora, Ill.

Charles Thomas,
St. Joseph, Mo.

R. Martin,
Galesburg, Ill.

Chas. Dean,
Chicago & Iowa, R. R.

G. W. Wheatly, Beardstown, Ill.
H. M. Martin, Keokuk, Iowa.
John Eckerson, Burlington, Iowa.
Geo. Fisher, Creston, Iowa
Wm. McClain, Brookfield, Mo.
E. B. Wadworth, Wymore, Neb.
Wm. Fowler, McCook, Neb.
Mat. Conners, Chicago, Ill.
C. H. Sanborn, Lincoln, Neb.
S. E. Hoge, Chairman, McCook, Neb.

COMMITTEE OF FIREMEN.

C. Pardieu, Aurora, Ill.
R. H. Lacy, Galesburg, Ill.
D. A. Sherman, Beardstown, Ill.
J. H. Snoddy, Brookfield, Mo.
E. J. Ebersol, McCook, Neb.
S. A. Eads, Burlington, Iowa.
J. F. Bryan, Creston, Iowa.
F. P. McDonald, St. Joseph, Mo.
W. Sphor, Lincoln, Neb.
W. F. Hackett, Wymore, Neb.
J. D. McCarty, Chicago, Ill.
H. F. Zinn, Plattsmouth, Neb.
M. L. Bixler, Chariton, Iowa.
J. H. Murphy, Chairman, Chariton, Iowa.

The union of these two committees was not a new departure. Engineers and firemen had met jointly from ten different roads, from Feb. 1887 to Feb. 1888, abolished classification on three roads and reduced one to one year, had effected many improvements, and reinstated men discharged without cause and in violation of contract. "It is the natural instinct of man to protect himself, and the limits of that protection are bounded by the golden rule. The ancient civilization neglected this; the personality of the citizen was lost; the individual was made an unlimited slave to an unlimited sovereignty, as it is now under some corporations of modern times. Man was reduced to slavery, and he, and all his interests, subordinated to state despotism. This is what man succeeded in reaching by losing the idea of our great Brotherhood under one common Fatherhood."[1] The belief in the justice of one's position lends courage, and these men composing these committees, although Mr. Arthur had shown them their difficulties and dangers, had the courage, and were convinced of the justice, of their position.

J. A. Cuykendall, an engineer on the C., B. & Q. road was discharged on January 20, 1888. His offense primarily was his being a member of the General Grievance Committee of 1886, and he was still acting as such at the date of his discharge. All the facts were laid before the Grievance Committee, just formed. It seems Mr. Cuykendall had a pendent set watch. As every one knows, in order to set the hands the stem winding pin must be pulled out to change the gear from mainspring to hands. Time was compared, according to rule, before starting, and was found to be right, but by some means while on the trip his watch became eight or nine minutes slow, supposed to be caused by a too easily working stem set. As he knew nothing about the derangement of the time it was reasonable to suppose that in taking the watch from

1 Extract from speech of Rev. Chas. O'Reilly, D. D.

his pocket, the pin was pulled out enough to catch the hands, and move them slightly—a very little makes several minutes. On his nearing West Burlington, where he expected to meet passenger No. 3, he was astonished to find the train was already there, when according to the time by his watch he should have been there first. He asked his fireman for the time and discovered to his astonishment, that his watch was wrong. Mr. Cuykendall, according to the rules, should have stopped and sent a flagman ahead, but by the time he was fully convinced that his time was wrong he was so near,—the trains being in clear sight of each other,—he concluded to pull in and so delay the passenger the least possible. His watch was then compared with the conductor's, and with others, and found wrong. There was no forgetfulness or carelessness claimed. Mr. Cuykendall and the conductor were both discharged—the conductor because he did not give better attention and see that the engineer did not commit such an error.

The Grievance Committee being satisfied that the penalty was too severe, took up the matter and asked an audience with Superintendent Brown, to see if they could not have it modified. The request was granted, and Mr. Brown appointed 10:00 A. M., Thursday, January 26, for the meeting. On January 25, the engineers and firemen met in joint session, and resolved to merge into one set of rules, the conditions desired by both Orders, and, as a joint body, present them to the officials of the company. Each article was then discussed pro and con, and decided by a joint vote. The committee at the appointed time, met Superintendent

Brown, in behalf of their discharged brother, Mr. Cuykendall. Mr. Brown said they must make an example; that it would not do to establish a precedent by reinstating Mr. Cuykendall. The extenuating circumstances counted nothing. The committee believed Master Mechanic West was the influence that prevented a rehearing of the case.

The work of the committee was nearly completed, and they desired to go to Chicago to meet the general officers. The chairman, Mr. S. E. Hoge, requested Superintendent Brown to furnish transportation, which he readily assented to, with the acception of Mr. Cuykendall, and he would try and get a pass for him, and would have all ready by 2:00 P. M. Passes were given for all, Mr. Cuykendall included. It is against the company's rule to give transportation to any employe suspended or discharged. To employes who are in good standing, the Burlington Company has always been fairly liberal. Some officers were more liberal than others, yet no fault could be found with the company in relation to transportation for their own employes. The article in the new rules as presented, was merely a request that they be privileged to show courtesy to traveling brothers who were known members, and worthy of their confidence and favor.

The committee believed that the general managers could not make a settlement without the consent of higher authority, and made their plans to obviate the long delay experienced in 1886. Accordingly they sent a message to President Perkins, before leaving Burlington, notifying him of their desire to meet him in Chicago, on Monday, January 30, 1888. They then adjourned to meet in Chicago.

The committee met at the appointed time in the parlor of the National hotel. S. E. Hoge, chairman of the engineer's committee, was made chairman of the joint committee, and J. H. Murphy, chairman of the firemen's committee, secretary. On Tuesday, January 31, a message was received from Mr. Perkins stating that he would be in Boston soon and would meet the committee in Boston the next week, if they so desired; but suggested that the committee meet the general managers and said he did not intend to come west very soon, as he had just come from there. The committee knowing it was useless to see the general manager, without his presence, or authority delegated by him to the managers, sent another message saying: "The General Grievance Committee of the whole system is here. Cannot make settlement with the general manager. Will you come?"

S. E. Hoge.

On February 7, a message was received from President Perkins, saying that he had written a letter to the committee from Boston, which was received by the chairman on the 2nd, in which Mr. Perkins requested that they meet with the general managers of the several roads composing the Burlington system. In compliance with this, an effort was made to obtain the desired interview. General Manager Stone was supposed to be in Washington, and on February 3, a message was sent to him asking an audience. On Saturday, February 4, agreeable to appointment with Superintendent Besler, the committee went to his office to make another effort in Mr. Cuykendall's behalf. They found Mr. Besler accompanied by Mr. Steward, assistant superintendent at Burlington, who read a long statement, going to show that Mr. Cuykendall had been careless on the whole trip. It was evident they were anxious to be rid of a member of the committee who tried to make the officers comply with the law. Mr. Besler was finally asked to say positively what he would do, whether he would reinstate him or not, and he answered, "No, I will not." The matter was referred to Mr. Stone, later.

Some of the engineers' committee of 1888 had been also of the committee of 1886. The long siege then, through the absence of the leading officials, and their inability at this time to secure a meeting, did not portend an easy solution of their difficulties. To have all the men along the line understand the situation, they reported progress, and requested that all members of the order should assemble and vote to sustain, or not, the action of their committee. Accordingly a letter was addressed to all points along the line, asking that all members of both engineers', and the firemen's Brotherhood should vote as to whether they would sustain the General Grievance Committee in demanding the enactment of such rules as seemed to them just and necessary. 1st, To sustain the committee, yes or no. 2nd, For total abolition of classification, yes or no. For one year classification, yes or no. Each brother to sign his own name. Each of the Brotherhoods of engineers and firemen has been called a one-man power, yet they have selected a man to represent their grievances, by ballot; they have voted upon the substance of the instructions to that representative, and they voted to sustain him in pressing for the concessions asked from the company; and they gave a separate and independent vote upon the all important subject of classification. The vote was almost unanimous on the first two propositions, "Yes." A few votes only were cast for one year of reduced pay.

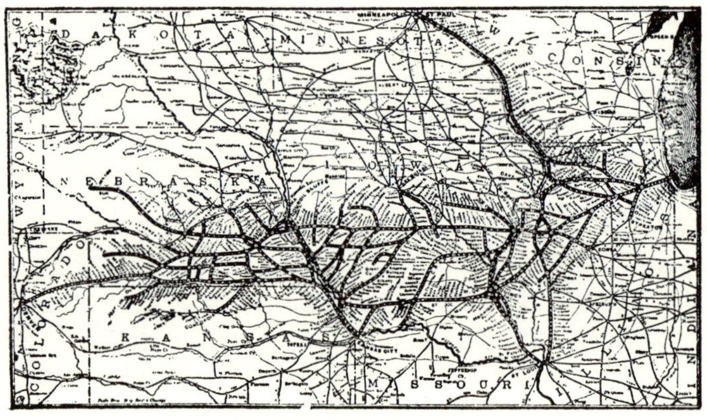

THE BURLINGTON SYSTEM.
SHOWING SCOPE OF TERRITORY OCCUPIED BY IT.

The above map is given to show the reader the immense territory covered, and the labor market controlled by this powerful corporation—the Burlington. The Chicago, Rock Island and Pacific; Chicago and North-Western; and Chicago, Milwaukee and St. Paul, control nearly all the roads shown above the south line of the Burlington.

CHAPTER XXV.

LOYALTY OF ENGINEERS AND FIREMEN.

The engineers of the Burlington were men of upright and unselfish character. They were of an independent cast of thought; they were generous and broad minded men. These qualities are clearly brought out at the close of the last chapter, but they are still better represented in the history of the Hannibal & St. Joseph railroad before it came into the possession of the Burlington. When Col. R. S. Stevens was general manager of this road—then a separate property,—the road was in a very bad financial condition. Mr. Stevens looked around for some means of retrenchment, by which he could tide over the depression. In pursuit of a method he addressed a letter to the engineers, stating the necessities that beset his management, and asked them whether they could not help him until such time as business should improve. To this appeal these men responded by immediately appointing a committee, who went to Hannibal, the headquarters of this road, and the members of the committee from Brookfield, Mo., joined those of the committee who lived in Hannibal, and with such interest as men feel over their own affairs, they consulted as to how much they could spare from their daily pay to help the general manager past his difficulties. They settled upon an amount of temporary reduction, met with Mr. Stevens at his office and gave him the result. Mr. Stevens was highly pleased, and gave them a letter of thanks and a written promise to restore the pay whenever business would justify it. In this he accomplished, by gentlemanly methods, and a due consideration of the second party, what he could not do arbitrarily, or by force.

In 1877, one G. B. Simonds became general master mechanic, who removed the division master mechanic at Brookfield, and put in one of his own kind, and a system of prosecution was inaugurated that culminated in an effort to secure the removal of this tyrant. Division 29, then located at Brookfield, appointed a committee who went to New York city to see the directors and have a stop put to the wholesale discharge, and the gross misuse of the men. This would have succeeded had it not been for a Benedict Arnold, in the person of George Jennings, who, on the promise of a place as division master mechanic, started a counter petition, and, securing a few names, succeeded in breaking up the harmony of the Order. Through this petition, G. B. Simonds held his place for the time being; and the consequence was that every Brotherhood man, not already discharged, was sent away with reason, or without. This tyrant was allowed full sway. The old and tried men were exchanged for any men not members of the Brotherhood. There were some good men among the new, but the average was extremely bad. The members of the division being discharged, their charter was surrendered and the organization ceased to exist at that point. Wreck and disaster followed. The company, through its petted and protected officer, had sown the wind and was about

WRECK AT CAMERON JUNCTION, JULY 31, 1888.—AN EDUCATIONAL EXPERIMENT.

to reap the whirlwind, as the natural outcome of its violence against justice and fair treatment. The company becoming convinced of the unprofitableness of this course, removed the master mechanic, and T. G. Gorman was appointed, who adopted a different policy. The Simonds bum element was weeded out, and many of the old men came back and took their places.

Peace and good order returned. Some who had been members of Division 29, which had been broken up by Simonds, organized what is now known as Division 79. In all this time, this company had forgotten that these men had reduced their own pay, on a written promise that it should be restored, and during the unorganized condition of the men, the company had ordered and executed another reduction. In 1883 the road was under the management of Mr. John B. Carson, a gentleman and a thorough business man. The traffic, under his management, had increased to the full capacity of the motive power of the company. The men were being paid less than were any of their neighbors. A committee was appointed by Division 79, to wait on Mr. Carson, and they took with them the written promise of the company, given by General Manager Stevens, and proceeded to Hannibal, Mo., the headquarters of the road. On their arrival they found General Manager Carson was in New York city, and they awaited his return, with entire confidence in his honor and integrity. On his arrival, he met the committee, and a settlement was made; classification was done away with, and they were paid the same rate as their neighbors, as will be seen in the following letter:

Hannibal & St. Joseph Railroad Company.

Office of Superintendent.

Hannibal, Mo., April 27, 1883.

Messrs. Burch, Leaphart, Rhodes and Smith,

Committee.

Gentlemen:

It has this day been decided, that from and after May 1, 1883, the wages of engineers shall be as follows: Engineers of passenger trains, 3½c. per mile. Engineers of freight trains, 4c. per mile on all classes of engines. Engineers of construction trains $3.50 per day. Engineers of switch engines, $2.50 per day, or $80 per month, a day's work to be twelve hours.

Engineers delayed over two hours shall receive 35c. per hour, after the expiration of the first two hours. The pay for short runs to be fixed by the undersigned on a mileage basis, the extra work, switching, etc., to be considered. The firemen's pay to be increased proportionately the same as engineers, taking as a basis, the pay as it was before the reduction by Mr. Carson. Yours Respectfully,

(Signed) W. R. Woodard, Supt.

(Signed) James Long, Supt. M. P. & M.

The best of feeling prevailed, as will be seen by the following correspondence:

John B. Carson, Esq.,

General Manager of Hannibal & St. Joseph R. R.

Dear Sir:

Appreciating the kindness shown us at our meeting with you, and feeling that you have placed us on an equality with other men of like calling, we wish to express our sincere thanks to you. We will endeavor by strict attention to your interests,—and through that the company's—to make restitution, at least in part, and we hope the friendly relations so long existing, and your able management of the road, may continue as long as it is your pleasure to remain with us. Again thanking you,

We remain respectfully yours,
(For the committee.) H. L. Burch.

Mr. Carson replied in the following:

Hannibal & St. Joseph Railroad Company.
Office of General Manager.
Hannibal, Mo., July 5, 1883.
Mr. H. L. Burch, Engineer H. & St. Jo. R. R.
Brookfield, Mo.
Dear Sir.

I beg to acknowledge receipt of letter from yourself and associates of the 30th ult. Permit me to thank you for you friendly expressions, and to assure you that they are fully reciprocated on my part, not only to yourselves, but to every employe of this company who has so thoroughly and faithfully performed his duties during the period of my management. Without such able and manly assistance as I have received on the part of the gentlemen associated with me in all capacities, I could not have succeeded in the creditable manner, so pleasantly referred to by you.

If you will kindly bear in mind that it is in your powei to make a saving to the company by the economical performance of your duties, equal to the additional compensation you receive, we will come out even in the end, and I have confidence in believing you will all try to accomplish this.

With best wishes I am

Yours Very Respectfully,

John B. Carson, General Manager.

Here is an instance of friendly intercourse, of mutual interest, which naturally comes of a considerate management. These relations continued pleasant during Mr. Carson's stay; but the Chicago, Burlington & Quincy Co. reached out its strong arms and secured the control of the Hannibal & St. Joseph railroad. Mr. Carson went to the Louisville, New Albany & Chicago railroad, and the Hannibal & St. Joseph railroad was placed under Burlington rules. A notice was posted that on and after November 1, 1885, all men promoted in the engine department would be classified, and the doors were suddenly closed upon the employment of engineers from other roads. This was a startling exercise of power. It was a widening of the domain of classification, which drove away contentment and harmony wherever it went. Their pay on the mileage plan was not disturbed. The General Grievance Committee was asking the Burlington to adopt the same standard of three and a half cents on passenger, and four cents per mile on freight: yet they were so much impressed with the evil of classification, that when they were asked to vote to sustain the General Grievance Committee, and vote on the abolition of classification, they voted unanimously to do away with a rule that had in it such an evil tendency. Their social relations with the officers were pleasant. Their pay was satisfactory to those who were past the year of probation. They deserve the credit of an unselfish devotion to principle, in lending their assistance, and risking their future by enlisting in a common cause, for a common good. Had the right principle of apprenticeship been adopted, these men could not have been so completely united as they were. Apprenticeship has always had defenders; it has yet. There is no question that the engineers and firemen would willingly accept a reduction of wages, equal to the difference between a tried man and an untried one. The Baltimore & Ohio road pays ten per cent less than first-class for one year, then full pay. Here are just principles. But on the Burlington, under classification, a difference of 33 per cent is demanded first year, and 16 per cent for the second year, then full pay; and employ no one who cannot be used at these reductions, consequently no engineers were hired.

CHAPTER XXVI.

JOINT COMMITTEE SEEKING AN INTERVIEW.

On Monday, February 6, having heard nothing from Mr. Stone, another message was sent him asking an answer by 1:00 P. M. Not receiving any answer, the committee concluded they did not intend to grant a hearing. They concluded to send another dispatch to Mr. Perkins, and tell him they had sent two messages to Mr. Stone and had received no answer, and that they would wait three days for him to come and meet the committee, and that if he did not come, then they would put the matter in the hands of the two grand officers, Messrs. Arthur and Sargent. To this Mr. Perkins answered on Wednesday, February 7: "S. E. Hoge: Message received. Mr. Stone probably did not get your message; he is on his way from Washington and will be in New York to-day, and I will talk with him."[1] The first dispatch sent to Mr. Stone might not have found him, the second one did. The Knights of Labor had a strike in Pennsylvania, on December 24, 1887. It was not a railroad strike, but it involved railroad men who were members of that Order. From subsequent developments it is reasonable to suppose that Mr. Stone did not desire to answer until he knew the purport of the dissatisfaction, and whether it could be made useful. A message was finally received from him and read to the committee on the 8th, and Mr. Perkins was so notified, and that

1 Minutes of member General Grievance Committee.

they would confer with him later. Mr. Holdridge was then heard from, and the chairman asked for an audience, and he was answered that they could not grant it until the next Wednesday. Five days more of waiting was no small item to this committee of twenty-eight men, yet the delay was accepted with good grace.

The committee believed the adverse railroad legislation in the state of Iowa was extreme, and that it would be detrimental to both the railroads and the common good of the state. They drafted a memorial to be presented to that legislature against the adoption of the two cent per mile rate. They then appointed a committee composed of F. P. McDonald, of St. Joseph, Mo., George W. Wheatly, of Beardstown, Ill., and Wm. Fowler, of McCook, Neb., who were instructed to present the memorial. This would indicate that while they were trying to secure equity of a railroad company, they were not unmindful of the interests of railroads.

On Monday, February 13, a committee was appointed to present the subject of the dismissal of their brother, J. A. Cuykendall, to Mr. Stone on the next day, and see if he would not reverse or modify the decision of Superintendents Brown and Besler. On Wednesday, February 15, this committee called and presented the matter, and Mr. Stone wanted to see the watch that had caused the discharge. In his decision, Mr. Stone said he could not reverse the decision of Mr. Brown on general principles. Not because the watch stopped and started again, losing eight or nine minutes, causing him to get on a passenger train's time, but he must sustain the decision because the engineer did not flag when he saw the train, and that he did not protect himself according to the rules. The committee believed that had Mr. Cuykendall never served on a committee, he would not have been discharged. Mr. Stone's decision is what every engineer expects for violation of rules. We only cite this case to show the liability of the engineer, and the extremely narrow path he must walk to keep his position. It will also serve for contrast in the future conduct of this company, in violating every principle enunciated in this decision. Mr. Cuykendall was still a member of the General Grievance Committee, and on receiving Mr. Stone's decision, he resigned. The committee asked Mr. Stone to give him a letter, which he readily did, stating cause of dismissal, and requesting whom it may concern to write to him for reference, as to character and ability, and he also gave him a pass over the Burlington. If his membership on the Grievance Committee did not influence the decision, and was in line with the Burlington's strict discipline only, Mr. Stone's action was more than usually considerate. The Burlington rule, as has been stated before, is that passes are not to be given to suspended or discharged employes; and usually when the discharged employe asks for a letter, he is told by the official, "You can refer to me when you find a place." Mr. Cuykendall went to the general manager of the Chicago, Rock Island & Pacific, and received a letter from Mr. St. John, which secured him a place without much delay. The extenuating circumstances in this case, no doubt influenced Mr. Stone to give the letter and pass, and perhaps secured a place for Mr. Cuykendall with the Chicago, Rock Island & Pacific; still it would seem that if he was a good man for Mr. St. John, he ought to be for Mr. Stone.

Mr. Merrill, general manager of the Kansas City, St. Joseph & Council Bluff, and Hannibal & St. Joseph Divisions, and Mr. Besler, general superintendent of the Illinois lines, were present at this meeting, and the subject matter which had convened the committee was taken up. Complaint was made of the violation of the rules of 1886 by the local officers. After considerable discussion upon the subject, Mr. Stone said he was glad the committee had come, that he was going to make some changes in the divisions of the road, and he would run the engines from Galesburg to Hawthorne, the freight yard in the suburb of Chicago. He said he expected it would make some dissatisfaction among the men and they could settle the whole thing at once. The reason he expected dissatisfaction was: The men lived in Aurora, and to run through Aurora to Hawthorne would oblige them to move to Galesburg, unless they would allow the crews to change at Aurora and the same engine go through. A protest was entered, not against the engines running from Galesburg to Chicago, but against being compelled to move away from Aurora. In discussing the schedule presented, the chairman, Mr. Hoge, told Mr. Stone that they wanted the pay fixed on the mileage basis. Mr. Stone answered that he did not have authority to make a full settlement for the whole system, until he could hear from Mr. Perkins. He then asked if the committee would grant him two days to look over the schedule and confer with his subordinates. This was granted. Mr. Hoge asked Mr. Stone if he would meet the grand officers, and he said he would. The business arrangements being completed, the committee retired. Mr. Stone, and the official force at hand, immediately set to work preparing the printed circular letter so widely circulated later. They succeeded admirably in showing up their side of the question; but one very grave oversight in the business of the committee, which future developments proved, was not preparing themselves with counter proof showing the justice of their position. While we are waiting for Mr. Stone to secure the authority he lacked, let us look at this letter with the light let in on both sides of the controversy. We shall see that this letter, prepared with such care and in such elegance, was not intended for the eye of the engineers and firemen only. It is evident it was intended for the use to which it was put. It was an appeal to the public. It was full of half truths well put and plausibly argued. It was evident that they did not dream of concessions to these protesting employes. The pamphlet contained twenty-four pages purporting to be a candid appeal to these disaffected men. It was filled with statements that were grossly unjust to the men and misleading to the public. We invite the reader to take a walk through it with a lantern in his hand. Its title page was a bold one.

CHAPTER XXVII.

THE CIRCULAR LETTER ANSWERED.

It will be remembered that the strike did not occur until February 27, and considerable time must have been consumed in the preparation of this document. It gives a statement of wages paid first, second and third year, on 166 different runs and conditions; four pages of this elaborate document are given to discussion of the company's side of the question, and giving a highly colored representation of wages paid, stating what men were paid without telling how much work was done for it. Below is a copy of the title page.

LETTER

TO

ENGINEERS AND FIREMEN

EMPLOYED ON THE

Chicago, Burlington & Quincy Railroad,
Burlington & Missouri River Railroad in Nebraska,
Hannibal & St. Joseph Railroad,
Kansas City, St. Joseph & Council Bluffs Railroad,
Chicago & Iowa Railroad.

CHICAGO, FEBRUARY 22, 1888.

It is evident they had two objects in view. One to dishearten any of the old men who might be weak, and to induce them to stay with the company. But the main object was to bias public opinion, and there is no doubt that it did very powerfully and erroneously affect the general reader. It was evidently intended for the newspapers, and to them it went, and thousands read it and formed opinions that to this day have remained unchanged. We propose to pay our respects to this document, and we shall leave the reader to characterize it after he shall have seen it dissected.

This document starts out by saying: A committee of your number presented, on February 15, 1888, for our consideration, a schedule, marked "A," attached hereto, providing for a new basis and rate of pay for enginemen. The schedule marked "B," also attached, gives rules of April 1, 1886, governing the pay of engineers and firemen in force upon all lines, and also the schedule of wages for the C., B. & Q. proper. The important changes which your committee suggests are as follows:

"'1st. Pay to be governed solely by the miles run, without regard to other conditions or circumstances,"

"'2nd. A large average increase in existing rates of pay.'"

"'3rd. The abolition of any classification based upon length of service, age, or experience.'"

You are requested to carefully consider the following objections to these suggestions:

"1st. That our present basis is in force upon many important railroads in this country, and is preferred because it is the best one to fairly provide for differences in the amount of labor, time and responsibility required of enginemen upon different runs and divisions."

"A branch passenger engine hauling two or three cars where there are two trains each way daily, is more easily handled than an important main line passenger engine where there are twenty or more trains each way."

"A branch freight engine hauling eight or ten cars, with easy and regular hours, and by daylight, demands less labor from enginemen than an engine on the main line with a heavy freight train, although the mileage may be the same."

"The trip basis, in view of all the varying conditions, covers value received. An arbitrary mileage basis disregards the value of the service rendered, and in the long run, we fear, would be unsatisfactory to the men and to the company." For example:

"On the Galesburg Division of the C., B. & Q. railroad, an engineer on a light passenger run of two cars between Buda and Vermont, under the present schedule earns in twenty-six (26) days, $123.50, and the fireman $74.10; under the schedule which you propose the engineer would receive $171.08, and the fireman $102.64."

One hundred miles constitutes a day's work on all roads, and the run being 188 miles, the enginemen run 4888 miles in the twenty-six days, and consequently work 48 and 2-5 days to earn $123.50, and the firemen $74.10. Had this letter been for the purpose of discussing the issue with the enginemen, the question of miles would certainly have entered into the discussion. Again they say:

"Upon the first division of the Cheyenne branch on the Burlington & Missouri River railroad, a passenger train of three cars, requiring six hours and ten minutes daily, is paying under the existing schedule, to engineers, $144.00 per month. Upon your schedule it would pay $189.00 per month."

Here again is 188 miles to run every day for thirty days in the month to get this $144.00, fifty-four days' work at $2.66 per day. We now come to the Villisca branch:

"On the Kansas City, St. Joseph & Council Bluff's railroad, on the run from Villisca to St Joseph and return, under the present schedule the engineer earns for a month of twenty-six (26) days, $143.00, and the firemen $72.80. Upon the schedule which you propose the engineer would receive $199.29 and the fireman $119.60. This is a three-car run, the engineer and fireman returning home every night; it is also a daylight run."

To earn this money, the enginemen run 219 miles each day, twenty-six days in the month, 5694 miles, nearly fifty-seven (57) days' work! Was the distance omitted to fool the engineers and firemen to whom it was addressed, or to mislead the public? This letter then quotes:

"On the Chicago & Iowa railroad, a light passenger run between Rockford and Aurora, which occupies four hours and fifty minutes in making the round trip, which leaves the engineer at home every night and every Sunday, and gives him the greater part of each day to himself, pays the engineer at present $104.00 per month. Under the schedule which you propose this run would pay $134.68 per month, which is out of all proportion."

Here is one hundred and forty-eight (148) miles to run every day, and instead of four hours and fifty minutes, the train leaves at 6:55 A. M., and returns at 8:35 P. M., thirteen hours and a half; 3848 miles in the twenty-six days, or thirty-eight and one-half day's work. This letter to the engineers and firemen closes these astounding statements with the remarks that:

"The above examples illustrate that some light runs are paid high at present in proportion to the heavy runs, where most of the men are employed. Other similar cases can be given to show that your schedule would create high paid runs, and that it disregards what is reasonable to the company, and fair to the men."

I have before me a book containing the schedules of over sixty railroads, of which forty-six contain a clause which says: "One hundred miles, or less, constitutes a day. All over one hundred miles will be paid for at regular rate per mile." Three of the other fourteen which pay by the trip, namely: the Southern Pacific, the Denver & Rio Grande, and the St. Louis & San Francisco, base their pay per trip, on the number of miles at three and one-half and four cents per mile, the Southern Pacific paying as high as $7.25 a trip. The Denver and Rio Grande for two hundred and seven (207) miles paying $7.90 on passenger train. There is no condition in any of these which specifies three cars or six, as requring less pay or more. We find better prices paid by the trip on the New York and the New England railway—a Boston road—than Mr. Stone was willing to concede, viz: one hundred and eleven miles run. Hartford and

Fishkill, on Hudson, $3.75 also; Hartford, Manchester & Fishkill, one hundred and twenty (120) miles, $4.00. Putnam to Hartford and return, one hundred and twelve (112) miles, $3.75. The first two are through trains, the last a local.

Let us compare some runs on other roads with Mr. Stone's main line fast mail, which is second to none in importance, as they are liable to $500 forfeit if the connections are missed. He pays from Aurora to Galesburg, one hundred and twenty-five (125) miles, $3.75, while if he paid the New York and the New England rate, he would pay $4.22. The local turn-around run of one hundred and twelve (112) miles, New York and New England, pays $3.75. The Burlington pays from Aurora to Streator and return, one hundred and twenty (120) miles, $3.65. If Mr. Stone paid the same rate as the New York and the New England, this run would bring $4.00. On the Norfolk and Western railroad, the pay of passenger engineers is based on three cents per mile, and at this rate Mr. Stone's Vallisca branch, quoted as paying $143.00 per month, would pay $170.82. I find the pay for passenger service from three cents per mile up to four cents, the country over, with a very few roads with such rates as the Burlington, and there are no roads in the west that could afford to pay better than it could before the strike.

The Burlington officials pick out the best month in the year to show the public what the men are earning. Below is their statement of earnings per month, of enginemen on the C., B. & Q., who worked during the whole month, taken from the rolls of November, 1887:

WRECK AT CRESTON, IOWA, APRIL 15, 1888, CAUSED BY GROSS NEGLIGENCE AND INCOMPETENCY, RESULTING IN THE DEATH OF FIREMAN SHORT, AND THE INJURY OF OTHERS.—TWO MAIL CARS THROWN DOWN THE EMBANKMENT AND BURNED TOGETHER WITH THE BRIDGE.—THESE MEN HAD BEEN ON DUTY 54 HOURS.

	ENGINEERS.		FIREMEN.	
	NO. MEN.	AV. RATE.	NO. MEN.	AV. RATE.
Chicago Division,	77	$105.10	94	$55.95
Galesburg "	68	113.56	77	63.34
St. Louis "	31	115.29	37	60.63
East Iowa "	26	110.69	33	58.22
Middle Iowa "	36	126.43	23	76.37
West Iowa "	50	128.76	53	72.51

Now, if we analyze this statement, we find that the firemen get in proportion to engineers' pay:

On Chicago Division,	65	per cent.
" Galesburg "	67	" "
" St. Louis "	63	" "
" E. Iowa "	68	" "
" M. Iowa "	38½	" "
" W. Iowa "	59½	" "

On the Middle Iowa Division the engineers must have fired for themselves part of the time, as there were fewer firemen by thirteen, and the total earned by them was only 38½ per cent of the engineers' earnings. We must conclude without further discussion, that this list was made up for effect; the schedule all through, on the average, showing the firemens' pay at fifty-eight per cent of the engineers'.

The third paragraph of this circular letter says: "At present we have one rate of pay for engineers just promoted from firemen, which continues one year. In the second year of service as engineer an advance in pay is given. On the expiration of the second year a further advance to full pay is given. The schedule proposed by the engineers' committee does away with this classification and insists upon full pay for every man as soon as he runs an engine." No, Sir! Not full pay for every man as soon as he runs an engine, but full pay as soon as the Burlington company puts him forward as a capable and safe man to be entrusted with a train valuable in property and life. If fully trusted to do the most difficult work, why not full pay? That is a question often asked, but never yet answered. If an answer had been within the horizon when this circular was indited, the powerful imagination of its authors would have brought it in. Capable and safe, means perfect, and if he is that, why degrade him in his pay?

"The classification arranging for lower pay for beginners is in force in other branches of service. There is no complaint about this system from any of the C., B. & Q. employes, except engineers. There seems to be no explanation offered that the classification of which you complain is not as applicable to the enginemen as to other employes."

The fact that brakemen and conductors work for their first six months at less than full rate, is not properly classification; it is an apprenticeship to which no class of laborers would object for a moment. To compare the probationary work of the engineers with that of brakemen and conductors and call them similar, as does the circular letter, is not only ridiculous to those who know better, but it is misleading to those who do not. It shows the want of candor in the writer, and of equity in their cause. It is a mode of attempting to make public sentiment, for which its authors must have felt ashamed in the dark for having committed treason against justice and logic. It makes the false issue that while engineers complain of classification for themselves, they do not complain of it as to brakemen and conductors, while the fact is that classification as it has been forced upon engineers, has never been applied to brakemen and conductors and the authors of this circular knew it.

"To mass all engineers into one common body and pay all alike, taking no account of superior ability or intelligence, seems to us unjust and unfair, and in direct opposition to the spirit of the times we live in, which tends to assure to each man whatever rewards are due to his own abilities and skill, and not to produce caste, all members of which are on the same level."

Let me quote from the Burlington schedule of pay, and show who creates caste, and whether ability is recognized and rewarded: "A passenger train between Aurora and Galesburg, one hundred and twenty-five miles, pays:

	FIRST YEAR.	SECOND YEAR.	THIRD YEAR.
Engineers,	$2.75	$3.25	$3.75
Firemen,	1.85	2.00	2.15

Is it caste to say that one man doing an equal amount of work shall do it for one dollar less than another? Is it rewarding ability? Does he have the ability? If not, why should the schedule quote a third-class man in first-class service? The position is positively inconsistent. If they are not equal to the service, they have no business in it; yet the schedule shows they are, and we know they are. The reason why there are not more third-class men running passenger engines is because the engineers have demanded that the oldest in the service shall have the preference of runs.

This letter says, "The spirit of the times we live in tends to assure to each man whatever rewards are due to his own ability and skill." Let us follow a passenger train from Chicago to Quincy.

		MILES.	1ST YR.	2ND YR.	3RD YR.	FIRST-CLASS.
Aurora to Chicago and Return........	Engineers Firemen	77	2.35 1.50	2.85 1.70	3.25 1.85	4½c per mile
Aurora to Galesburg..	Engineers Firemen	125	2.75 1.85	3.25 2.00	3.75 2.15	3c per mile
Galesburg to Quincy..	Engineers Firemen	100	2.45 1.70	3.00 1.85	3.50 2.00	Trains 101, 102, 103. 104. 3½c per mile
Galesburg to Quincy..	Engineers Firemen	100	2.40 1.65	2.90 1.75	3.37½ 1.90	Trains 105, 106. $3.37½

The last trains specified, 105 and 106, are local between Galesburg and Quincy, and make twenty-six (26) stops, making an average speed greater than either numbers 103 or 104. Mr. Stone says it is because they do not pull so many cars, consequently there is not so much profit, so he must take twelve and one-half cents from the engineer and ten cents from the fireman; not because he lacks ability, nor because the risk is any less or the work either, but that he may be made to share the loss or the difference between these two trains—one five or six cars, the other eight or nine cars. When we state from their own report of 1886, that the locomotive service east of the Missouri river only costs one and nine tenths of one per cent of the expense account, it looks very small. It looks still more niggardly when we look at their report for 1866 which says: "Excess of income over operating expenses and taxes, $12,016,452.56 for the whole line operated east and west of the Missouri river."

The next clause in this letter is very valuable, as it outlines what the Burlington considers their rights and what the public demands. It says: "The company must reserve absolutely the right to ascertain, by whatever examinations it may think advisable, whether its employes of all classes are capable of fulfilling the duties they undertake, and the public also demand that the railroad company shall take every precaution to employ only those men who can safely perform the work entrusted to them." This is right unless the examination is only meant to arrest and discharge old employes, as was done in the color-blind test. In that matter, as all know who know anything about it, the men were tested with all the various and delicate shades of color so that an expert in colors would hardly pass. Our engineers of the first and second years held in regular work, but with inferior pay, have requested any, reasonable examination, but could not obtain it. The best of work was required for two years at degraded rates of pay, while steadily refusing a fair examination as to ability and skill with reference to promotion, and this by a company that is laboring to prevent others from creating caste. Now read the evidence taken before the Illlnols and Iowa rallroad commissioners concerning the kind of men which later took charge of the company's property, and its patrons' lives, without a particle of either qualification or examination, and the authors of this circular are "hoisted on their own petard." This letter closes with these words: "In conclusion, we would say that, while we cannot see our way to accepting your committee's proposals, we expect to pay as much as our neighbors for similar services, and we are ready at any time to take up the question of wages and adjust any inequalities in our schedule that may be shown to exist. We cannot, however, attempt to adopt a basis which says that one 100-mile run should be paid the same as another 100-mile run, regardless of the effort and ability required and the difficulties to be overcome on each. Believing as we do, that these are matters of great importance, we will print for distribution copies of this communication, so that these questions may be fully considered by all concerned."

Yours Truly,

HENRY B. STONE,
General Manager, C., B. & Q. R. R.

H. S. HOLDRIGE,
General Manager, B. & M. R. R. R. in Neb.

W. F. MERRILL,
General Manager, H. & St. J. R. R. and K. C., St. J. & C. B. R. R.

H. D. JUDSON,
General Superintendent, C. & I. R. R.

"We expect to pay as much as our neighbors for similar services." I will quote some of their neighbors:

Chicago & Alton.—Passenger service, three and one-half cents per mile. One hundred miles or less to constitute a day's work. Classification is abolished from March 1, 1888.

Atchison, Topeka & Santa Fe.—No classification;

three and one-half cents on passenger, and four cents per mile on freight. One hundred miles or less make a day's work.

Chicago, Milwaukee & St. Paul.—On all runs of less than ninety miles, $3.50 will be allowed. In case actual mileage on such runs exceeds one hundred miles per day, actual mileage will be allowed at the rate of $3.70, three and seven-tenths cents per mile.

Louisville, New Albany & Chicago.—Passenger 3½ cents per mile. Freight, eight (8) wheel engines, 4 cents per mile, and six (6) wheel with connected engines, 4 2-10 cents per mile. No classification.

Union Pacific.—$3.85, both freight and passenger, and one hundred miles a day's work.

Wisconsin Central.—$3.70 per one hundred miles, freight and passenger. One hundred miles a day's work.

Minnesota & North Western.—same as Wisconsin Central. No classification.

Wabash.—3½ cents, passenger; 4 cents, freight. One hundred miles a day's work. No classification.

Chicago, St. Paul, Minneapolis & Omaha.—$3.70, freight and passenger.

Northern Pacific.—4 cents, freight and passenger. One hundred miles or less a day's work. No classification.

Chicago, Rock Island & Pacific.—Engineers, passenger, $3.60 per hundred miles; firemen, passenger, $2.15 per hundred miles. On freight, for one hundred miles, $4.15, and firemen in proportion.

The engineers on fast mail, Chicago, Burlington & Quincy, 125 miles per day, receive $97.50 for 26 days' time. The engineers on the Chicago & North Western railroad, for the same service, receive $120.00. No proof is necessary to show that men are not rewarded in accordance with merit and ability, which Mr. Stone says the spirit of the times demands. It is never ability on the Burlington, but time, that advances the engineer's pay. If the engineer just promoted has the ability, why should he be kept at reduced pay if it is ability that is to be rewarded? And if the older engineers have ability equal to the North Western engineers, why should not this ability be recognized, and be paid as much?

These quotations prove that the Burlington pays less than its neighbors, and yet it is the best able to pay—or was at that time. It is easy to see that there was no intention to make a settlement. The officers had made up their minds to fight it out and win laurels for great generalship, not considering the interests of the "10,000 stockholders in Illinois alone."[1] The London advertisement, in November, with its false representations, and the advertisements in New York, Pittsburg and Philadelphia, as early as the 26th of February, are ample proof of what was intended, so that all the negotiations were only a means of making time for the Burlington officials to be better prepared. Here is an event of the day before the strike: "Reading, Pa., February 26, 1888. It is learned here to-night that an agent of the Burlington has been in this vicinity for several days, recruiting striking engineers and firemen from the Reading road, whose places were taken by Brotherhood men."[2]

[1] Railroad Commissioners' report. [2] Kansas City Journal, Associated Press report.

CHAPTER XXVIII.

THE END OF NEGOTIATIONS.

Grand Chief, P. M. Arthur, and Grand Master, F. P. Sargent, with a joint committee of engineers and firemen, were in Chicago on February 15, to meet an engagement with the officials of the Chicago & Alton railroad, on Friday, the 17th of February, 1888. This committee had presented a joint schedule, similar to that formulated by the Burlington committee, asking for the abolition of classification and the adoption of the mileage basis of pay. After two half days of consultation, their schedule was accepted and signed. It is rather strange that the Chicago & Alton found so little that was objectionable in this, and the Burlington found so much. While Messrs. Arthur and Sargent were in Chicago on this business, the Burlington committee advised with them in relation to their committee work, and were instructed by the two grand officers how to proceed, and were told, if they failed to come to an understanding that they should send for them and they would add their efforts to those of the committee.

On the 17th, Chairman Hoge received a letter from General Manager Stone, appointing 10:00 A. M., Saturday, February 18, for a meeting with the committee at the Burlington General Office. The committee had been in Chicago twenty days. The first seventeen were consumed in an effort to procure an audience, and the next three they were waiting for the Burlington officials to prepare their famous letter. On arriving at headquarters they met General Manager Stone, of the Illinois lines, General Manager Holdridge, of the Burlington & Missouri, and General Manager Merrill, of the Kansas City, St. Joseph & Council Bluffs, and Hannibal & St. Joseph roads, and General Superintendent Besler. The only business of importance at this meeting was the presenting to the committee the carefully prepared document containing the schedules and rules of 1886 and 1888, as shown in chapter XXVII. They were asked to look it over and consider it. There was great skill in the preparation of this document, and no doubt the officials would have been highly pleased if it had created a division in the ranks of the committee, for which no doubt they hoped. The committee accepted the circular letter, and adjourned to meet at their own quarters, not that they expected to find anything in it to change their minds, but they could hardly do otherwise with reasonable civility. They saw in it time—the dragging along of the issue without meeting it. There is not much doubt that this document was intended to do demoralizing work in the committee, and if it should fail in this, then to use it, as they did use it, to bias public opinion. There was no evidence of a disposition to meet the men and discuss the points at issue; but every move by Mr. Stone called for time. Each day of delay brought a warmer sun, and drove jack frost—the known enemy of ignorant engineers,—farther away. The committee were becoming disgusted with procrastinating evasions, and after considering the circular letter, and seeing no point in it where the company proposed any reform, they concluded to notify President Perkins that unless an audience was given the committee in three days, the men would stop work. A message was received from Mr. Stone at 6:00 P. M. saying he would meet the committee on the following Monday, February 20, at 3:00 P. M.

On Monday the two chairmen, Messrs. Hoge and Murphy, were sent by the committee to see Mr. Stone and tell him they would limit the time to three days in which to give them due consideration. Chairman Hoge said Mr. Stone became very indignant, but told them he could not settle until he heard from Mr. Perkins.

On Tuesday, February 21, Mr. Stone sent word to the committee saying he would meet them, but that he had not heard from Mr. Perkins. Mr. Stone finally obtained the authority, and the committee met him on Wednesday, February 22, at 11:00 A. M. After the usual courtesy Mr. Stone opened the subject by making objections to some of the articles in the proposed rules. Mr. Stone did not seem to understand them as they were intended, and the chairman explained them. Mr. Stone said that if the committee had considered the matter and could see any certain article in the schedule in any different light he was ready to listen. The committee readily understood the import of this remark from word and manner, and the chairman told Mr. Stone they were of the same mind as when they last met. Mr. Stone then said, "If that is the case we cannot make a settlement, as there are things in the schedule which I could not allow."

No effort was made to discuss them separately, in an effort to come to an understanding, and the committee retired and sent for Messrs. Arthur and Sargent to come immediately, saying that they had done all in their power to come to some understanding and without result. These gentlemen arrived on an early morning train, February 23, met with joint committee and found that they had, in anticipation of the necessity, obtained the vote of the whole system on the subject of the controversy, and as the vote had been so unanimous for the committee to stand their ground until they had obtained some substantial concessions, nothing was left them but to proceed with the effort.

At 10:00 A. M. the committee, headed by the leading men of their respective orders, proceeded to the Burlington headquarters. On entering they found assembled Vice-President Peasly, General Manager Holdridge, General Manager Merrill, together with a large number of superintendents and master mechanics. After various introductions all were seated. Mr. Stone had not yet arrived. It must have been an auspicious moment to the mind of Mr. Stone. To have the superior authority of a great railroad, representing as it does, "property aggregating over $192,000,000; the interests of eleven thousand six hundred and sixty-eight stockholders,"[1] and the employes of this vast holding; to have in his hands this vast power to be used for good or evil, was indeed a momentous epoch in a man's life. The magnitude of this responsibility in the mind of a conscientious man must weigh heavily. But Mr. Stone weilded a power emanating from a Boston directory. "When slavery

[1] Railroad Commissioners of Ill., 1888.

still wielded its lash, the merchants of Boston mobbed William Lloyd Garrison, and hissed Wendell Phillips, because they cared more for their trade with the south than for the poor slave."[1] Again, in this case, they cared more for money than for justice.

A few moments after the committee were seated, Mr. Stone entered. An eye witness says: "His greeting was cordial, yet his every act showed that he was determined to make an obstinate fight, and that his answer would be, now, the same he had given to the committee at their previous meeting: "I give nothing." A few preliminary remarks were made by both Mr. Arthur and Mr. Sargent and the work was taken up for which they had assembled. Article I was read. This article was discussed for nearly two hours; proposition after proposition was made in an effort to meet Mr. Stone's objections, but he was not in a mood to be suited, and it was finally passed. The second article was taken up. This, like the first, did not suit Mr. Stone. Substitutes were offered, but, like the first one, no proposition met with his approval, and it also was passed. Then the meeting adjourned for dinner to meet at 2:00 P. M. The two rules, which by no possible means could be made to suit Mr. Stone, are in force on nearly all the trunk lines in the country, and it was evident he did not wish to be suited.

Promptly at 2:00 P. M. the work was again taken up. Section 2 of Article II was read. This, like the other propositions, did not suit Mr. Stone. Mr. Arthur read rule after rule which had been adopted by other companies, but none suited. Finally, Mr. Stone made one himself. Mr. Arthur said, "We will accept that Mr.

[1] Rev. C. O. Brown, in Labor Troubles.

Stone." He replied, "I did not mean that to be accepted; I want to consult with my associates." General Managers Holdridge and Merrill recommended that it be accepted by the company; but Mr. Stone did not want his own proposition after he had made it, and it was finally passed without agreement or action. The real intention of Mr. Stone was evident in what followed.

Section I of Article III was read, which calls for the mileage basis for engineers, 3½ cents on passenger and 4 cents per mile on freight trains, and Mr. Arthur said, "What do you say to that, Mr. Stone?" "I say, No, Sir, I will never concede it." Mr. Arthur said: "That is frank of you, Mr. Stone; when a man says 'No, Sir, never,' some one will have to yield or there will be no settlement." Concessions were again attempted on Mr. Arthur's part, and rates were quoted from other roads. Mr. Arthur proceeded to show the number of roads that were paying the rates asked for by the committee. He showed where the Rock Island and Northwestern, running through the same region as that of the Chicago, Burlington & Quincy railroad, was paying more than was asked by the committee, and more than 90 per cent of the roads were paying what was asked. He read a clipping from a newspaper which stated that the Chicago, Burlington & Quincy had over a million dollars surplus on hand, and then asked Mr. Stone whether the Burlington was not able to pay as much as its neighbors? Mr. Stone hesitated a moment, and answered, "That they might be able to do so, but that the basis on which they paid their engineers and firemen was working satisfactorily to them, and they did not propose to make any change."

Mr. Arthur, having exhausted all known resources, and seeing that it was useless to waste more time with him, then said: "Very well, Mr. Stone, if you will not consider that proposition, if your men decide to quit work, I will sanction a strike on your road." The sanction of Messrs. Arthur and Sargent carried with it the support of all members of the Brotherhood of Locomotive Engineers and the Brotherhood of Locomotive Firemen. Neither could order, but they could advise and consent, and in the position of this joint committee, it meant a strike. It was evident from Mr. Stone's demeanor that he was prepared for the conflict, as he evinced no surprise when Mr. Arthur informed him what he might expect. The committee withdrew, and on their way to the hotel Messrs. Arthur and Sargent revolved in their minds what further could be done to obviate the disaster of a strike. They knew that Mr. Stone had been delegated full power to do as he pleased, but Mr. Arthur thought that if President Perkins, who was still in the east, knew the situation, he might intervene. Accordingly, Messrs. Arthur and Sargent formulated, and sent the following message:

To President Perkins:

"Unable to settle the grievances of your engineers and firemen with General Manager Stone, men are determined to strike. We want to prevent it. Will accept the same terms as made with the Chicago & Alton, and Atchison, Topeka & Santa Fe; three and one-half cents per mile on passenger, four cents per mile freight service, sixty per cent for the firemen. Answer quick!"

No reply was made to this until Friday afternoon, February 24; then a message was received from President Perkins, stating that "he had given the authority to Mr. Stone to settle with the men. He said he was not familiar enough with the case to form an opinion, but he hoped the men would do nothing rash; that he would be in Chicago some time the next week." The coldness and the indifference embodied in the wording of this message, considering the importance of the occasion, is most un-American, and could only emanate from an autocrat in disposition. It showed utter indifference towards the men employed upon the Burlington system. The committee, together with their grand officers, had done all in their power to avoid a conflict, and there was nothing left them but a dignified maintenance of their position, or to withdraw and leave their future to the tender mercies of a power that had discharged the committee in 1883, and had demanded of its employes a withdrawal from the Knights of Labor in 1886.

Grand Chief Arthur reviewed the situation, and placed a strike before them in its worst possible form, showing what the result might be. Grand Master Sargent also pictured the possible future, telling them that "no sooner would the news go forth that there was a strike inaugurated than men would come by the score to take their places; that even men bearing the badges of their Order would come to take the places they would make vacant; that the company would use every means in their power to defeat them; that men

J. A. BAUEREISEN.

who had become incensed at the Brotherhood of Locomotive Engineers at something said or done, would take this opportunity to get revenge."[1] This had no effect upon their determination to receive consideration from the company, or take the consequences, whatever they might be. Nothing was said by the grand officers to induce the men to strike, but they each told the committee that if they concluded to do so, the men would be paid as their respective constitutions provided—$40 per month for three months, if the strike was not successful. If it was, they would get nothing; and that money would be raised to buy or hire, if possible, such men as were worthy. After mature deliberation they concluded to stop work, and the time was set for four o'clock A. M., February 27, and the committee were instructed to go home and inform the men, and make all preparation for what seemed inevitable—a strike. Grand Chief Arthur's instructions were, unless otherwise notified: "When the appointed time arrives, those who are at terminal points will quit, and those who are on the road with a train, will run the engines to the end of their trip, leave them in good order, go home and remain away from the company's property, and commit no lawlessness or overt act." "If," he said, "we cannot win this strike honorably, we will acknowledge defeat." This ended the conference. Chairmen Hoge and Murphy remained in Chicago, and the rest of the committee departed to carry out their instructions.

One more effort was made by Chairmen Hoge and Murphy for peace, but Mr. Stone was as relentless as ever, and they then told him the men would quit in a

1 Living Witness.

body, at 4:00 A. M., February 27. Mr. Stone said: "Forty per cent of the old men will stay with the company."[1] This estimate I have been credibly informed, came from the local officials' estimate of the men at each point along the line. It is hardly to be doubted that Mr. Stone was deceived, or misled by erroneous information, and had he known the true character of the situation, that instead of having forty per cent he would have none,. that he must depend upon strange faces and unknown characters for success; he would not probably have felt such assurance, nor would he have given at this last meeting the answer he did. Had Mr. Stone shown any disposition, the conditions asked for could have been modified, peace would have been preserved and millions—not of Mr. Stone's money—but of the stockholders, saved. His disposition and intentions are very manifest in the following interrogation by a reporter:

February 26.—"The spacious rooms occupied by the general officers of the Chicago, Burlington & Quincy railroad company are generally vacated Sundays. Yesterday was an exception to this rule. The leading officers of the company were at work at their desks, and hard at work. Several consultations were held during the day between General Manager H. B. Stone; Vice-President J. C. Peasly; General Freight Agent, E. P. Ripley; General Passenger Agent, Paul Morton; General Superintendent, J. D. Besler; and Division Superintendent, Howland. Hundreds of telegrams were sent out to the various points liable to be directly affected by the strike; a half-dozen stenographers were kept busy with important correspondence."

[1] Chairman.

"General Manager Stone was closeted about 11:30 o'clock with S. E. Hoge, of the engineers, and J. H. Murphy of the firemen. The conference lasted about ten minutes, and when questioned upon what transpired Mr. Stone said: These men called upon me this morning and gave me the first official notification that there would be a strike. They asked me if the Burlington was willing to meet them in conference upon the points discussed at the last meeting, and I told them most emphatically, No. I informed them that we were willing to consider the question of wages, but did not care to talk about abolishing the system of classification. They then said that every engineer and fireman belonging to their respective organizations would strike at 4 o'clock tomorrow morning. That ended the interview."[1] (It will be remembered by the reader that the mileage basis was what broke off the negotiations, and not classification.) "Did not Chief Arthur inform you Thursday that the men would strike unless their request was complied with!" "No, he did not; he said that he would give his consent to a strike. All the information we have had since then up to this forenoon was derived from the papers." "Is there any chance now of averting the strike?" "None whatever unless the men recede from their declared intention. We are making every preparation in our power to prepare for the worst."[2]

When Messrs. Hoge and Murphy met Mr. Stone, and received his answer, "Most emphatically, No," the last act was performed, and the answer severed all diplomatic relations between these two powerful factors. The engineers and firemen, representing as they did a

[1] [2] Chicago Tribune, February 27, 1888.

body of 50,000 men, when they received the sanction of their grand officers, could not, with any dignity, recede without having any of their requests granted, when so many roads were giving all and even more than they were asking. It was left to be seen after the ultimatum had been given, whether radical measures would bring about what peaceful negotiations had failed to effect.

Mr. Arthur said: "It is the first instance where I have failed to effect a peaceable settlement of the grievances of our men with a railroad company. Mr. Stone absolutely refused to meet us on the mileage basis; he would not touch the wages question at all. I was willing to make all honorable concessions, and had already made some when he abruptly told me that he would listen to no proposition to treat on the mileage basis. This of course ended the negotiations. Why the Burlington people decline to entertain it, they alone can explain." In answer to the question of why they selected so early an hour, Mr. Arthur said: "We selected that hour because there are fewer trains on the road at that time, and we do not wish the traveling public to be inconvenienced any more than we can possibly help. Remember that this affair is none of our seeking and I regret exceedingly that Mr. Stone has forced us into it. It has always been our policy to avoid strife, and particularly strikes. What we ask is that we are entitled to the same consideration by the Burlington road that we have received from other roads." Grand Master Sargent said: "The die is cast and the public should understand that it is not a move of our own choice. We have engaged in this contest fully prepared. There will be no intimidation, but we shall claim the right to buy any locomotive engineer that we please. We may decide to go to a locomotive engineer and hire him ourselves; no one can question us that privilege." "Mr. Stone admitted that few men could be pressed into the service from Chicago and based his hopes upon the smaller towns and cities along the road. He said an attempt will be made to press into the service the older and more experienced machine shop men. The company also expected considerable help from the firemen. There are hundreds of firemen, it is claimed, who are competent to run a locomotive engine, who would jump at the chance to secure a good job."[1]

The Burlington management had said in their circular letter that the public demanded that the railroad company should take every precaution to employ only those men who can safely perform the work entrusted to them. What a sudden change! They refused to modify the tests for fear they would employ some one not up to their standard. Then within a week, we find them groping in the dark, with a bid for all comers, without regard to kind or character, giving a glad welcome to the refuse from all other railroads, as well as from their own. Local committees were appointed by the general grievance committee men, at each point along the whole line, and they were instructed to enter the field on the principle enunciated by Mr. Stone in 1886—"supply and demand;" and to persuade, if possible, or hire if necessary. That honorable warfare was confined to the side of the striking men the following pages must convince the most sceptical.

[1] Interview with Tribune reporter, February 26, 1888.

CHAPTER XXIX.

THE BURLINGTON STRIKE.

The difference between the Burlington managers and the engineers and firemen employed on the system was chiefly in this: that the enginemen asked for a change of the basis of wages from the trip to the mileage plan, and the managers refused to make any change.

The ultimatum was given on Feb. 22, 1888, leaving the Brotherhood the alternative of retreating from its position, or of endeavoring to enforce its request by a strike. The latter alternative was adopted by the two orders of engineers and firemen. The men of the grievance committee were instructed to return to their respective constituents along the line, and notify them that unless the managers had consented to treat with them before 4 o'clock A. M., Feb. 27, every man should leave his engine on arriving at its terminal point. Meanwhile the managers were making preparations for the coming conflict. The enginemen hearing nothing from them at the appointed time vacated their places over the whole Burlington system, six thousand miles of road. Manager Stone said, "Only one man of the whole 2000 remained."

The company was unusually active on Saturday and Sunday clearing the tracks and getting everything passible to its destination. The men were as obedient to order, and as careful of the company's interests as though they expected to continue in its service. At four o'clock all engines at terminal points were run into their roundhouses and housed with the usual care. All trains on the road were run to the end of the division and left in good order. In fact the deportment of the old employes was unexceptionable. Evidently the men believed that their places could not be filled. They did not dream that the great Chicago, Burlington & Quincy road, proud of its efficiency in every department, demanding high intellectual and moral qualifications of its employes, would disregard its own rule, held to be inflexible, under which no novice could run an engine.

The officers of the road were astonished at the unanimity of sentiment which they perceived in the men. So entire was it, that not half a dozen engineers and firemen were left in as many states and territories to serve the company. Two thousand men scattered over several thousand miles, united in giving up their honest and reputable employment, their good prospects, their certainty of home and friends, for principle. They began the strike, not alone to secure better terms for themselves, but to give laboring men everywhere a better chance,—a just share in the proceeds of capital. Their loyalty became a sublime spectacle when it was seen to be the trait of men vowed to practice, "Sobriety, truth, justice and morality." They believed that the contest on which they had entered would be no trifle, but they did not believe their opponents would be willing to destroy millions of other people's property to gain a point.

At four o'clock on the morning of Febuary 27, the

officials of the road who had been in their offices all night, called in each man as his engine came in and urged him to stay with the company, but without success.

All business came to a standstill. The few passenger trains on the road were abandoned by the men as soon as they came to the terminal point, where the engines were changed. It became necessary for superintendents, master mechanics, road masters, foremen in shops, machinists, anyone who could start and stop an engine to be ready to fill the vacated places. Danger to the property of stockholders or patrons did not deter the officials from entrusting such persons with the trains.

At Chicago a few moments before four o'clock, the C., B. & Q. yards at Canal and Sixteenth street presented their usual appearance. The early morning train had left on time, and the switch engineers were at work as usual. Just before four o'clock Train Master Pope issued an order that no trains should be moved west of Chicago. This was taken by the few trainmen in the yards to mean that the company had secured no men worth mentioning, and that the road would be in a few moments practically tied up. Exactly at that moment the switch engineers stopped work and run their engines into the roundhouse and the strike was on.

The first surburban train to come in was manned by Master Mechanic Smith with Superintendent Howland acting as fireman.

The through passenger trains that were on the road were stopped at division points, and there being no engineers to man the engines, the passenger trains from the west were left at Galesburg, and those from the Illinois Central managed to get to Aurora. "The fast mail being for the benefit of Uncle Sam, was not interfered with, and went as usual. No. 18, leaving Aurora at 6:10 A. M. was taken to Chicago by T. S. Pope, the train master of Chicago. No. 20, at 7:15 A. M., was taken in by F. M. Paris, master mechanic at Streator. No. 33, at 7:20 A. M., the milk train, by G. W. Rhodes, superintendent of motive power at Aurora. The Mendota passenger train was run by Dick Nixon, master mechanic, at Mendota." [1] The Brotherhood's blow fell with paralyzing effect. At the Western avenue round house the most profound quiet prevailed. The round house was full of engines without steam. At 7 o'clock only one engine had left, and that was for the stock yards which was not involved in the strike.

The Burlington sent out the following circular:

"It will probably be a week or more before this company will be able to receive freight from you, and it will therefore be advisable, and for the public interest, for you to deliver all freight consigned to us and destined to competitive points, to such other roads as in your judgment can most promptly take it to its destination. We shall also be obliged for a few days to decline to receive freight for local points. But as soon as we are able you will be advised of our ability to handle freight."

At noon six hundred freight handlers were laid off, and every freight office in the city belonging to the Burlington was shut down. "The great freight house, fronting on Canal street and south of Harrison, was

[1] Aurora, (Ill.,) Express, February 27, 1888.

deserted. There was no trace of the hundreds of trucks with their immense loads of outgoing freight, and each of the twenty receiving doors was adorned with the following sign. 'No freight will be received to-day. Lot. Brown, Agent.'"[1]

Out of fifty-four suburban trains run daily by the Burlington, only four were run, and on a canvas of the opinion of the patrons on one of these trains, it was found that nearly all were in sympathy with the enginemen, and were willing to put up with the inconvenience. They all seemed to think that the Burlington could pay by the mile as well as other roads.[2] The train that should have left Chicago at 10:15 A. M., did not get started until 3:00 P. M. At an evening visit to the Union depot in Chicago at night, as far as the Burlington was concerned, passenger traffic was decidedly blocked and solemn. Not a train left after six o'clock P. M. Passengers holding tickets over that road were obliged to sit in the depot all night on the hard benches. A throng of applicants was at the company's office for the places vacated by the outgoing men, and fifty-three were reported as examined by eleven o'clock. The examination must have been very limited. Mr. Stone said when interrogated, "You see there are plenty of men ready for the places." When he was asked who they were, and where they came from? he answered: "I don't know."[3]

At Aurora the shut down was complete, all operations ceased by the hour set. Several trains came in just before the time, and each was quietly abandoned by the men. Nothing was stirring, and the company's premises were silent and gloomy in the gray

[1] Chicago Tribune. [2] Chicago Times. [3] Associated Press.

light of early dawn. Later in the morning could be seen a motley crowd about the company's grounds, made up of curious citizens, old employes, and the officials of the road, the latter trying to grapple with the difficulties of the situation. The officials were appealing to every man they thought could be induced to come up and fill the vacant places, and the old employes were as watchful and persistent in trying to keep them away. The engine for the Chicago & Iowa, called the Chicago & Dubuque train, was run out of the roundhouse about 11:40 A. M., and Master Mechanic Morris was making a desperate effort to find some one to run the engine. The officers were just beginning to learn that the men were in earnest. The men told Mr. Morris and the train master that they could obtain an engineer and fireman upon application to the engineers' committee, but they spurned this offer, saying they would like to know who was running the Chicago & Iowa road—the Brotherhoods or the officers? Failing to get any one to go, they finally sought the committee, who readily assigned an engineer and fireman, but they were enjoined not to take anything but mail cars. That seemed to be satisfactory, and the men went on the engine and started up. Seeing all the cars were still attached, the engineer stopped. and told them they must cut off the coaches. This they made a show to do, and again gave a signal to go, and the engineer finding they had not cut them off, stopped again. At this the fireman got off and told Mr. Morris to fire the engine himself. They then gave a signal to back up into the yard, with another demonstration of cutting them off, and when the engineer saw this he got off the engine, leaving them with no alternative but for Master Mechanic Morris to go himself, which he did. The next train was number 2, due in Aurora at 6:45 A. M., which arrived at 2:00 P. M., with A. O. Taylor in charge of engine. The engines were changed, and engine 403, manned by Mr. Fred Geyer, foreman of the machine shop, who had never handled an engine in his life, and Seth Parsons, a farmer from Plano, Illinois, acting as fireman. When Foreman Geyer backed the engine up to couple on the train, he could not control it, and ran into the train so hard that it ran back a car length, and it was composed of eleven cars. Geyer remarked then that he could build an engine better than he could run one. They finally got started with the train, and when seven or eight miles from Aurora, they got out of steam, caused by the farmer fireman filling the fire box with green coal. Geyer said he thought to run up and down the track would help make up steam, so they ran away from the train about half a mile east of the train, partly up grade, and in coming back Geyer lost control of the engine, which was going at a rapid rate and struck the train, telescoping the mail car, the whole tank and part of the engine going into it. Expert Geyer was taken out of the side door of the mail car, cut, bleeding, nose broken, and badly injured otherwise. Farmer Parsons, the fireman, had his leg and collar bone broken, and is a cripple for life. One of the mail clerks was very badly injured and has never worked since. Geyer was confined to his house, and Farmer Parsons was at the city hospital for several weeks. The evidence in this case before the Illinois railroad and warehouse commisioners will be given later.

A collision occurred at the Chicago, Milwaukee & St. Paul crossing. William H. Pierce, assistant engineer of tests in the C., B. & Q. shops at Aurora, upon learning of the strike, with several other young men, signed a letter to Mr. Rhodes, superintendent of motive power, offering to go out in any position the company should deem advisable, and Mr Pierce was detailed by the master mechanic at Aurora to go to Mendota, Ill., and take a train to Fulton, as engineer. Mr. Pierce had never run an engine; never was examined for one; was obliged to wear glasses to see and was quite deaf. However, regardless of all interests, and with an eye single to the defeat of the striking engineers, this man was assigned to pull a passenger train.

He started at Mendota and things went fairly well until he arrived at the crossing of the Chicago, Milwaukee & St. Paul railroad. Unfortunately, there was a train on that road just crossing the Burlington track, and this novice failed to stop as he should, and ran into them, going at the rate of forty-five miles per hour, striking the back trucks of the Milwaukee engine tender, throwing it and the Milwaukee mail car into the ditch. The Burlington engine and mail car were also thrown in the ditch, as shown in cut, injuring Mail Clerks Wilhelm and Brown, Express Messenger Morrison of the Milwaukee, and Mr. Pierce, the new engineer, Road Master Seegers, and the conductor of the Burlington train.

In the evidence before the Illinois railroad commissioners appears the following evidence, Superintendent of Motive Power, G. W. Rhodes, being asked:

"Do you know Mr. Pierce?"

"Yes, Sir."

"What is his business?"

"Mr. Pierce is assistant engineer of tests in our laboratory at Aurora."

"Is he an engineer in the employ of the Burlington road now?"

"He is not an engineer."

"Was he ever at any time an engineer in the employ of the Burlington road?"

"He was never examined as an engineer for the Burlington."

"You say he was not?"

"No, Sir. He was not."

"Did Mr. Pierce ever run a locomotive engine before?"

"Mr. Pierce had handled a locomotive engine. Yes, Sir."

"The question was, did he ever run a locomotive engine before. Please answer that."

"I am not able to say whether he did or not."

"Are you in the habit, when exercising your best judgment to select engineers, to put a man on the road to run a locomotive engine when you do not know whether he has ever run one before or not?"

"In a case like this when our trains were"——

"In any case?"

"We do so. I would do so again."

"When the lives of the public are in peril you will take a man without knowing whether he has ever run an engine before or not, and put him in charge of an engine?"

"No, Sir; Mr. Pierce's education and training justified me in believing that he could handle the train properly."

"Do you believe any technical education in the shop witbout practical experience fits a man to be placed in charge of an engine to which is attached a passenger train?"

"Properly guided by a pilot and conductor, I say so, decidedly."

"You would do so at any time; if there had been no strike, you would select a man of that experience, would you?"

"I would do that under the circumstances we were"——

"Only under emergencies!"

"Yes, Sir."

"You would not say, generally, it is a wise thing for a railroad to do, would you?"

"I would say under circumstances such as we were left in, it was a wise thing for us to do."

What does the public think of this manifest indifference to any thing but "our" interest. The public interest must be subordinated to that of railroads, is the motto.

At Galesburg, similar conditions could be seen. The passenger trains from the west stopped according to agreement. The engines were vacated by the men, and there were no enginemen ready, in spite of the strenuous efforts of the officers. The passenger waited seven hours, and finally got started with Conductor Dewey at the throttle. The next train following this was also a passenger train, pulled by mogul engine No. 135, manned by one Chapman, who had been delivering engines for the Baldwin locomotive works. When he got about two and a half miles east of Galesburg, he stopped and stood there for about an hour and a half, when Master Mechanic Colville took the switch engine and went to see what was the matter, and got him started again and they reached Buda about 4:30 P. M., using more than six hours in making a distance of forty-five miles. Here he gave up the train and put the engine in the round house where it remained for three days, said to have been burned.[1] Zeb. Sammis was put on an engine pulling a passenger train between Galesburg and Quincy, so drunk he had to be helped on the engine. His son, W. C. Sammis, tried to persuade him not to go, and the officers of the company, Master Mechanic Colville and James Lindsey, road master, laughed at him and called Marshall Ennis, who told the son to go away or he would run him in.

[1] See evidence before Ill. Railroad Com.

THOMAS BRODERICK.

CHAPTER XXX.

THE STRIKE ALONG THE LINE.

At Beardstown as early as February 24, before the committee got home, the master mechanic and superintendent called the engineers all in to the master mechanic's office and asked them what they intended to do. The men being still in ignorance of what had happened in Chicago, they asked the superintendent what he meant, and he answered: "Don't you know that we are on the eve of a big strike?" and then produced the famous circular letter and tried its influence on them, but their only answer was, "We have nothing to say. We sent a man to Chicago to attend to our business, and whatever he did, we propose to stand by." This effort evidently did not prove very satisfactory, yet it furnishes further proof of the company's intentions. Business moved on as usual until Sunday, February 26, when Master Mechanic Wallis sent for the committee representing the engineers and firemen, Messrs. Wheatley and Sherman, and he wanted to know if they would furnish an engineer and firemen for the mail trains, and he was answered: "Certainly, if a government officer requests it; but will only pull mail cars, no coaches." Then Master Mechanic Wallis and Superintendent L. E. Johnson sent for the chief engineer of Division 127, P. J. Murrin. These officers told him they would appoint him traveling engineer, creating the office for that purpose, and it soon became evident that the officers thought by capturing the presumed leader they would break up the solidity of the men, but they were mistaken. When the hour came all business ceased, and on the morning of the 27th, they called every engineer and fireman to go, but all refused, and about 7:30 o'clock A. M., they got a machinist to run the engine, with the new traveling engineer to pilot and to educate. This train was for Rock Island. In their dire necessity, they took into their family one W. K Hollis. This man was in the employ of the company before at East St. Louis, as foreman, and General Manager Stone declaredin 1886 that he was a thief, and that he stole coal by the car-load and forged time checks. What a fall was there in a day, when the great C., B. & Q. takes back into its service the false, the disreputable and dishonest, recently branded as thief and drunkard!

At Beardstown, as elsewhere, all officers were brought into service. The shop foremen at Rock Island, East St. Louis, Monmouth, and other places, taking a new role with a bound. At East St. Louis, about forty engineers and firemen notified the officers that they would not resume their places on the engines of the C., B. & Q., at the same time telling them that no opposition would be made to men filling their places, nor would there be any obstacles to the movement of trains. However, the company secured Sergeant Langley with three policemen, to guard their property. The men on duty in the yard at East St. Louis began at midnight to make preparations to abandon their engines, and as there was little doing, several of the engines that ought to have been in the yard, were run into the roundhouse and deserted, and at four o'clock the shut down was complete. At Keokuk not a pound of freight was handled, and every engineer and fireman quit his post, and the St. Louis, Keokuk & Northwestern was tied up, with the exception of a passenger train which started from St. Peters, with a fireman named Burns, as engineer.

On the morning of February 27, the bulletin board at Creston, Iowa, contained the following: "Owing to the strike of the engineers and firemen, and consequent abandonment of all freight trains, this company will refuse to receive freight of any kind until further notice." The official energy on the whole Burlington system was centered on the effort to man the passenger trains. The first train to move was passenger No. 15, which went west, piloted by Traveling Engineer George Brown, engine No. 295, with Ernest Fritse, engineer, and Ernest Higgins, fireman, with two extra men in reserve. Train No. 61, south bound passenger, which should have gone out at 4:20 A. M., pulled out at 9:00, with ex-fireman J. C. Shoemaker as engineer, and Brown as fireman. No obstacles were placed in the way of any man who desired to work, and the enginemen said no force would be used or countenanced. All honorable means were employed to persuade the new men to stand with the Brotherhood, and they were empowered to hire them so to do. Passenger No. 8 was abandoned, and passenger No. 4 came in about 2:50 P. M. with only the mail cars, and the Brotherhood furnished Wm. Vangent to take them to Ottumwa. The coaches which should have been attached to No. 4, were brought in a second section and arrived at 4:30 P. M., with the engine manned by Conductor A. K. Stone, and Ed. Sheridan firing. Train No. 7 came in at 5:00 with only the mail cars, with Will and Chas. Flint as engineer and fireman, both Brotherhood men furnished on account of the mail. At the rear of No. 7 was attached Superintendent Brown's special car No. 50. On arrival at the station, Superintendent Brown entered the cab of the engine that was to pull No. 4, which had been deserted by the Brotherhood men, his car being placed in the rear of No. 4. A great crowd had gathered at the depot, and as Superintendent Brown pulled the throttle out, the condensed water from the cylinders and dry pipe went out through the stack, carrying with it all the soot and dirt and splashed over the bystanders, and the pounding and sputtering of the engine was great fun for the boys. Train No. 7 which arrived at five o'clock, did not get started until 6 P. M., when it left with Conductor Lon Stroud at the throttle. The next passenger came in about 8:20 P. M., with Mike Johnson, an ex-bartender of Ottumwa, as engineer. This train stood in the yard for two hours and finally was pulled out by Conductor Will Patten, with engine 210. No. 5 passenger came in on the morning of the 28th, with an ex-brakeman named Burnham running the engine, and two middle division conductors, Frank and Cloyd, firing for him. The effect of the strike at Quincy was disastrous to its business interests, it being practically cut off from railroad travel and traffic, except by the Wabash, and the Quincy Missouri and Pacific, which was through the northern countries of Missouri, and these roads were seriously affected, because the switching at this point was done by the Burlington engines. The system there embraced the main line, viz: Galesburg to Chicago, the Hannibal & St. Joseph, the Carthage branch, the St. Louis, Keokuk & Northwestern, and the Louisiana line. A desperate effort was made by the officers to get passenger trains through, the freight business, as at other points, receiving no attention. At Brookfield, the headquarters of the Hannibal & St. Joseph railroad, the superintendent's office was kept open all night, and each crew of engineer and fireman as they arrived, were called into the office and asked whether they would stay with the company, and all but one gave the same answer, whether they were members of either organization or not. One lone man, Wm. Hannum, had evidently entered into some contract, and on the morning of the 27th, he, with some other firemen, came into the hall occupied by the engineers and firemen and said: "He hoped God would paralyze his right arm if he ran an engine in the strike. The men did not believe him to be sincere, and they followed him to the depot and he acknowledged he was going, giving as a reason that he was in debt. The firemen offered to pay his debts, but to no purpose; he was willing to perjure himself before God and forsake his friends for the sake of getting an engine to run. He was a fireman, but not a member of that organization. He was the only man they obtained and he went out as engineer on the next fast passenger train. Superintendent Crance and Master Mechanic Wilber, of Brookfield, General Master Mechanic Paradise: and Traveling Engineer Johnson of Hannibal, and Foreman Thompson of Kansas City, did the work of engineers in the passenger train service. All officers, station agents, and some of the conductors, were searching in every direction for men; men who had been discharged, no matter what for, or what their character was. The road master was even looking among his section men for capable men to be put on the locomotives.

They agreed to give them protection and board them at some good hotel at the company's expense, during the strike. The officers, having watched the situation all night, and then during the day having to go on the engines themselves, were getting tired out and began to feel that they had got about to the end of their rope. About all the engineers and firemen on that road were located at Brookfield, and the officers found it a pretty hard matter to get an engineer or fireman to go out, for as fast as a new man would appear the men would induce him to go up to their room and he was not likely to withstand the appeals of the strikers. The officers ran in about thirty section men of all sorts and paid them for coming, in an effort to tire out the vigilance of the old men, but they did not succeed in this, as the old men put them through an examination which few could stand without some knowledge of the business, and they would soon give themselves away. Master Mechanic Wilber went out on No. 15 and met engine No. 4 manned by Foreman Thompson from Kansas City, when they changed; Thompson going back to Kansas City and Wilber back to Brookfield. General Master Mechanic Paradise ran from Hannibal to Quincy, and Traveling Engineer, Horace Johnson, ran from Palmyra Junction to Bucklin, where he met Superintendent S. E. Crance on No. 4, when they changed; Crance going back to Brookfield, and Johnson back to Palmyra Junction. No. 3 was without an engineer and there being no other road at Brookfield, the chances of hiring men at that point were very poor, owing to the incessant work of the old men to keep them away- On account of their inability to obtain men, their fast train had to be abandoned, and the officers finally con. cluded to run the engines through from Quincy to Kansas City, with two firemen and one engineer—226 miles. In this way they thought they could keep the strikers from getting a chance to talk to them. Trains No. 5 and 6—Cameron to Kansas City—were abandoned, and also Nos. 61, 62 and 64—Cameron to Atchison. Foreman Frank Johnson at Atchison, a carpenter by trade, was urged to take the engine on No. 63, but refused. He had never been fireman or engineer, and knew nothing about one. No. 64 was finally got off with a switch engineer from the East Tennessee, Virginia & Georgia railroad, Mr. Shetla. At Kansas City, all the men quit at the appointed time and put their engines in the roundhouse in first-class order; the hostlers quit also. The first attempt to run was passenger train No. 4, with Foreman Thompson acting as engineer, who knew nothing whatever about running an engine. The regular fireman refused to go, and a man was secured to go whom they called Cow Boy. He was dressed in cow boy style, with broad brimmed hat and belt. They finally pulled out after much chafing and delay, and on arriving at Brookfield the cow boy was treated to some Sam Jones argument and the company lost his services. The first train into Kansas City came on the Kansas City, St. Joseph & Council Bluffs road, with the engine manned by one Dudley. A squad of police immediately surrounded the engineer, but there was a large crowd gathered, and Dudley was greeted with: "Show your face!" "You will be afraid to face your own family!" etc., but no violence was offered. The Burlington advertised in the Kansas City papers.[1] "WANTED.—Competent engineers and firemen will be given permanent employment upon the lines of the Burlington system. Men entering our service will be paid full pay as per our schedule. We will give full protection and guarantee employment as long as they fulfill our requirements and prove competent. G. E. Fish, assistant superintendent of Hannibal, St. Joseph & Council Bluffs railroad." Mr. Fish evidently forgot that their company required three years' service to obtain these conditions of their old men, and Mr. Fish offers in this advertisement just what the men asked of the C., B. & Q. company; three and one-half cents per mile on passenger, and four cents per mile on freight. The Chicago, Rock Island & Pacific stopped the freight business of their road, which runs over the Burlington to Cameron Junction, because the latter was trying to get this freight handled by the Chicago, Rock Island & Pacific engines, by putting the cars in their trains. The Chicago, Kansas & Nebraska, also a part of the C., R. I. & P. system, when the men were asked not to run into a yard where scabs worked, tied up their road for about four hours. Finally the following dis-

[1] Kansas City Journal.

patch was received from P. M. Arthur: "Do not interfere with the Rock Island engineers and trains, so long as they maintain neutrality."[1] "Train No. 6, passenger, backed down to Union depot at five o'clock, an hour late, with an unknown man at the throttle, and the officials of the company said they did not know who he was. When it came to a stand-still, not less than three hundred people gathered around the engine, of all ages and classes. Several attempted to get into the cab but were driven back by the officers. Then they indulged in remarks at the expense of the engineer, a bearded old man who sat in the cab with the fortitude of a martyr. "What does he look like?" shouted one. "Does his mother know he's out?" "Look at his whiskers!" said another. "Come down and show yourself, pap!" "Let me have your photograph," etc. These and many similar remarks were made, and even the police had to laugh at the puns and good nature of the crowd."[1] The Eli train was abandoned, and the Eli and No. 2 passenger were made one train, not having any one to run the engine for the fast train. The same motley crowd of three hundred or more were there to see the fun. The official report of this occurrence is as follows: "No. 2 delayed at Kansas City, caused by about three hundred men around engine before train was due to leave, putting links in guides of engine 18, blocking wheels, throwing rocks at engine cab and coaches; train will be delayed here a short time doing work on engine. All pressure possible should be brought to bear on city authorities, in getting them to furnish officers to protect the company, and prevent strikers

[1] Kansas City Journal.

from hurting men who are willing to work." This is hardly just to the strikers, as there are none but switch engineers live in Kansas City, and there were but few road engineers there; yet it is in direct line with the following from Superintendent Fish who says: "In fact, many men have been turned away. No engineers have been hired who have not had charge of an engine at least one year, and the same rule was adopted for firemen. This rule was adopted by the company to prevent its trains from being intrusted to incompetent men, and to insure the customary safety to the passengers."[1] It is a notorious fact that Mr. Fish was taking whoever offered themselves, as did the officers at all other points. At St. Joseph City at the appointed hour, every engineer and fireman quit their post—about two hundred. The Burlington has several lines here; Kansas City, St. Joseph & Council Bluffs; Hopkins branch; Villisca branch, etc. It looked like Sunday at the Union depot and around the freight yards. The B. & M. Cannon Ball arrived on time, but was deserted by the engineer and fireman, and it was delayed two hours or more before it pulled out for Kansas City. No more trains arrived until 3:35 P. M., when No. 2 pulled in from Omaha, with Master Mechanic Bridenstein, of Council Bluffs, on the engine. When No. 2 pulled in, a striker stepped forward to speak with Master Mechanic Bridenstein, but was promptly pushed aside by Joseph Hanson, superintendent of the Union depot. When Chief of Police Broaden said: "The man had a perfect right to speak to the engineer on business," and allowed him to do so. He wanted to pursuade Bridenstein to leave the

[1] Kansas City Journal, Feb. 28, 1888.

engine. There was no loud talking among the strikers, but they were determined, and said that no violence would be used in the matter, and if they could not win in a peaceable manner, they did not want to win at all. General Manager Merrill stated that the company would not give an inch, as the demands of the strikers were unjust. "Morning of February 28: the report says of the previous day: passenger train due at 7:00 A. M., arrived at 2:00 P. M., with a Rosedale section foreman as engineer."[1] This train was from Creston, and the engine was manned with Shoemaker and Brown.[2] Conductor Lowridge said they reneged on him and the trip was continued with a section foreman from Rosedale as engineer, and brakeman Omer as fireman. Hannibal & St. Joseph No. 3 came in with Shetla, Atchison dummy line engineer in charge, who was induced to leave the engine. Kansas City, St. Joseph & Council Bluff's train came in four hours late, with Pat. Brown, a fireman, as engineer. No. 1 went north with Master Mechanic Steiger, of the St Joseph & St. Louis road as engineer. No. 11 came in nearly on time, and the engineer and fireman were induced to leave the engine, and they joined the strikers; then the hostler of the roundhouse was sent for and took the train out, two hours late.[2] "Joseph Hayward, road master, got his brother, Ben Hayward, out of the calaboose, and they put him on a passenger engine.[3] Men were put on engines at this point who never drew a cent of salary from any company as enginemen in any capacity; yet Superintendent Fish says: "No man is hired who has not had charge of an engine at least one year."[4] The officers em-

[1] Associated Press report. [2] Creston Advertiser. [3] Statement of citizens.
[4] Kansas City Journal.

ployed by the Burlington railroad put forth all their energies to save that company from defeat, and the company ought to be at least satisfied with their services. Their statements for the public were manufactured to suit the occasion, regardless of facts. "At Lincoln, about eighty trains, freight and passenger, depart daily over the Burlington system from this place. There are two hundred Burlington engineers and firemen who reside here."[1] "All these men quit, and the tie-up was complete from Chicago to Denver. The latter part of the day some trains were running, manned by conductors, train masters, dispatchers, master mechanics, and others who could be pressed into service, regardless of their fitness. One train was got out of Nebraska City, the engine being in charge of Road Master Filbrick. No trains arrived. The Kansas City passsenger train got as far as Pacific Junction, and the engineer and fireman refused to go farther. They were using mule teams instead of switch engines to switch with. A desperate effort was made to run all passenger trains except the Eli. which was abandoned."[2]

"At Denver, Colorado, February 26, the officers were notified that the strike would take place at 4:00 A. M. the 27th, and they made special effort to move eastward all the loaded coal cars for distribution along the line, in order that the people who depend upon the road for their fuel supply, might not suffer. No through passenger was sent out on the evening of the 26th, and the officers of the company questioned every passenger, and when they held through tickets over the Burlington, these were taken up and Union

Chicago Tribune. 2 Kansas City Journal.

Pacific tickets were given in place of them. Way passengers had no alternative, and had to take their chances. The Narrow Gauge, Denver, Utah and Pacific road, a branch of the Burlington, was also tied up. One train was finally got off from Denver, with a man named Dickerson as engineer, who consented to take it as far as McCook."[1]

[1] Kansas City Journal.

CHAPTER XXXI.

"MEN OF EXPERIENCE AND TRUSTWORTHY."

We have considered the conditions now at most of the important points from Chicago to Denver. The survey shows that the Burlington has succeeded, to some extent, in handling its passenger business, by putting into harness any man who would lend himself to help crush labor. Let us return as far as Creston, and see how much this company digressed from its own rules of highest practical requirements. In considering this question, we should remember that the C., B. & Q. company has required of their men from three to five years as firemen, and three years as engineers, to obtain that proficiency demanded by the Burlington system. At their general office at Chicago, a meeting of President Perkins, General Manager Stone, Paul Morton, and Chester M. Dawes of the legal department, decided to send out the following bulletin notice along the whole Burlington system: "Post immediately upon your bulletin boards, and in all conspicuous places, in and out of all depots in your division, the following notice: 'All engineers and firemen recently in the employ of this company, who do not apply for positions by noon of Wednesday, February 29, will be considered out of the company's service. Every man who has not applied by the above hour, can get all pay due him upon application to the master mechanic of his division.'" This notice had no effect whatever upon the men at any point, unless it was to strengthen them in their determination to stand fast. In speaking of this, the Creston Advertiser said: "There was no undue commotion here, and it is hoped there will be none. The Brotherhoods realize that any rashness or violence on their part would be in a measure, fatal to their cause, and any inclination on the part of hot-heads or impulsive members, will be promptly suppressed by the thoughtful and conservative men who are largely in the majority." Instead of going to any extremes, or doing anything unseemingly, they realized they were being introduced to a surprising kind of violence by the officers; violence against the rules under which they had been made to live, and that the officers were assigning any one to be engineer who would go. They then appointed a committee to go to Des Moines and wait on Governor Larrabee, and lay the subject before him, and ask that none but competent men be allowed on passenger engines.[1] To meet this, Superintendent W. C. Brown, of the Iowa division, telegraphed the following instructions to the general solicitor of the Burlington, who was then at the capital, watching the course of adverse railroad legislation:

Burlington, Iowa, February 28, 1888.

J. W. Blythe, Des Moines.

"I understand that a committee of engineers from Creston have gone to Des Moines to petition the governor not to allow incompetent and irresponsible men on passenger engines. You may say to Governor Larrabee if you think best, that our passenger engines

[1] Creston Advertiser.

are being run by men of experience, perfectly trustworthy and competent, and can give him a full assurance that no man will be put on passenger engines, or any other engine, except those possessing these qualifications. We think we are better calculated to judge in regard to the character and ability of men we employ, than the striking engineers, and we have certainly a great deal more at stake."

(Signed) W. C. Brown.

The facts obtained from personal acquaintance of the men assigned, and from the evidence before the Iowa railroad commissioners, do not bear Mr. Brown out in this statement, but on the contrary, they place his statement in a very bad light. We will describe briefly here, the men referred to as being unqualified: "First comes A. K. Stone, who has been employed on the West Iowa division for several years as conductor. He has never had any experience whatever as a locomotive engineer, and has acknowledged that he knew nothing of running an engine. L. H. Stroud, another conductor, has been pulling passenger trains, never having had any experience as an engineer. George Loughridge, C. A. Drake, Dempsey Ethridge, Dick Allen, John Erbert, Dan Hackett, and William Patten, all conductors of the Burlington, have been pulling passenger trains, and all of them have admitted that they know nothing of running a locomotive, and they are not reliable or efficient engineers. Mike Johnson, in charge of a passenger engine, was a bar tender at Ottumwa, and his experience consisted of a few months braking. Frank Mertz, a farmer, had been employed

GEORGE GODING.

about six weeks as fireman; was given a passenger engine to run. Ed. Sheridan, also from a farm, was employed only a few weeks as fireman; was placed in charge of an engine on passenger trains, and is one of those efficient men of Mr. Brown's. Chas. McClelland, a brakeman, had some experience as fireman, but was discharged two years before by the Burlington for incompetency, but has been considered equal to the occasion as an engineer. E. J. Sperry was a fireman for this company but was discharged for color blindness, but the officers having modified their conditions, he is accepted as a competent engineer. Richard Price, whose only experience as a railroad man was a few months as brakeman, and with no other experience, owing to the scarcity of competent men, he passed muster. Chas. Connet, whose only experience was as a baggageman, was given a passenger engine, with the promise of a life job. Ed. Young, a yard master at Pacific Junction, run the yard engine and succeeded in getting it on the Kansas City railroad crossing, and not knowing how to handle air, could not get off from it, and the Kansas City passenger train came along, with Master Mechanic Bridenstein at the throttle, and not stopping as he should for the crossing, ran into it, smashing up both engines. Bridenstein was arrested, but when trial came, by some magic, no one appeared against him and the case was dismissed."[1] And now, what does the reader think of Superintendent Brown's letter, wherein he says: "You can tell Governor Larrabee that our passenger engines are being run by men of experience, perfectly competent and trustworthy." The reader will remember, that up to three days

[1] Creston Advertiser.

before this, the Burlington required from three to five years as fireman, and then three years as an engineer before he became perfectly competent and reliable. They made the possession of this experience so important that no engineer's knowledge could be taken on testimony, but all men were required to go through these years of experience on the Burlington system. But now, if a man is willing to become the tool of this corporation,—one laboring man to grab at the throat of another—he is promised first-class place, regardless of his qualifications. He is even promised for the work of engineer, $4.00 per day and board, and for fireman, $2.25 per day and board, and Pinkerton protection thrown in. This is a sudden change. It guarantees pay, and certifies as to qualification, both in advance. No further evidence is needed that classification is not necessary, and is, as our men claim, wrong in principle. Every effort possible was made by the officials of the Burlington to bias public opinion, and the liberties taken with the truth were marvelous. "From Lincoln, no trains moving west of McCook. Superintendent Calvert said he had men, but he was unwilling to send them out unprotected, because he had reason to fear violence on the western division, and he also said the trains would soon be running as usual, if the people would show the company the sympathy they really felt."[1] The reader will see later how much sympathy there was for the Burlington in Nebraska.

[1] Kansas City Journal.

CHAPTER XXXII.

WHO CAME.

To return to Aurora: Division Master Mechanic Forsyth sent the following telegram to General Manager Stone: "The firemen and engineers have boycotted stores from selling our men provisions; can't get anything to eat. Have dining car sent. Can't you make arrangements to get us provisions from Chicago?"

From the *Aurora Express*: "A BIG LIE SOMEWHERE. LET US LOOK FOR IT.—An *Express* representative called on all the Main street provision stores, and showed them the above, and they said there was not a word of truth in it as far as they knew, and said it was an outrage to publish such a thing. He showed it to the leading members of the Brotherhood who said they had never thought of such a thing and did not believe Forsyth had sent it.

Mr. Forsyth himself was next seen and when shown the dispatch said it was *correct*. A reporter, in further tracing the facts, discovered that the only foundation for the story is that Grampp, who keeps a saloon and hotel near the depot, had told two of the new men that he thought it was not to his interest to keep them." A concerted effort was made along the whole line to make it appear that an armed force was necessary to prevent the destruction of property and loss of life, and thereby turn the tide of public opinion against the old men The local papers along the whole line evidence the fact that the conduct of the old men was beyond reproach and whatever hoodlum element there was afloat was brought in by the Burlington. The *Chicago News*[1] said: "At the General offices this morning the rush of applicants for positions was even greater than yesterday. Not less than a hundred men crowded and hustled each other outside G. W. Rhodes' office. The crowd was of the same motley character as that of yesterday. Some of the men were respectable looking, well dressed fellows. Others were men of gray beards and venerable mein, whose only commendable qualities would appear to be that they were veterans at the business, if they were ever in it at all. There was another class, whose bearing, dress, and general deportment bespoke the genus Bum."

"The false and sensational reports from Aurora, published in the Chicago daily papers, deserve the most severe denunciation. The strikers have been peaceable and orderly; have made no attempt to interfere violently with railroad traffic, and are numbered among our best citizens. But, while they enjoy the esteem of the public, there is on the other hand, no ground for the report that the people of Aurora are hostile to the Burlington road. Aurora deplores the strike because of its injurious effect upon the business of the city. We should be glad to see the difficulty speedily adjusted on the basis of mutual concessions and compromise to prevent further losses, not only to the community directly, but indirectly through losses suffered by the road, and the enginemen who are residents here."[2]

This is a fair sample of public opinion all along the line outside of Chicago, and it furnishes proof that the

[1] February 28, 1888. [2] Aurora, (Ill.) Beacon.

desire for selfish leadership characterizes the officials to a greater degree than the strikers. The utter disregard of gentlemanly dealing, and the violation of the rules of their own making, by the officials, became an aggravation to the men. The Burlington men passed from the strictest enforcement of discipline to an utter disregard of their own laws, so as to be able on one hand to take on unqualified and disreputable men, and on the other to make it impossible for their former employes to return. Their motto seemed to be: "We stoop to conquer."

The engineers and firemen kept their halls open day and night. Every strange face that appeared on the scene secured their attention. If he was inclined to work for the Burlington, his manliness was appealed to, and if that appeal did not succeed he was hired if possible, and most of those who came first, came under a misconception of the situation and could be easily persuaded to go away and leave the battle to be fought by the interested parties. Many of these were given something for expenses, while others were void of principle and put a selling price on themselves, ranging from $10 to $50. Hundreds were in various ways persuaded to leave.

The picture was filled with all phases of humanity, from the appearance of high respectability to the level of the gutter; Knight Templar, Knight of Pythias, Odd Fellow, B. of L. E., B. of L. F., G. A. R., K. of L., and the man of every known order, who had sworn allegiance to his fellow man, converted into a lie his solemn oath, taken before God and man, and took the place of those whom he had sworn to protect.

It was an astounding picture of human depravity. The legal and moral right of unobligated men to take the places made vacant was not questioned, yet when men had taken an obligation, solemn as a marriage vow, no man could take his brother's place, and retain his character. An occasional grain of gold however, was mixed with the dross. A letter was received at Brookfield, and enclosed was the following message:

BROOKFIELD, Mo., Feb. 28, 1888.

WILLIAM FULTON, Chapin, Ill.

Do you want to take position on the Hannibal & St. Joseph R. R, on regular engine? If so, answer and say if you will report here or at Quincy, at once.

S. E. CRANCE, Supt.

The following is Mr. Fulton's letter:

CHAPIN, ILL., March 20, 1888.

MR. C. H. SALMONS,

Dear Sir:—I hope you will excuse me for taking the liberty of writing you. I wish to send you a dispatch I received from Superintendent Crance, February 28. I do not know where he got my name, neither do I care. I have been out of work six months, but Mr. Crance knows now that he addressed the wrong man for a scab. I would rather have the good will of my fellow man than the great monopoly—C., B. & Q. road. I am not a member of any labor order, and whether my action is appreciated or not, I shall feel that I have done as I would be done by. Wishing you success, I remain, Yours Truly,

WM. FULTON.

It was a pleasant relief from the nauseating duty of appeal to honor, and from the purchase of the souls and the bodies of men, to realize that hundreds who received offers of places from the company had, nevertheless, sufficient integrity to practice the grand truth uttered by the Italian patriot, Mazzini: "It is around the standard of duty, rather than the standard of self-interest, that men must rally to win the rights of men."

"Thousands of years ago, monarchs were everything, and the masses were nothing. Millions of men could be herded to fight the battles of a king, or to pile the pyramids which should be his tomb; the lash was over them; they could only obey. They might wail, it was nothing; they might die, there were other millions to take their places beneath the burdens and the lash."[1] And so it seemed then, as though the educational forces of the age had been inverted, and the bettering of the conditions of labor, through Mazzini's principles, was to be destroyed by the very element which created it. The striking enginemen were astonished at the number of persons who, blinded by greed and selfishness, were willing to lend themselves to the Burlington monopoly, to violate all principles, and accept a place that was made possible only by the sacrifice of others.

Many said they had come for bread, others for revenge. Every one had an excuse. I never met one who defended his action, because he thought the Burlington was in the right. The vigilance of the strikers, their presevering appeals, their money and their friends, made the situation anything but agreeable

[1] Rev. C. O. Brown.

for the officers of the company. They were tired out trying to get the passenger trains over the road themselves. They were hunting in every direction for some one who would lend their assistance. Letters and ·messages were sent to old employes who had been discharged for drunkenness; men were accepted without experience, from prison, from the gutter; yet the market was open on Mr. Stone's principle of supply and demand. The persuasion of the strikers, and their money, were always diminishing the supply. The officers said: "As fast as we get them, the gang (meaning the strikers) gets hold of them, and they are gone." There came a corner on the market of supply and demand.

The company gained control of state and municipal authority to accomplish their purpose. Officers along the Burlington were notified by the managers, to see the sheriff, have shop men, carpenters, and others that could be used, sworn in as deputies, and to keep the strikers away, and to post notices of warning in all conspicuous places. Sheriffs, without regard to the necessity, readily responded. At Brookfield, one hundred and forty-seven men were sworn in as deputies Their character and fitness were not known by the sheriff, who is responsible for their acts. They were taken from a list of names furnished by the Burlington company. Not the slightest disturbance had occurred to create a necessity. The city marshal had not even been spoken to on the subject, and none existed so far as the public was aware. But the company wanted a demonstration, for two reasons: "1st, to keep the strikers away, so they could not entice or hire their new men. 2nd, a demonstration to make people believe violence was threatened." Kansas City, St. Joseph and all the cities along the line, were appealed to to furnish a police force to guard the company's property.

The officers did not make any direct charge that the strikers were trying to destroy their property; yet whatever demonstration was made by them which had the appearance of guarding against violence, naturally reflected upon the old enginemen, in the minds of the public. Accordingly, the greater the demonstration the better for the company. "At Chicago a suburban train which stopped at the C. C. and I. C. crossing, was reported as having been boarded by four men, who got on the engine, said a few words to the engineer, and got off, and this crew reported that a coupling pin was put in the engine's guides for the purpose of breaking it down. There was no proof that it was the strikers. An old conductor who had been with the company for years, was on the engine, and knew none of them." "At 9:30 A. M., as the preliminaries of starting were being arranged, half a dozen police officers kept jealous watch over the engine. No one was allowed to approach it except those in charge. The cause of this extra vigilance was due, it was claimed, to the attempt on the suburban train. However, the half dozen or so who witnessed the departure of the train, did not seem inclined to destroy things, and kept a respectful distance without the persuasions of either fists or batons."[1]

At 12:01 P. M. another train was started. "The engine was guarded by a squad of police as before,

[1] Chicago Evening News.

and no one was allowed within three yards of the engine. A small crowd witnessed the departure of the train, but no attempt was made to interfere with it in any way." "The crowd of applicants, so far, had been in no way interfered with or molested by the strikers, the latter having been, in fact, conspicuous by their absence from the precincts of the offices and depot ever since the strike was inaugurated," yet every demonstration of this character carried with it a supposition in the minds of the public that the necessity existed, and it was naturally laid at the doors of the strikers, and the greater the demonstration, the greater the reflection. The laws of both engineers and firemen prohibit the molestation of property under penalty of expulsion. The weeding out process, the effect of their rules, would naturally leave men of character, and they were greatly annoyed to have it traduced by such demonstrations which later became monotonous, both in number and kind.

We have said before, that whatever of the radical was found among the strikers later, was an outgrowth of the feeling that their character was being unjustly traduced. The war of the rebellion produced a Booth; politics produced a Guiteau. It is simply impossible to have a strike like the Burlington, with one side all honor, every man living up to the standard of equity and good deportment, and every man on the other side a miserable fraud—the motto of one side: "Do as you would be done by;" the other: "Might makes right." It is a known fact that the two orders of engineers and firemen deprecated all acts in violation of the true principles of good citizenship. No degree of vigilance, however, can dissever every evil element. The act of an individual, in violation of the principles of the institution of which he is a member, should not be charged as emanating from that institution, but he should be tried as an individual offender, and when convicted, if the society of which he is a member does not purge itself by expulsion or punishment, it can reasonably be charged as an accessory. But the Burlington's deputy sheriffs, Pinkerton bullies, with their repeating rifles and their court proceedings, menacing the interests of the public and usurping its powers, were meekly submitted to without protest. The public hardly seemed to notice the ready submission of sheriffs, police, and courts to the will of a corporation.

Nor was the public mind at all shocked at the violation of moral principle in the Burlington's defence of its bums and drunkards, which had been gathered up to man their engines. Even reputable newspapers, which ought to be the channels of truthful information, and by means of which the public mind is educated, seemed to be as indifferent as a railroad official to either justice or truth. They were closed to the discussion of the points at issue. I have been credibly informed that a leading newspaper charged as high as forty-five cents per line for space for the defense of the much assailed men. Some newspapers, just at the first, discussed the question of rights and the relation and duties of railroads to the public, but very soon something closed their pages against anything not emanating from a Burlington official, directly or indirectly. As an effort to buy silence, we append the following sample of letter sent to the newspapers along the Burlington system to control the public press:

Creston, Iowa, April 6, 1888.

Chicago, Burlington & Quincy Railroad,

Mr. E. J. SIDEY, editor Commonwealth:

Dear Sir:—If in unison with your views, give the company some nice editorials commenting on the strike. It occurs to me our citizens ought to shield the company as far as possible, as their interests are identical with our people. While our people give the company considerable cash in return, the company, through their different avenues, keep a volume of money flowing through the arteries of Creston industries. In return will endeavor to get you value received, but do not turn the flag of truce on me in return."[1] Very Truly,

(Signed) G. W. FOGG.

The allurements of such bate, so nice and tempting, no doubt led many editors to believe that the Burlington was in a bad way, and needed defending. Yet for all the influence used, there were some editors who stood for justice and discussed the question fearlessly. It is a notable fact that most of these editors were personally acquainted with the striking enginemen and the circumstances surrounding them. The editor of the St. Joseph, Mo., *Gazette* was true to his convictions, as were also the editors of the *Railway News Reporter*, Omaha, Neb.; Wymore *Democrat*, Neb.; *News*, Atchison, Kans.; *Railway Service Gazette*, Toledo, Ohio.; *National Car and Locomotive Builder*, Chicago; *Railroad and Engineering Journal*,

1 Chicago World, May 20, 1888.

New York City; Elmira, New York, *Telegram*; the Creston, Iowa, *Advertiser*; Chicago. *World;* and St. Joseph, Mo., *Patriot;* also a few labor papers. But the great majority of the papers were on the side of monopoly regardless of public interest. This placed the strikers, not by direct charges, but by implications in a very unfavorable light, going so far as to say that "If chief Arthur, or Chief Powderly, or chief anybody else, inveighs against interference or violence, he is guilty of willful hypocrisy."

Such inferences carry with them in the mind of the reader—unacquainted with the character of the men alluded to—the idea of socialism, and other issues that are abhorrent to the honest laborer, and more so than to any other class. What class would do what the laborer did at Cleveland? "In the great parade on labor day at Cleveland a few anarchists scorning the flag of the union, hoisted the hated emblem of anarchy. This insult to the glorious flag of the republic fired the loyal hearts of the patriotic sons of toil, and as a result the anarchists were most unceremoniously fired from the grounds with broken heads and bloody noses." Some of these papers seemed to express surprise that these laboring men should have been so prompt to resent an insult to the public. More loyal and patriotic hearts do not beat in America than those beneath the broad chests of the men whose strong arms have made the republic what it is, and who in the machine shops, upon her railroads and in her fertile fields, are still clearing her pathway to greater future glory. In the late war between the north and south, was it the representatives of capital alone that offered their blood for the cause they believed to be just?"[1] The Burlington strikers were as honest in their convictions, and were as ready with their sacrifices to maintain them, as were the men of 1861 to 1865.

But the weight of all this pressure bore heavily upon these men, and as we look at it now, after the smoke of battle has cleared away, we wonder at the unanimity with which they stood the test, and held steadfast. Very few were affected sufficiently to turn back to the company, which was no doubt greatly desired. I am reminded of one man—James Johnson, of Galesburg, Ill.,—who said "He did not expect to live long enough to live down the disgrace of being a C., B. & Q. striker." Such men as this have lived in all ages, and in all countries. They are the enemies of progress. They are, however, always ready to accept the benefits earned by others, and this man no doubt, influenced partly by the newspapers, more by his inane greed, forgetful that his vote and voice had been joined with his brothers, turned his back upon them and honor, and joined that company better suited to his nature—"the scabs." To more fully show the one-sided character of the controversy as presented in the leading newspapers, we give in the next chapter, quotations from the Chicago Journals.

[1] Railway Service Gazette,

CHAPTER XXXIII.

PUBLIC OPINION MADE TO ORDER.

The famous Creston letter is made the foundation for the following editorials on March 3:

The *Chicago Mail* said: "The fact must not be overlooked that the striking engineers have assumed a grave responsibility, and that among those who will suffer, are thousands not interested in the fight between the railroads and its employes. It is a serious thing to cripple business, to interfere with the movements of the traveling community, and possibly, in the end, to have caused violence and bloodshed. If the strike now on becomes otherwise than peaceable in any of its features, the public will not be tolerant. It requires a great deal of patience on the part of the community at any time to endure a strike where the crippled employer is a public servant, for the first evil effects in such a case are felt by the people at large. The present strike is of the sort referred to. It hurts the public at once, and seriously. The public will not submit to it if the fight is greatly prolonged. If, as in the great strike of 1877, there is violence from any source the sentiment of chafing endurance will change at once to one of earnest aggressiveness and somebody will be punished. It is well that those conducting the warfare should bear the attitude of the people in mind."

The Chicago *Evening Journal* said: "The unbiased and disinterested person who examines the existing controversy between the Chicago, Burlington and Quincy railroad and its striking engineers and firemen, will find it difficult to reach a conclusion justifying some of the demands of the strikers. Their requests are in some respects extraordinary and indefensible. How much the general public may be disposed to sympathize with the engineers, who as a class are intelligent, courageous, and self-sacrificing men, yet they cannot reasonably expect public support in unreasonable demands. The sooner this entire controversy shall be submitted to intelligent arbitration, and adjusted upon a basis of reason and justice, the better for all concerned. Even if the demands of the engineers are worthy of favorable consideration, and the object of arbitration should be to ascertain and pass on the actual merits of the case, no time should be lost by either side to bring the unfortunate contest to a speedy termination by all rational and practical means in their power."

The *Chicago Tribune* said in an editorial article: "Taken in connection with the vital and fundamental demand for a leveling up of wages and leveling down of general efficiency, individual merit and the incentive to personal effort and ordinary ambition on the part of the employes of the road, we should say, without further light upon the subject than we now possess, that the Brotherhood have crowded the company to the extreme limit of endurance. It may be that there is some supplement to this correspondence that has not been given to the public and that the Brotherhood has offered to recede from some part of the orig-

J. J. KELLEY.

THE INFORMER.

inal programme; as the reply of the railroad company, however, is dated only last Wednesday, this does not seem to be probable. If there has been no modification since Wednesday, we risk nothing in saying to the representatives of the Brotherhood, that whatever the issue of the strike may be they will not be sustained as to the justice of their course by public opinion. It will be said everywhere that they have attempted to impose the intolerable despotism of an outside labor council upon the manager of this great property, going so far as to suggest interference with them in the discharge of legitimate and necessary duties. If the case is susceptible of no further explanation, the managers will be upheld by impartial men in resisting, by every means and all the resources at their command, such a proposed invasion of their rights."

The Chicago *Daily News:* "There can be no question that the system which recognizies a difference in ability of men and in the kind of service required of them is right, and that the demand which classes all members of the Brotherhood as of equal ability, and all kinds of service of equal value is wrong. In its application of its system to individual cases the company may possibly be seriously at fault. In principle, however the system itself is fair and right. In view of its long and honorable career, it is a suprise and a disappointment to all true friends of organized labor to find the Brotherhood of Locomotive Engineers taking a position so inconsistent with all the prevailing conceptions of American manhood. It must abandon so untenable a position or lose not only the present fight, but more important still, the respect and confidence of the American people."

The Chicago *Inter Ocean* and *Herald* were conservative and just, but the Chicago *Times* said: "The last general strike of the Locomotive engineers inflamed the nation to the verge of revolution. Scores of lives were wantonly sacrificed. The people were appalled by the sight of blood and fire, and Pittsburg paid an indemnification bill of $13,000,000 and even then was not fitly punished for the demagogical countenance it lent to the lawless. The Brotherhood has "lived down" the responsibility for the calamity of ten years ago. Chief Arthur has been commended for his sterling sense. The past has been forgotten and forgiven, and the heroic duties performed by the engineers have elicited, from all classes, unstinted admiration."

"No great strike, after what has taken place, can bring anything but defeat, unless it shall invoke a universal spirit of revolution, and the American people have given their final verdict against revolution and rebellion. Mr. Arthur says they have a right to stop work, and that they have no intention of interfering with persons employed to take their places. He knows that the object of the strike would be negatived by orderly withdrawal and non-resistance. Such action would be equivalent to resignation. A strike means but one thing; to refuse to work and to make sure that nobody else is permitted to work in your place, and when Chief Arthur, or Chief Powderly, or chief anybody, inveighs against interference or violence, or aids to the cause, he is guilty of willful hypocrisy. Chief Arthur has called this strike. If it shall prove harmful to commerce, and shall invite disorder and loss of life, the public will hold him and his co-adjutors to a strict accountability."

The opinions of the *Mail*, *Journal*, and *Tribune* are no doubt the result of the seed sown by the Burlington circular letter. But that of the *Times* is a wonderful exhibition of bigotry and untruth, and if it was not written by some official of the Burlington, the writer must have had some inducement other than that of a desire to guide public opinion to the truth. The charge that the engineers were responsible for the Pittsburg strike and its consequences, and the allusion to the people of Pittsburg, was adding insult to untruth. These lines from the *Times* betray an underlying baseness and disregard for truth and fairness that is astounding, and after reading them, nothing in or about the paper should surprise us. The Chicago *Herald*, of July 24, 1889, had a column and a half of discussion of the character of the editor of the *Times*, J. J. West, not even sparing accusations of obtaining money by false representations and of bribe giving, and it is no wonder, if there is any foundation for such charges, that articles vituperative and malicious, written either for him or by him, should appear in his paper. Yet they were read, and exercised a powerful influence in forming public opinion. They created difficulties, if not dissensions, among men in the interest of organized labor, weakening conservative men, and abating that heroic defence of their principles which is so essential to success.

It is greatly to be regretted that the engineer's side of the question was not before the people as well.

It is a sad reflection upon the public educators of a great country, as our newspapers undoubtedly are for good or for evil, that they should become such violent partisans on one side, when the facts in the case were so easily obtainable, and were so contradictory to the statements which they made. It is not unreasonable to believe that the literary ability employed in writing the famous circular letter, to which we have given respectful notice, was quite equal to the writing of any of the editorials which are honored with quotation in this chapter.

CHAPTER XXXIV.

THE USAGES OF OTHER ROADS.

It is very curious that the requests upon the Burlington should call forth such vehement denunciation of the conditions asked, when so many companies had acknowledged their justness with their signature. We append portions of the Atchison, Topeka & Santa Fe schedule, with like conditions which the Burlington objected to, and were so roundly condemned by these editors.

ATCHISON, TOPEKA & SANTA FE RAILROAD COMPANY.

SOUTHERN KANSAS RAILWAY COMPANY.

MECHANICAL DEPARTMENT.

"The following schedule of rates, rules and regulations, are hereby agreed upon on behalf of the above specified companies and the engineers and firemen employed thereby."

ARTICLE I.—"No engineer or fireman shall be suspended or discharged upon any charge whatever, without first having a fair and impartial hearing and his guilt shall be established, with the exception of aggravated cases, such as serious collisions or intoxication."

"There shall be a board of inquiry, composed of the division superintendent, division master mechanic, and one disinterested engineer from the division on which complaint may arise, whose duty it shall be to investigate all charges of misconduct on the part of the engineers and firemen. The right to appeal from local to general officers, as also the right of the engineers or firemen to act as a committee on conference, will be duly recognized, and leave of absence from duty will be granted for that purpose."

ARTICLE II. "Engineers entering the service of the company for the first time shall be employed by the superintendent or assistant superintendent of machinery."

ARTICLE III. "All firemen who are to be promoted to the position of engineer will be examined by the superintendent or assistant superintendent of machinery. The division master mechanic may recommend for examination and promotion such firemen on their respective divisions as they believe will make good engineers, always giving the oldest firemen the preference."

ARTICLE IV. "It being important to the company that every engine in service shall be worked to its fullest capacity, and in order that there may be no misunderstanding between the transportation and mechanical departments as to what is the working capacity of an engine in service, the rating as to the average load to be hauled will be fixed from time to time, as necessities may require, by the general superintendent and superintendent of machinery, who will jointly furnish the division officers all necessary instructions pertaining thereto."

ARTICLE V. "The compensation of engineers and firemen in passenger service shall be as follows: Engineers—On all classes of locomotives, $3.50 per 100 miles, or less, per day; all over 100 miles, three and one-half (3½) cents per mile; except on engines hauling passenger trains over the mountains, which shall be three and three-fourths (3¾) cents per mile. Firemen—On four-wheel coupled engines, fifty-three (53) per cent of the engineer's pay, and on other than four-wheel coupled engines, fifty-five (55) per cent of the engineer's pay. Eight hours shall constitute a day's work for engineers and firemen in passenger service, and no overtime will be allowed until those hours are exceeded. When the schedule for any train exceeds eight hours, all delays of more than one hour beyond the schedule will be paid for at the rate of eighteen (18) cents per half hour for engineers, and ten (10) cents per half hour for firemen."

ARTICLE VI. "The compensation of engineers and firemen in freight service shall be as follows: Engineers—On all classes of locomotives, $4.00 per 100 miles, or less, per day: all over 100 miles, four (4) cents per mile: except on engines hauling freight trains over the mountains, which shall be four and one-third (4⅓) cents per mile. Firemen—On all four-wheel coupled engines, fifty-five (55) per cent of the engineer's pay: and on other than four-wheel coupled engines, fifty-eight (58) per cent of the engineer's pay."

ARTICLE X. "Ten hours shall constitute a day's work for engineers and firemen in freight service, and no overtime will be allowed until those hours are exceeded. When the schedule for any train exceeds ten hours, all delays of more than one hour beyond the schedule will be paid for at the rate of eighteen (18) cents per half hour for engineers, and ten (10) cents per half hour for firemen. Ten miles per hour shall be considered the running time of extra or irregular trains and all scheduled trains that do not reach ten miles per hour. A delay of fourteen minutes over the hour shall not be counted: a delay of fifteen minutes over the hour shall be considered a half hour."

ARTICLE XIII. "When an engine is ordered out and not used on account of train being abandoned, or other cause, the engineer of such engine shall be allowed one-third of a day's pay for the division and class of engine, and stand first out on the board."

ARTICLE XV. "Engineers and firemen shall not be required to go out when they need rest, and are expected to judge for themselves whether they need rest. When engineers or firemen feel that they require rest, and will be unable to go out, they must report same to roundhouse foreman when they register their arrival. Eight hours shall be considered sufficient for rest."

ARTICLE XVI. "Engineers and firemen shall be promoted according to seniority and ability on their respective divisions, unless incapacity is established. Engineers having engines and runs they are not entitled to according to the terms of the agreement made between the company and engineers July 1, 1886, shall be removed, and said engines and runs given to the men according to seniority on their respective divisions. The foregoing to apply to all roads covered by said agreement. In case of a dispute between the company and the engineers as regards seniority, the engineers shall furnish a list, which shall be accepted unless proven to be in error. Seniority of engineers

FRED GEYER, FOREMAN OF THE BURLINGTON LOCOMOTIVE DEPARTMENT, AT AURORA, ILL., MAKING HIS FIRST AND LAST EFFORT TO BE AN ENGINEER, FEB. 27, 1888.

shall be reckoned from the time of entering road service on their respective divisions."

ARTICLE XVII. "Engines will be run 'first in first out,' except when the superintendent of machinery finds it necessary to assign engines to certain fast runs, which will be done only when absolutely necessary."

ARTICLE XX. "Engineers' and firemen's time will commence at time of the departure of train, as designated in caller's book, and trip tickets will be dated accordingly. In cases where the roundhouse register and train sheets conflict as to arrivals, the matter will be investigated, and, if proper, the time of engineers and firemen taken from the roundhouse register."

ARTICLE XXIII. "Hostlers shall be provided at all terminal stations, whose duty it is to take engines on arrival. Engineers or firemen shall not be required to put away engines, clean fires, or blow out fronts at terminal stations."

ARTICLE XXIV. "Engineers and firemen, after being permanently located on a division, who shall be transferred at the request of the company, shall have the privilege of returning to their respective divisions before any others are hired or promoted on the divisions from which they were transferred."

ARTICLE XXV. "The company on its part, and the engineers and firemen on their part, agree that they will perform the several duties and stipulations as provided for in this agreement until thirty days' notice has been given by either party to the other requesting a change in the same."

ARTICLE XXVI. "In case a difference of opinion

as to the construction of this.agreement shall arise between the engineers or firemen and division officers, a written state of the questions at issue must be submitted by the engineers or firemen, as the case may be, to the general manager, through the division officers, and superintendent of machinery, for his construction. Grievances, to be considered, must be presented within sixty days after their occurrence."

ARTICLE XXVII. "On the adoption of the foregoing schedule, rules and regulations, all previous schedules, rules and regulations shall become void. This agreement shall be in affect from and after February 1st, 1888."

For Atchison, Topeka & Santa Fe Railroad Co.,
GEO. HACKNEY, Supt. of Machinery.

For Southern Kansas Railway Company.
GEO. HACKNEY.

For Locomotive Engineers and Firemen on A. T. & S. F. R. R. and So. Kas. Ry.

I. CONROE, Chairman. WM. M. HAMILTON, Secretary.

This is a Boston company, and the president, Mr. W. B. Strong, said in an address to the stockholders: "Wise leaders, honest and intelligent counselors, working with and for the welfare of the workers in any branch of industry, can accomplish much for the advancement of its members, but a demagogue is as bad in one place as in another; wherever he is, he does harm, but in my judgment the interests of the engineers and of whom they serve, as well, also, of the public, who are primarily most concerned, have been, and will be promoted, by maintaining the organization and following the just, fair, and conservative policy, which has generally characterized the Order." This high compliment was paid the engineers and firemen, after they had shown such loyalty to their Orders as to stop work in sympathy with the Burlington men, who were so severely condemned by the Chicago papers.

The request for changed and better terms, as made in the schedule presented to the Burlington authorities, was not new in railroad usages. It was only the rate generally in vogue which was demanded. Here is a short list that could be extended for pages, of leading trunk lines with the dates affixed at which they made distinct and formal orders covering the same contract rates of pay, demanded by the engineers of the C., B. & Q. road.

Union Pacific, April 1, 1887.
Chicago Milwaukee & St. Paul, Dec. 16, 1887.
San Antonio & Arkansas Pass, Jan. 1, 1888.
Southern Pacific, Jan. 15, 1888.
Fort Scott & Gulf, Mar. 1, 1888,
Chicago & Alton, Feb. 1, 1888.
Atchison, Topeka & Santa Fe, Feb. 1, 1888.
Southern Kansas R. R. Co., Feb. 1, 1888.

Necessity has compelled combined action in railroad service, and the increase of magnitude of the corporate holding has increased the necessity.

I have before me a pamphlet emanating from seventy-five engineers of the Michigan Southern railroad, bearing date, January 13, 1886. It is a protest to the directors and stockholders of the road. It says: "Our trouble dates from a few weeks after the appointment to the road of a new officer, that of General Master Mechanic, Mr. Segley, who had not been here long before he decided that the engineers—to use his own language—"know to much." He seemed to think it very necessary for the interest of the company to employ men who know less; and in order to bring this about, he commenced a system of petty annoyances. Mr. Segley, without giving any notice that the rules had been changed, under which the engineers and firemen of your road had been paid for years, made a new departure as to extra time. By the rules of the road, extra time was allowed in all cases, after a man had run over one hundred and thirty miles in twenty-four hours. An engineer on the western division ran his engine one hundred and eighty miles within twenty-four hours, and Mr. Segley told the time-keeper not to allow the usual extra. We had always been allowed five engines, to runs number 1, 2, 3 and 8 on the western division. Mr. Segley decided that they must be run with four engines, and no pay for Sunday work. The men, on drawing their pay, found the time from four to six days short of the time that should have been allowed according to their agreement with the company. On the Air Line, engineers have had to run their engines thirteen times over the road—the distance is one hundred and twenty-three miles—within seven days.

The collision on the Air Line at Millersburg, between passenger train No. 9, and a freight engine, in which engineer Charles Dunewell was killed, was one of the results of forcing tired out men to go beyond endurance. If a man refused to go out, on account of being completely used up, he would have to lose the time. We tried to have an interview with Mr. Segley but he would not listen to any "committee," or that he would not be questioned, and we found it impossible to induce him to give us a hearing. He would say, "If you do not like it, leave." Mr. Segley discharged four men from the service on the western division without giving any reason for it except that they were not wanted. No fault was found with them, neither was it pretended that any duty had been neglected, but that the falling off of business necessitated a reduction of staff. At the same time Mr. Rice of Chicago was, by the instructions of Mr. Segley, hiring men to fill the places of these old and tried servants of the company. One of our engineers obtained a leave of absence for one day. It came to the ears of the master mechanic that he was doing it in order to try and lay our grievances before the higher officers of the road. His leave was recalled, and he was ordered to go out, which he refused to do, and he was discharged. Another engineer came into La Porte completely tired out. His engine had to go on through, and he was ordered to go on with her. He told the officer that he had fallen asleep twice before arriving at La Porte, although he had taken all the precaution possible to prevent it, not even allowing himself to sit down. It was still insisted that he should go. He said that he would not endanger the lives of the passengers, by running an engine while asleep, for the whole southern road, and positively refused to go out again until he had some sleep. He was immediately discharged. These facts were testified to by seventy-five men, and when these facts were presented, the president, Mr Phillips, answered: "I decline to interfere with any action taken by my subordinates." S. H. Egerly. of the Michigan Central railroad, in 1877 and 1878, is another startling instance of this personal management, of browbeating, of arrogant assumption, demanding even the manhood of the men under him, while the higher officers looked on complacently, and declined to interfere with any action taken by their subordinates. This kind of men can be found in every branch of railroad service, and probably always will be found, and the smaller the official position the greater the aggravation. If these editors cannot defend such men as Messrs. Segley and Egerly, who are identified with nothing but themselves and their salary; then these great deprecators of organized labor, and defenders of corporations, must acknowledge that organized labor conducted upon right principles, has been a necessity, and has affected a cure, at least in a great measure, by securing laws to govern the avarice and personality that enter so largely into corporate authority. The counterparts of Mr. Segley live to-day; and are in place along the line of the C., B. & Q. railroad. President Perkins, like President Phillips, refused to intervene. The officials are privileged to squander millions of other people's money in an attempt to foster a wrong, and the Chicago papers are helping by publishing one side of a contest that involves the rights of thousands; while many of the newspapers, in their editorials, are defending corporations and making incisive allusions to the engineers and firemen, giving them to understand that violence will not be tolerated. And that, if the strike shall prove harmful to commerce, and shall invite loss of life, Chief Arthur and his co-adjutors shall be held to a strict accountability. But while they gave so much space to condemn and advise the enginemen, no word was spoken against the usurpation of state and municipal authority by the Burlington officials, with their deputy sheriffs and armed force of Pinkertons and scabs,—the direct cause of the Brookfield tragedy, given in the succeeding chapter; which touched the hearts of all fair minded people.

CHAPTER XXXV.

THE MURDER OF GEORGE WATTS.

George Watts, one of the striking men, was the first engineer who fell directly by a murderous hand. There were too many irresponsible men suddenly raised to positions of influence, to little pinnacles of petty power, to make life safe about the depots and roundhouses. Accordingly the instructions from headquarters were, always to keep away from crowds, and from all assemblies of idle men. The words of Grand Chief Arthur were well remembered: "If we cannot win honorably let us submit to defeat." If violent partisans in a contest are clothed with the authority of policemen or deputy sheriffs, the public danger is not abated but increased. There are men who love the distinction of striking a fatal blow when they have a shadow of authority to hide behind. When such men, becoming murderers, are protected from punishment by citizens, or shielded by the courts, there is great cause for alarm as to the safety of both property and life. On the morning of Saturday, March 3, 1888, just before daylight, the passenger train from Quincy, Ill., pulled in to the depot at Brookfield, Mo. Granger was the name of the engineer and he was attended by a deputy sheriff named George H. Bostick, who had been sworn in as stated in last chapter. George Watts was at the depot at that early hour to take the train for St. Joseph, where his mother resided. It was the custom with the striking engineers everywhere, to induce other engineers on the same system, to join them. This had been done all along the line, and it had not been called in question anywhere, nor was it then. Young Watts stepped on the engine as it stopped at the platform, and entered into conversation with the engineer. While he was thus occupied, the engine was uncoupled and driven some distance away from the train and platform. When the engine stopped, young Watts was driven off by the deputy sheriff, Bostick, and he started at once, with a quick step, back towards the platform, with his back to the engine and to those upon it. He had hardly taken a rapid step or two away, till Bostick called out to him to throw up his hands. Evidently, he could hardly believe his own ears that such words were uttered, but without stopping his walk he looked around, as if to see the cause of such an order, and with his right hand up he reached the attitude at which the fatal shot was fired, striking him in the right temple. He must have looked along the deliberately drawn pistol barrel, for at the moment of looking, the brave deputy fired, the ball cutting the right front of the hat band and piercing the brain. The employes present carried the body into the baggage room.

The news of the frightful tragedy spread rapidly. The chairman of the engineers and firemen at that point, went at once to the scene of the murder. Immediate preparation was made for an inquest, and for appropriate expression of the pent-up feelings of all who knew the facts.

George had lived in St. Joseph, Mo., from his youth

up. His mother was a widow, and from his boyhood, she had depended on George for her living. Nobly did he respond to her faith in him. From the time, when a little boy he blacked boots at the depot, he always carried his earnings to his mother. He did the same when he became a wiper in the roundhouse in St. Joseph. His mother was not his treasurer, but he earned money only for her, after scantily providing for his food and clothing. At an early age he became fireman on a switch engine, then he was the attentive fireman on a road engine with the writer of these lines for eighteen months, working in all weather and in all hours, when he was promoted to be engineer in November, 1885, at the age of nineteen years. He was a cheerful, hopeful, happy spirited boy, loved most by those who knew him best, but chiefly by his mother, for whom he lived, and in whose smile he was the happiest.

Why should a murderous weapon be turned on such a boy? No one who knew him will ever believe that any word, or look, or thought of his, warranted violence in return. There are in the world great, strong, brutal men, who never lift a hand against an equal, but who will whip their wives and beat their children; not for any ill-doing of the helpless ones, nor for any counterfeit manliness of their own, but to gratify the devil that is in them. And this they try to do in a way that will not expose them to the deserved punishment in return. They trust to the very gentleness which they outrage to escape prosecution. Once in a while such a man discounts his manliness enough to say that the woman or the child assaulted him, and that he committed a homicide in self-defense!

Messages were sent in various directions, and among others, one to a friend in St. Joseph, to go to the house of George Watts' mother and tell her the terrible news. The resident, striking engineers carried the body of the murdered youth to the city hall, where a coroner's jury was impaneled to investigate the cause of his death. While these preparatory steps were being taken the following notice was printed and circulated in the city:

TO THE PUBLIC:

"The unfortunate shooting of George Watts need give the public no uneasiness, as far as the engineers are concerned. Vigilance, not violence, is our watchword."

C. H. SALMONS.
Brookfield, Marcn 3, 1888. J. H. SNODDY.
Committee.

A meeting was called in the strikers' hall at ten o'clock, to which the acting mayor of the city, Hon. John Ford, was invited. He evidently expected to hear revengeful expressions, but he heard nothing but words of inexpressible grief, as when brothers speak of a brother untimely stricken down. Of the hundred or more brothers present, there were no threats or thought ot revenge. Without exception, they were law abiding men, and whether wisely or not, they trusted that the law of impartial justice would be vindicated.

A newspaper printed at Linneus, the county seat, to which the slayer of George had been taken, printed the following under date of March 3:

"The sheriff brought George H. BOSTICK, who shot

George Watts at Brookfield, to this place for safe keeping. A force of forty armed deputies has been sent from here to Brookfield to assist in preserving peace. The excitement there is high, and lynch law is talked of. The strikers and sympathizers are determined, and they feel outraged at this useless attack."

No grosser injustice was ever done the good name of the city and the people who compose it, including the strikers. That they felt the shooting to be an outrage, there is no question, but that lynch law was thought of, is a positive untruth, and none knew it better than the mayor of the city. This piece of news was widely circulated, and it cast such an unjust reflection on the city that the mayor was urgently requested to deny it officially. This he would not, and did not do. So potent is the interest of a great corporation to retard justice ! So readily does the highest municipal office lower its dignity, and offend its own law abiding citizens rather than risk offending a great railroad corporation !

When the coroner's jury assembled at the city hall, the railroad superintendent and the company's attorney met with them. The strikers, not seeing the necessity of this, then secured also a legal advisor. Immediately strenuous objections were made to the presence of lawyers. A member of the jury, instead of limiting himself to finding the cause of death, and instead of listening to the evidence, argued the case as if he was Leviticus himself. The verdict of the jury accorded with the facts and requested the holding of George H. Bostick to the grand jury.

Preparations were then made by the strikers for the last act of good will and brotherly love for their unfortunate comrade, George Watts. Superintendent S. E. Crance evidently felt the shooting to be a most unfortunate occurrence. He was kind and cordial in his offers of service. He tendered the free use of a coach for the bearers, including the relatives, to attend the funeral at St. Joseph. He also asked for and paid the undertaker's bill of upwards of $40. Mr. Crance had always, and deservedly, stood well with the men. On Sunday, March 4, the friends and the members of division 79, of Brookfield, joined by members of division 107 and lodge 43 of St. Joseph, buried their friend and brother with affecting ceremonies. About one hundred engineers and firemen were in line, in regalia, led by Pryor's military band. The Ladies' Auxiliary Society attended in open carriages, presenting many beautiful floral emblems. A fine burial lot was presented to the family. The entire community was profoundly moved.

At the preliminary trial of Deputy Sheriff Bostick, before the justice, he testified in part:

"I told him to put up his hands. He raised his right hand a little way, not higher than his shoulder, with his fingers partly shut, with his other hand in his overcoat pocket. I says, 'Put up the other one;' told him to do it twice. He still had his back on me. Just then I heard a noise to my left and back of me; turned my eyes that way; seen a man; heard a click to the south of me and back of me; turned my face a little bit that way; seen a man with a pistol in his hand, not more than eight or ten feet away from me. Just at that instant

I felt somebody catch me by the right hand, which was down about my waist. Jerked it upward; as it went up the pistol went off. He (Watts) hung by my waist a second or two and then fell with his head toward the north, with his feet outside the rail, and towards the rail. As soon as I could see—for the flash blinded me a second—I looked for the man on the right of me and behind me. They were both running toward some box cars in a south-westerly direction. I stood for half a minute, then I starts and walks south in the shadow of some cars. Dewitt Boyd came to me; I gave myself up to him. We started towards the roundhouse, but I wanted him to take my pistol. He said he would rather not, or something to that way. We had not gone far when we met Beeler. (Mr. Beeler is chief train dispatcher.) He says who is this, or something that way. I says, is this you, Beeler? He says yes. I says, there, take my pistol. I guess I have killed one of those little engineers. He says how? I says, I was crowded, and had to do it in self-defense. He takes my pistol, and Boyd and I goes to the roundhouse. Boyd did not go all the way to the roundhouse with me. He told me to go and get on one of those engines,—No. 51, I believe. He goes back some place, and gets the sheriff and brings him up, and turns me over to him. I believe that is all, except what has been told. Here are the marks on my wrist where he caught me, (showing some scratches on his right wrist where the head of the radius makes a protuberance.)

(Signed) George H. Bostick.

The reader will notice that he claims to Mr. Beeler

that he did the shooting in self defense; when he had before described it as an accident. But it is not our business to try this case, but to show what was done to prevent the trial, and evidently done to prevent the conviction. The evidence above quoted was presented to the grand jury, and an indictment was found for murder in the first degree. Judge Burgess being called away, had assigned an ex-judge to the bench in his absence, a man who was at this time attorney for the railroad company, and for the accused as well as being his bondsman, yet the verdict of the grand jury indicting his client was presented to him, or rather he accepted a position where he knew he must receive that verdict, as a judge, and decide the question as to admitting to bail, and then fix the amount. We do not cite this to cast any reflections, yet to the average person not familiar with the ways of the world, these evasions of trial predict acquittal of the prisoner, if not actual discharge; unwhipt of justice. The idea that men have of a judge is taken from the idea of impartiality and rectitude of the Supreme Being, who is just, and true, and righteous altogether. For a thousand years it has been the custom of courts, where the judge is at all a party or partisan, that he shall come down from the bench, and wash his hands of all decision for himself or for his client. It would seem hardly possible for one so encumbered to follow a direct line of justice, and it brings to mind with startling emphasis the "impartial" conditions demanded of a juror, and the conditions permissible in a judge. The bail was fixed at $3,000 for appearance at court, to answer the indictment. The prisoner, out on bail, went back to the Hannibal division of the Burlington, and took his place as an employe of the Burlington system. The case was docketed for a special term, then put off to the December term, when the Burlington's legal advisers came into court and said "not ready." The case was then continued to the June term of 1889, at the company's cost. At the June term, the first day of court, the case was called, and both sides answered "ready." The judge then continued the case for one week in order to give time to summon a special jury.

When the trial day arrived it was found that three of the most important witnesses for the state were absent. Among them was Granger, the scab engineer, with whom George Watts was talking when driven off the engine. This man had said that Watts conducted himself like a gentleman, and if there ever was a murder committed that was one. Granger had been discharged but had not yet left Brookfield at the beginning of the term of court, but at trial day he was gone. It is said he was given transportation to California by the Burlington company; at all events he was missing when wanted, as were the other two who were employed by the company. But the superintendent, road master, chief train dispatcher, etc., of the Burlington were on hand ready for the trial. This necessitated the state calling for a continuance on account of absence of main witnesses. Then the trial was postponed again to the December term, 1889. If the man is innocent why not let the law take its course, and free him from the stain of murder? If he is guilty, why

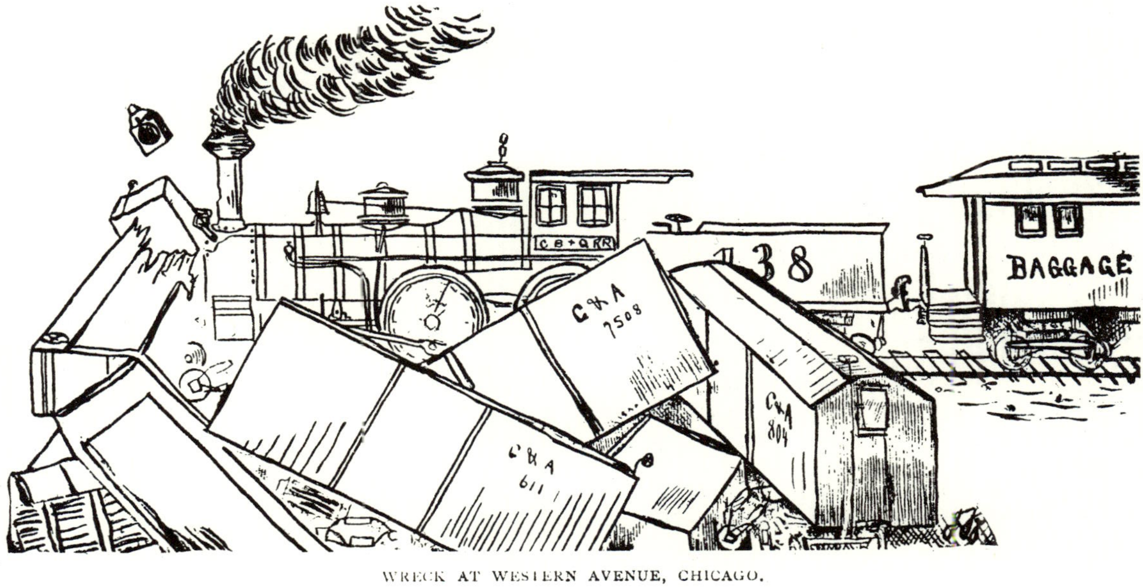

WRECK AT WESTERN AVENUE, CHICAGO.

does the Burlington Company resort to every means to defeat justice? If the Burlington Company does not assume the responsibility for the act of this man, what is the incentive for his defense by them?

The great philanthropist, John Howard, said that it was his own personal experience and observation that kindled his compassion for those of his fellow men who had no one to stand between them and the arbitrary will of unwatched officials. The world has produced no duplicate of John Howard in the benevolent work of prison reform; yet his powerful and persistent talents often stood appalled at the evils that emanated from the courts and kings of the old world. It is just as necessary that both court and king, in these times, shall have on them the restraints of responsibility and of public opinion, as it was when John Howard, unexpectedly to them, turned upon them the light of noonday.

CHAPTER XXXVI.

THE RAILWAY PROBLEM.

When the power of wealth takes the place of fidelity to principle it is an unhappy omen for the majesty of the law, and the rights of the people. In the year 1874, in a speech in the lower house of Congress, in discussing the railway problem, the lamented President James A. Garfield said, in part:

"We are so involved in the events and movements of society, that we do not stop to realize what is undeniably true, that, during the last forty years, all modern societies have entered upon a period of change, more marked, more pervading, more radical, than any that has occurred during the last three hundred years. In saying this I do not forget our own political and military history, nor the French Revolution of 1793. The changes now taking place have been wrought, and are being wrought, mainly, almost wholly, by a single mechanical contrivance, the steam locomotive. Under the name of private corporations, organizations have grown up, not for the perpetuation of a great charity, like a college or hospital; not to enable a company of citizens more conveniently to carry on private industry; but a class of corporations, unknown to the early law writers, has arisen and to them have been committed the great power of the railroad and the telegraph, the great instruments by which modern communities live and have their being. Since the dawn of history the great thoroughfares have belonged to the people, have been known as the King's highways, or the public highway, and have been open to the free use of all on payment of a small uniform tax or toll to keep them in repair. But now the most perfect, and by far the most important roads known to mankind, are owned and managed as private property by a comparatively small number of private citizens.

"In all its uses the railroad is the most public of all our roads, and in all the objects to which its work relates, the railway corporation, is as public as any organization can be. But in the start it was labelled a private corporation, and, as far as its legal status is concerned, it is now grouped with eleemosynary institutions and private charities, and enjoys similar immunities and exemptions. It remains to be seen how long the community will suffer itself to be the victim of an abstract definition."

"It will be readily conceded that a corporation is strictly and really private, when it is authorized to carry on such a business as a private citizen may carry on. But when the state has delegated to a corporation the sovereign right of eminent domain, the right to take from the private citizen, without his consent, a portion of his real estate, to build its structures across farms, gardens and lawns, into and through, over or under, the blocks, squares, streets, churches, and dwellings of incorporated cities and towns, across navigable rivers, and over and along public highways, it requires a stretch of the common imagination, and much refinement and subtility of the law, to maintain the old fiction that such an organization is not a public corporation."

"In view of the facts already set forth, the question returns, what is likely to be the effect of railways and other similar combinations upon our community and our political institutions? Is it true, as asserted by the British writer, that the state must soon recapture and control the railroads or be captured and subjugated by them? Or do the phenomena we are witnessing indicate the general breaking up of the social and political order of modern nations so confidently predicted by a class of philosophers whose opinions have hitherto made but little impression on the public mind? The analogy between the industrial conditions of society at the present time and the feudalism of the middle ages is both striking and instructive. In the darkness and chaos of that period the feudal system was the first important step towards the organization of modern times. Powerful chiefs and barons entrenched themselves in castles, and in return for submission and service gave to their vassals rude protection and ruder laws. But as the feudal chiefs grew in power and wealth they became the oppression of their people, taxed and robbed them at will, and finally in their arrogance defied the kings and emperors of the medieval states. From their castles planted on the great thoroughfares, they practiced the most capricious extortions on commerce and travel, and thus gave to modern language the phrase, to levy black mail.

"The consolidation of our great industrial and commercial companies, the power they wield and the relations they sustain to the state and to the industry of the people, do not fall far short of Fourier's definition of commercial or industrial feudalism. The modern barons, more powerful than their military prototypes, own our greatest highways and levy tribute at will upon all our vast industries, and as the old feudalism was finally controlled and subordinated only by the combined effort of the kings and the people of the free cities and towns, so our modern feudalism can be subordinated to the public good, only by the great body of the people, acting through the goverment by wise and just laws.

"I shall not now enter upon the discussion of methods by which this grand work of adjustment may be accomplished. But I refuse to believe that the genius and energy which have developed these tremendous forces, will fail to make them not the masters, but the faithful servants of society."[1] Fourteen years have been added to intensify the picture, as seen by the mind of one of our greatest thinkers, and who shall say that the evils pictured by him have been mitigated? The inter-state commerce law has done something for commerce, but where are the laws to mitigate the evils of necessary "submission and service?" Who have undertaken to amend the "rude protection and ruder laws" for their servants? And has not state, and even national legislation, at least in a great measure, been subjugated to the aggressive greed of private corporations?

[1] Life of Garfield.

CHAPTER XXXVII.

ANTAGONISM.

The Burlington people were beginning to understand that none of the old men worth mentioning would return to work, instead of having thirty-five or forty per cent stay with them. Mr. Stone, realizing the value of their services, made an effort through the local officials to regain them, and his instructions were complied with, as thoroughly as it was possible. The wives of one class of employes were sent to the wives of strikers to get them to induce their husbands to return to the company, but the wives were as loyal as their husbands, and in many instances, they were the very power that held them. The letter is as follows:

Chicago, February 28, 1888.

"Dear Sir:—The time is not far off when our men must necessarily decide whether they wish to permanently sever their connection with the company or not. We have purposely proceeded somewhat slowly in employing new men in any great numbers, in order to give the men who have been in our service, time for reflection; but a considerable number of men from the Reading district and other parts of the east, will be here within a day or two and will go to work, and any new men employed, who are competent, and of good character, will not be discharged in order that we may take back the men who have left the service.

We are extremely anxious that such of our old men as are competent, sober, and industrious, should come back to the service. We know perfectly that many of them, probably a majority, have entered into this strike at the instigation of hot-heads and agitators, and that it is impossible that they should sincerely and seriously desire to leave the service where they know, as well as we do, that they have always been well paid and well treated."

"In a strike of this kind, and in the excitement of the moment, men are led to act hastily, and with a vague impression that they are going to force the company to yield to their demands. The time is at hand therefore, if it has not arrived now, when a great deal can be done by personal talk to induce good men to return to the service, and give up what must inevitably be a contest full of disaster to them if it is proceeded in. Many of our men have grown up in the service, and their homes are on the line of our road; their property, if they have accumulated any, is here with us, and our interests are identical. Aside from the interests which the company has as a matter of business in having these men returned to the service in preference to getting new men, we very much desire to save the men themselves from the consequences of fighting this matter to the end, and forcing the company to man the road with new hands."

"We realize fully the situation; we know the difficulty of filling the places of good men who know the road, and we know the losses to the road of a prolonged conflict."

"All this has been fully considered and is taken into

account, but you can see, and any man who will stop to think can see, that it is simply impossible for the company to yield to the demands which have been made. We must, as a matter of self preservation, fight it out, no matter at what expenditure of time and money. I hope, therefore, that you and others holding positions in the service which enable them to do so, will use the utmost exertion to convince our men by personal persuasion, by pointing out to them the inevitable consequences of a continued contest, to induce the men to come back into the service, satisfied to let the company and its officers manage their own property. It is obvious that men who are receiving $4 and $5 a day cannot expect public sympathy in any demand for more, which is carried to the extent of a strike."

"This contest can have but one end, and that end is just as easy to see now as it will be perhaps when it will be too late to do the old men any good. I hope you will do every thing in your power to make them appreciate the situation by talking to them singly, and impressing on their minds the truth of what I have said above."[1] (Signed) HENRY B. STONE.

Mr. Stone says: "Many, probably a majority of the old men, have entered into this strike at the instigation of hot-heads." It would hardly seem probable that a few hot-heads could hold, against their will, nearly every man, not only for a day but for months. From my own knowledge, the men who did go back, were the "hot-heads," in nearly every case. The men who were most ready with vituperation at the beginning of the strike, were the hardest to keep in a line of gentle-

[1] Chicago Daily News, March 1, 1888.

manly deportment after the strike was fairly on; were first sought after by the Burlington, and first to secure a place. They remind me that in the war for the Union, a pugilist would always hunt a safe place out of range of danger. It was the every day thinking man, in office and out, who held all in line. But Mr. Stone said they were "holding off to give the old men a chance to come back, but that a considerable number of men were coming from the Reading district and other parts of the east." Let us see if we can analyze the nature of this demonstration from the east, of which Mr. Stone speaks. How did he know so soon that these men were coming?

Who were all these men who so readily loaned themselves to the Burlington company? Where did they come from, and what was the incentive? What was their character? "More men went in and out of the offices of the company, at Chicago in one day, at the beginning of the strike, than probably any time since they were built. The great majority of them claimed to be engineers or firemen. They had heard the rumbling and threatening of war; it had come; so had they. The passage way leading to the general superintendent's office was crowded from early morning until sunset. In answer to questions put to a number of these applicants they all represented that they had more or less of experience as either engineers or firemen. Some appeared to be quite intelligent, while others were either reticent or ignorant. A few among them belonged to the Knights of Labor, but none of them, as far as could be ascertained, belonged to the Brotherhoods. One of the Knights said, 'I went out with the southwestern strike of engineers. One of the Brothers took my place. I have not been able to get any work since and I am trying now to get a Brother's place. When a man has been slapped on the face it is not unreasonable that he should return the blow."[1] There had been no strike of engineers in the southwest. The stories that the motley multitude told were stereotyped. The men who were hired or bought, or appealed to by the strikers, all told very much the same story, and there was one feature that strongly marked almost every narrative, the story had stamped on the face of it, "lie." I do not say they all did this; many of them came to the Burlington apparently indifferent as to anyone's opinion of their conduct, and had no need to lie to preserve their reputation. Some of this kind had been in the business of scab before. "Most of these applicants were respectably dressed, although here and there, the marks of having been out of work were plainly visible; there were nearly 200 of them."[1]

The examination as to their fitness was entrusted to G. W. Rhodes, superintendent of motive power, and Mr. J. V. Murray, traveling engineer on the Chicago division of the road. These officers were occupied the whole day, and, at the conclusion of their labors, the following men were among the thirty who had been selected after they had satisfied their interrogators as to their competency: Engineers, Charles Riggs, H. Botham, M. Jenks, H. C. Cass, Geo. Graham, "Doc" Merriam. Firemen: Martin Lane, Chas. A. Phurow, Robert Hoey, O. D. Skiff, W. D. Smith, Louis Eott, A. G. Patten, W. McDennot, Albert

[1] Chicago Tribune, Feb. 28, 1888.

Fitch, H. C. Lefont, John Hogan." The last named engineer, "Doc" Merriam, is known by hundreds of railroad men. He was discharged from the Burlington as a worthless drunkard, and washed spittoons in Aurora to get drinks. The traveling engineer, J. V. Murray, who assisted in the examination of these men, was a member, (at that time) of Division 127, of Brotherhood of Locomotive Engineers, Beardstown, Ill., and for the sake of a place entered into this work for the company with great zest, and he was expelled by his divison for violation of obligation.

From all the reports circulated about the Reading railroad men, and others from Pennsylvania, it would look as though half of the population of that state were engineers and firemen, and all out of work, and had a personal grudge against the Burlington engineers and firemen. The only instance within our knowledge of official interference, is in the following:

"Reading, Penn., Feb. 26, 1888. Capt. Geo. L. Eastman, national organizer of the Knights of Labor, is authority for the statement that the executive committee of the Reading railroad strikers have notified General Manager Stone, of the Chicago, Burlington & Quincy, that in the event of a strike on his road, and a failure of Chief Arthur to withdraw the Brotherhood engineers who took their places on the Reading road, they will send him three hundred engineers tomorrow morning."[2]

It will be remembered that a strike of the Knights of Labor occurred on December 24, 1887. The Reading engineers being members of the Knights of Labor, were ordered out, to assist in coercing the Reading company. It is a known fact that

1 Chicago Tribune, Feb. 28, 1888. 2 Associated Press Report, Feb. 27, 1888.

the miners and coal handlers of that company, which controls the greater part of the coal fields of Pennsylvania, are, and have been for years, steadily ground down until the condition has become un-American and indecent. It could only exist under such a combination as the Reading railroad made with the coal and iron interest. A committee of Congress investigated this matter in 1887 and 1888, and showed up the manner in which the mine owner, the railroad officials, the Pinkerton coal and iron police, and the officials of the commonwealth, combined to defraud labor of its just reward, to force the public to buy coal at a factitious price, and to gamble away the rights of the people.

Harper's Weekly of June 16, 1888, in describing the coal mines of Pennsylvania, has this to say of the wages and life of miners:

"Wages are very low in the coal regions. Laborers receive from sixty to eighty cents a day. Year in and year out, for the last ten years, during which time the cheap foreigners have been coming to this country in great numbers, the average daily wages for a common laborer has probably not been more than seventy cents a day. With the stopping of work very few laborers make more than $12 a month the year round, and a third of this must go as rent for the shanty. Eight dollars a month is very little in the expensive coal regions for food, clothes and medicine."

"There is many a miner who goes without dinner day after day, and who tightens his belt when noon comes."

"A piece of fresh meat is a luxury for holidays, and

two or three cold potatoes are the usual contents of the dinner pail. There is no allowance made by the employers for accident or illness. When the doctor is needed, each visit must be paid for when it is made. When the rent day comes, the rent is taken from the month's earnings, and if the head of the family can work no more, the family is turned out with all the bitter cruelty of business."

Wholesale evictions take place in Pennsylvania, as in Ireland, and scenes of brutal indifference to human suffering, may be seen in the one country, as in the other."

It is not surprising that those men were aggravated to think that any other class of labor should refuse to assist in bettering these conditions, instead of, (as they claim,) filling the vacated places, and thereby breaking down the only power they possessed to make the conditions better. Yet it is not reasonable to charge any labor organization, as such, with the responsibility of the acts of individuals beyond their control. They might be members, and be commanded as P. M. Arthur commanded in 1886: "Keep your hands off! Do nothing which belongs to another to do,—in fact, mind your own business!" It was the position occupied by the Brotherhood of engineers in 1886, and it was all they asked at the beginning of the strike in 1888. They did not ask any help from any other Orders. The engineers and firemen were willing to go it alone, and only asked, hands off.

The conductors and brakemen were told to keep at work, but to not do anything that did not belong to them to do. Was that not consistent with the position they took as an institution in the southwestern strike? That individuals violated this principle of non-interference, there was never a better illustration than in the Burlington strike. Messrs. Arthur and Sargent both deny that they had any knowledge of members of their respective Orders taking the Knight's places. That there was much feeling against the engineers, there can be no question, and it evidently emanated from the isolated position they have always occupied of "no amalgamation." They have been patted on the back from year to year, for occupying this position, by the leading representatives of capital. In fact, capital usually has one class of labor to use as a club to break down the power of some other organization whose members are trying to better their condition. It appeared to be the Knight's turn to have their backs patted. The Burlington had, in 1886, ordered the Knights of Labor off their premises, but in 1888 they were gladly welcomed and many came, but not with the sanction of the Knights of Labor as an institution, as the following chapter will show.

CHAPTER XXXVIII.

ATTITUDE OF THE KNIGHTS OF LABOR.

Richard Griffiths, the grand worthy foreman of the Order said: "There is absolutely no foundation in the report that our Order will interfere with the striking Brotherhood, nor will any attempt be made by the Order to supply the Burlington people with engineers to enable them to defeat these men. The best of feeling exists between Mr. Powderly and Chief Arthur, and the Order, as an Order, has no grievance whatever against the Brotherhood. Of course, there may be individual cases where men have griefs. If they go to the Burlington road and apply for work, they will do so as individuals, and not otherwise." "It is true," said Mr. Griffiths, "that in the strike of the Missouri Pacific, Chief Arthur asked his men to leave our Order, but that did not create any bad feeling. You may state authoritatively that, not only will the Knights of Labor Order not assist the Burlington road, but that its sympathies are with the Brotherhood first and last."[1]

"T. B. Barry, a member of the general executive board of the Knights of Labor said: "I don't think any of the engineers from the east, now en route to Chicago, are members of the Knights of Labor. Our Order will not send any men to take positions there, or advise them to go, but there is such an intense feeling against the Brotherhood of engineers, that

[1] Chicago Tribune, Feb. 29, 1888.

some of our engineers cannot be restrained from going." [1]

The following was adopted at Chicago on Feb. ary 28: "To the members of the D. A. 24, Knights of Labor; Greeting: During the last twenty-four hours the public press has been lumbered down with reports of the strike of the Brotherhoods of engineers and firemen of the Chicago, Burlington & Quincy railroad. In connection with this, many rumors have been set afloat, that this monopoly of a corporate power would be aided in their contest against their company, by members of the Knights of Labor, who are reported as being anxious to take their places, actuated by feelings of retaliation for bad conduct the Brotherhood is claimed to have been guilty of towards our Order during similar contests in the past. Without going into an examination as to whether this charge against the Brotherhood is false or true, the executive board of D. A. 24, Knights of Labor, unqualifiedly protests against any of its members taking the places of these striking workers."

We call on the members of our Order everywhere, to refuse under any and all circumstances, to become the tools of this corporation in their hour of trouble. If the members of the Brotherhood have been guilty of any wrong towards our Order, this wrong cannot be righted by committing another. By the exhibition on our part, of a higher and nobler manhood in the cause of struggling labor, we may prove to them our worth as Knights, thereby sowing the seed of that higher fraternity that should exist among all bodies of organized labor. Let no Knight fire an engine or

[1] Chicago Tribune, Feb. 29, 1888.

CLIMBING A TELEGRAPH POLE AT MORGAN AND JOHNSON STREETS, CHICAGO.

pull a throttle on the C., B. & Q.

The Executive Board, D. A. 24, Knights of Labor,

GEORGE SCHILLING, Chairman,

WILLIAM TURNBULL, Secretary.

District Assembly 79, which includes the state of Minnesota, issued an order on February 28, advising against interference: "To the Order in District assembly 79, Knights of Labor; Greeting: The District Executive Board fully endorse the sentiments in the manifesto of District Assembly 24, of Chicago, advising all knights to refrain from taking the places of the striking engineers and firemen on the Chicago, Burlington & Quincy railroad. By taking this position, the board believes that it will show to those who seek to sow discord between the different labor organizations, that we are above the low spirit of revenge that has so often thwarted the efforts of organizations in the past. While the Brotherhood, may, in the past, have taken a stand in opposition to our efforts, yet by retaliating on them in their hour of trouble, nothing will be gained, and the antagonism will become more bitter. It is by showing our manhood under such circumstances, that we will ultimately bring about the complete realization of our object, viz: to bring together in one organization, and bind by one fraternal tie, every man and woman who toils for a living."[1]

On the 29th of February, twenty-five men, said to have been Reading engineers, were quartered at the Briggs house, Chicago. One of them, on being interrogated by a reporter, said: "We are the advance guard of a small army of engineers who will fill the

[1] Chicago Tribune, Feb. 29, 1888.

places of the Burlington strikers. We were not selected by any agent of the Burlington road, but are some of the men who were made the victims of the Reading strike. I am not empowered to speak for the others, but I intend to go to work to-morrow morning."[1]

"What is the general feeling of the Knights of Labor throughout the east in relation to this strike?" They desire the defeat of the Brotherhood. I am not here as a Knight of Labor, but as a first-class mechanic, out of work. A Brotherhood man is now running my machine, and if I pass examination to-morrow, I expect to return the compliment. In doing so I shall not consider myself 'a scab,' but shall hold that I am fulfilling my duty to myself and to my family. The Brotherhood started this fight and must stand the responsibility." When asked if there were more from the Reading road who felt as he did, he said: "You bet your life, there are! The Reading engineers went on a strike in company with forty thousand miners, who were the only support of thousands of families. When the result was trembling in the balance, the Brotherhood of Locomotive Engineers came forward and filled our places. They claim that it was done as individuals. Perhaps it was. We are here as individuals. You have not heard that the Knights of Labor have declared against the strikers, have you? I feel sorry for the striking engineers of the Burlington as fellow craftsmen, but I have no use for their organization."[1]

This man does not consider himself a scab. Some one, he claims, has done him an injury in Pennsylva-

[1] Associated Press dispatch.

nia, and he comes to Illinois to get even with the man in Pennsylvania, by doing what he acknowledges was a mean thing for the other man to do. While he is doing this, he is filled with sympathy for the men whom he comes—for the sake of vengeance—to harm. "Two wrongs never made right," and as it has been said before, nearly all of these men had an elaborate excuse to offer for coming. When a man says he comes filled with sympathy for his intended victims, that man should join the socialists, and no labor organization should be held accountable for his acts. If he had said "I hold I am fulfilling my duty to myself and family," and stopped there, he would not have exposed the fact that he came to the Burlington to do what he condemned as an outrage on the Reading.

General Master Workman Powderly, of the Knights of Labor, defines very forcibly what he thinks of such a man as the above, no matter what he belongs to. He said: "I have been asked what my opinion is concerning the strike of the engineers on the Burlington system. An expression of opinion is requested as to whether I favor Knights of Labor taking the places of Brotherhood men. I do not know the particulars of the strike question, but if true men are making an effort to do away with the European custom of grading men up and down, regardless of merit, they are right for making a fight for equality. My opinion is, that the man who takes the place of another struggling for his rights, deserves the contempt and scorn of every man who loves justice. The man who takes the place of another when that other engages in a struggle with a corporation, is a "scab," whether he is a member of the Knights of Labor, or the Brotherhood of Engineers. Knights of Labor, if you take my advice, you will stand back and allow this struggle to go on.

Let the Brotherhood demonstrate its power to stand alone, 'without entangling alliances with other trades.' The spectacle presented by men of labor, who belong to different organizations, rushing at each others' throats when strikes occur, must be a gratifying spectacle for employers of labor. Knights of Labor, from Maine to California, stand back! Keep hands off! Let the law of retaliation be disregarded and let the men of the Burlington road run this strike if they can!"[1] Samuel Gampers, president of the American Federation of labor said: "The Brotherhood of Locomotive Engineers is an excellent organization, although it has done wrong in isolating itself on labor matters. In the present strike, the Trades' Unions are with them."

1 Associated Press Report.

CHAPTER XXXIX.

NEGOTIATIONS FOR HARMONY.

For all these strong expressions from the chief men of the Knights and kindred orders, there seemed to be a concordant movement on the part of the ex-Reading employes, to come to the Burlington. The press of the country took it up, and with great energy magnified not only the numbers, but the presumed grievances of the Knights against the Brotherhood of Engineers and Brotherhood of Firemen. They quoted sayings of Grand Chief Arthur, and doings of individuals, in order to help to widen the breach. All the antipathy so created was in the direct interest of monopoly. All the vast railroad interests were interested in making this the wedge to divide the power of organized labor. The more they magnified the picture of wrongs done, the wider the breach, and the better for the Burlington.

It is evident from Mr. Stone's letter in a preceding chapter, that he had been notified of their coming. When they began to arrive they were met by the strikers' committee. They were reminded that they came to injure men who had in no way injured them, and who could not be held accountable for the acts of some individuals in Pennsylvania. A few were found who had a spark of manliness left, and the earnest appeals of the committees would sometimes help them to see how much they were violating the principles that should actuate one laboring man towards another. How generous and considerate, and how chivalric do all men believe a knight, a true knight to be. If they were true knights, why did they come ?

By such appeals a few were induced to agree to return if transportation was furnished, and many did return, or at least went elsewhere. Many of them were no doubt impostors. But such things cannot be avoided in such times. When excitement is at boiling heat the scum is sure to come to the surface. The human vultures, like the other kind, are always ready to take whatever falls in their way, whether the means to be used are false or fair. The strikers had expected men would present themselves for the places vacated, in some numbers, but they did not think any members of labor organizations would come, and it was evident something must be done to check, if possible, this movement.

At this time there appeared upon the scene, one who claimed to be the leader of this army of Reading men.

"Joseph Cahill, secretary of the executive board of the Reading employes, brought Chief Arthur and Grand Master Sargent official information that 150 members of their Order had taken the places of the Knights of Labor on the Reading road."

"Both Chief Arthur and Mr. Sargent have denied repeatedly that they knew that these men had taken the places of the Reading striking employes. They assured Mr. Cahill that they had no knowledge other than newspaper reports that this thing had occurred. Both gentlemen expressed a willingness to play fair with the knights, and an agreement was entered into by which Mr. Arthur and Mr. Sargent agreed to request their men to quit the Reading road's employment."

"In return for this Mr. Cahill agreed to keep the 150 to 200 Reading engineers and firemen in the city from taking places on the Chicago, Burlington & Quincy road. These men will be held here twenty-four hours. If the Brotherhood men obey the request of their chiefs and quit the Reading road the Knights of Labor men here will return to Reading and other points along the Reading lines whence they came. Mr. Cahill telegraphed other contingents of Reading men to remain where they were. He estimated the number of engineers out of employment along the Reading lines at six to eight hundred."

"Chief Arthur, about five o'clock, on the evening of February 2, sent the following telegram to Mr. Edward Kent, chairman of the executive board of the Brotherhood of Locomotive Engineers of the Philadelphia & Reading railroad company:"

"'Go to Philadelphia and use all your influence to have the members of the Brotherhood of Locomotive Engineers on the Phildelphia & Reading road who have taken the places of the men who went out December 27, 1887, to leave the service ot the company, furnishing them with the financial support of the Brotherhood. The Chicago, Burlington & Quincy company is striving to use Reading strikers to defeat us in this conflict. We must use all honorable means to checkmate it.'"

"Mr. Kent was at Sparkhill, Rockland county, N. Y.

He at once telegraphed Mr. Arthur that he would go to Philadelphia immediately."

"Grand Master Sargent sent a similar dispatch to Harry Walton, chairman of the executive board of firěmen at Philadelphia.

Chicago, March 3, 1888.

HARRY WALTON:

"See all members of the Brotherhood on the Philadelphia & Reading railroad that have taken the places of the men that went out December 27, 1887, and request them to sever their connection with the company, and I will pay them untill they can find employment elsewhere, and allow the men now out to return to work. By doing this, the ill-feeling now existing will be obliterated, and will assist us to win our struggle with the Burlington."

(Signed) F. P. SARGENT.

Mr. Sargent promised the men support until they could find employment elsewhere. Mr. Walton responded by telegraph that he would at once issue the necessary orders. Messrs. Arthur and Sargent thought these men would obey their requests, as they both thought the men were in the wrong in taking the places of the organized workmen. In order to insure greater success in this movement it was thought best to secure the services of some one who belonged to the Knights of Labor and was directly interested in the strike on the Burlington. Mr. J. J. Delaney, who was a member of the Brotherhood of Locomotive Firemen and also a member of the Knights of Labor, was secured, who proceeded to Philadelphia to co-operate with the others.

It is said, George E. Detwiler of Chicago, a member of the Knights of Labor, and editor of a labor paper, rendered valuable assistance in this effort to dissuade the knights. While these negotiations were pending, nearly one hundred new arrivals reached the city of Chicago, and were quartered at the Briggs house. They claimed that they were all Reading men. The Brotherhood's committees, ever watchful, were on hand, and "knots of excited men gathered around the leaders and the war of words waged thick and fast. The Reading men openly accused Chief Arthur of causing the troubles on that road, but despite all the gesticulating and loud talk many were in favor of a settlement. The Brotherhood delegates told the new-comers of the settlement between Arthur and Powderly. 'We won't go back unless we are recalled by Corbin himself,' shouted several of the Reading men. 'If Chief Arthur calls the Brotherhood men off the Reading road will you go back and fight your own battles?' A few said they would. The committees were aided materially by two Knights of Labor from Reading, said to represent Mr. Powderly. They knew the men and placed a chalk mark on every good man." "A number of the Reading men were not skilled engineers. A large percentage of them were firemen, and a great number were incompetent men who were given free transportation to Chicago. The Brotherhood's committees were after the competent men and hired about half of the entire number."[1] These were furnished free transportation, and they returned to Pennsylvania. At the Brotherhood's headquarters at the Grand Pacific hotel, there

[1] Chicago Evening News.

was a scene of exciting activity. Men were there of all kinds, nationalities and interests, scores of them. The deceived, some were deceivers, and others were repentant. Said one of these men: "I came here on my own responsibility. I do not belong to the Brotherhood, neither am I a Knight of Labor. I was out of work and came from Reading here. I didn't want to go farther west than Chicago. They wanted me to go to Nebraska, though I have a contract for work here. Five others came with me and we want to get transportation back home. I don't like the looks of the situation."

The committee sent to the Reading road by Messrs. Arthur and Sargent, had a meeting with the Reading strikers, who repudiated Mr. Cahill's authority to speak for them, and insisted upon the ordering out of every Brotherhood man on the Reading road. This meant another strike on the Reading, which the grand officers of the two Brotherhoods had no power to effect. Their constitutions only gave them power to sanction a strike when the men had voted it. The Reading road has 800 engines, and at the time of this strike it is said there were not more than twenty Brotherhood men employed on that road.

Nearly all those who had taken the places of the striking knights, were not members of any organization. Many of them were said to be the dissipated refuse of other railroads and of the Brotherhoods. Some of them were the men who struck against President Gowan's order to withdraw from the Brotherhood, or from the service of that company in 1877. When that strike came, their places were filled, and

[1] Chicago Evening News.

by some of these same men who struck in 1887 as Knights of Labor. These men, many of whom were still in Pennsylvania, and had not run an engine since 1877, and being bound by no labor ties, went back to the Reading company. This committee, which was sent to negotiate peace with these knights, only found eleven engineers and seven firemen who belonged to these Orders, at work on the Reading road. It must now be evident to the reader that when the Reading men claimed that the Brotherhood as an Order, had filled their places in 1887, they were entirely mistaken. It is also plain that they used this pretext for an excuse for doing what they evidently felt was as mean in themselves to do as it had been in those who, it was said, took their places. Everything was done by the officers of the Knights of Labor to prevent any members of their Order coming to the Burlington, and they should in no way be held responsible for the acts of these men as individuals. The good will of the Order was shown on every hand and in the west they made the Burlington feel their power in a depleted business and encouraging words to the strikers.

CHAPTER XL.

FEINT, FOR EFFECT.

It is evident that the Reading men were grossly misrepresented. Where there was one Knight of Labor who did come, there were one hundred who claimed to be Knights who never had seen the Reading road. The officers of the Burlington road were glad to call everything that came in the shape of an engineman, "direct from Reading." On March 1, Master Mechanic J. W. Rhodes, from his headquarters in Chicago, sent out the following:

"To all Master Mechanics:

We have a large number of engineers just from the Reading road; can furnish you any number of engineers you want. Let me know as soon as possible how many you want."[1] J. W. RHODES.

Here is another sample:

St. Joseph, Mo., March, 2 1888.

A. C. DAWES, Kansas City.

"I have a message from Chicago saying that reported arrangements between P. M. Arthur and the Knights of Labor to take Brotherhood men off the Reading and send Reading men back, have no effect whatever upon those who have come to us from the Reading road. They seem to be more anxious to find out how they can get their families west than to talk about going back to Pennsylvania. They say

[1] Creston (Iowa) Advertiser.

they will have nothing to do with the Brotherhood of Locomotive Engineers and are well satisfied with their prospects. One hundred and fifty odd went to Nebraska, and one hundred and fifty more than we expected arrived this morning."[1]

W. F. MERRILL,

General Manager.

Much of this talk was no doubt intended to frighten the strikers, and create a stampede among them. The Burlington officials were too wise not to want the old men back if they could get them without receding from their position. The notice to apply on or before Wednesday noon of February 29, had done no good; if anything it had increased the strikers' determination to fight it out; they would not accept their salary, and did not go for it until the pay car come out at its regular time. The great news dispenser for the Burlington, during the strike, was Mr. Paul Morton, general ticket agent, who was formerly a reporter on a newspaper in Nebraska. Having been educated in the newspaper business, he knew how to work the machine for all it was worth. He was a terse, forcible writer, and was always ready to dish up news in any quantity to whomsoever might come, and he never forgot the coloring.

"Mr. Morton said 250 competent engineers and firemen had been accepted by the company, and had been sent out to man engines on various divisions of the road. These men were principally ex-employes of the Reading, whose places had been filled with Brotherhood men. Mr. Morton said that several other large bodies of competent man were on the way to

[1] Kansas City Journal, March 3, 1888.

Chicago from the east, and he read dispatches from several points, announcing that delegations were on the way to Chicago. He said that the company would not discharge its new men to make room for the men who had quit work in case the latter wanted to come back. "The position" said he, "on this question is exactly similar to that of Mr. Corbin in regard to the Reading strikers, which is fairly illustrated by the following extract from the proceedings of the Reading investigating committee before the House at Washington: Mr. Corbin said—'If there is no more coal mined from the Schuylkill until we are compelled to mine it by discharging men who have come to us in our trouble, and stood by us, to make way for the strikers, no more will ever be mined while I have influence to prevent it.'"

PAUL MORTON AND THE REPORTER.

"Do you mean to say, and go on record as saying, that for that and that only, you will not take them back."

"Yes, emphatically, I want that to go on record.

They left me, and I gave them notice. It will be a pretty cold day when I discharge men who stood by me when I needed help, for men who concerted and attempted to ruin me."

Here are three hundred and fifty more ex-Reading men, all within twenty-four hours !

"Great excitement was occasioned at the Union depot on the evening of March 1, upon the departure of the 5:35 P. M. train, known as the Denver express. The engine of this train was manned by a Reading engineer and fireman, who had an old brakeman, for a pilot, in the cab with them, and all were armed with revolvers. The train was composed of a mail car, three baggage cars, four day coaches, two chair cars and two sleepers. There were but three passengers in the chair cars, and none in the sleepers. A great crowd had collected in the vicinity, for the train was unusually long. About 5:30 Lieutenant Fitzpatrick, with a detail of eight men, and Lieutenant Ross, of the Desplaines street station, came down leading a procession of over 200 men. They were Reading engineers and firemen who had come to help out the road in its difficulty. With them was a large pósse of Pinkerton men under the command of Lieutenant Lane, and every one of the large body was armed with a 44 caliber revolver, ready for any emergency which might arise on the way The 200 men were placed in the four day coaches, each in charge of four Pinkerton men. The crowds thronged about the engine in the depot, but four stalwart policemen drove them away from the locomotive. General Manager Stone, Superintendent Howland, and Superintendent of Motive Power Rhodes, were all on hand to see the crowd, and even Freddy Gebhard was attracted to the spot by the excitement. He was especially conspicuous on the platform, with the bunch of blue violets in the left lapel of his coat, and his exceedingly small derby hat on his very large head, until somebody yelled, "Get onto the bloke!" when he vanished. The train started off very slowly, and there was a good deal of feeling shown by the crowd as it passed under the Van Buren street viaduct, but no person attempted or offered to do any violence."[1] And this is not all. On the same day one hundred more new arrivals of "fine looking fellows" were heralded, far and wide.

Mr. Morton said: "We first heard from the Reading men through committees appointed by them, and that they were ready to take the places of our striking engineers. The story that they were misinformed and supposed they were to work on new lines, is untrue. Our agents were instructed to inform them just what they were coming for."[2] It will be seen by the following that the number was greatly exaggerated.

"One hundred more of the Reading engineers and firemen arrived last evening. Of these fifty-eight came on from the East over the Pennsylvania lines and arrived at 6:45 o'clock, and the remaining forty-two came in at 9:30. This body of men is by far the best looking, from a respectable standpoint, that has yet arrived. There were no guards with these men, as they insisted that they needed none, because they were able to take care of themselves. The first batch lingered about the Union Depot for a half hour, and

[1] Chicago Tribune. [2] Chicago News, March 2, 1888.

WRECK AND FIRE AT 16TH & WOOD STREETS, CHICAGO.

were then taken to the Briggs house. The others also came in later, and found no one to meet them except a delegation of brotherhood engineers who endeavored to proselyte them. This work was in vain."

"We would not have come here to take these places" said one of the men, "but we are forced to it. There is no place for us in Pennsylvania. We have been driven out by the Brotherhood of Locomotive Engineers. That is true, every word of it. Our men who were working in blast-furnaces at $1 a day, were driven away like vagabonds to wander over the earth because they were strikers. Yes, we are Knights of Labor, but we are men and we can stand up and defend ourselves. We leave starving families. Three of our party leave at home dying wives to earn for them the very necessities of life of which they stand in need. If the Brotherhood engineers had not interfered with us we would not have been here to-day. But they displaced us; now we displace them. There is no room for argument here. The facts are there, and we will abide by them."

"This morning at seven o'clock, March 2, 150 more Reading men will arrive at the Union Depot by the Fort Wayne road."

"Twenty of the new men who were sent out on the 5:35 train last evening deserted after going out a short distance and returned to the city at 6:40 last evening. They said that they had had all they wanted of railroading. They only wanted a chance to see Chicago, and had taken advantage of the opportunity offered by the strike." [1]

Philadelphia, March 2.—General Superintendent

[1] Chicago News.

Swigert of the Reading railroad company, said: "The entire number of locomotive engineers who left the service of the Philadelphia and Reading company during the recent labor disturbance was 109." [1]

The nineteen Brotherhood men who took places on the Reading must have been a power indeed to have displaced forty thousand miners, and blast furnace men, beside all this army of men who call themselves Reading Knights, who are coming for vengeance. To the reading public who found the newspapers filled with this astonishing exodus from Pennsylvania, and the wholesale charges of our labor organization against another, it must have brought vividly to mind the Irish, traditional duel:

> There was once two cats in Kilkenny,
> And each thought there was one cat to many;
> So they quarrelled and fit,
> And they gouged and they bit,
> Till, excepting their nails,
> And the tips of their tails,
> Instead of two cats there wasn't any.

The grand officers of the twin Brotherhoods, as they were very appropriately called, from their information, did not believe these stories, and they sent out the following to all points along the line:

Grand Pacific Hotel, March 1, 1888.

To Engineers and Firemen.

Dear Sirs and Brothers:

"We are informed that a number of men are being distributed by the company, on the system, with a view to demoralize the ranks of our men along the

[1] Associated Press report.

line and give the appearance that a sufficient number of engineers and firemen have been secured to resume operations. Pay no attention to such reports or to outward appearances. The outlook is better than ever before. Success is practically in sight. Do not, under any possible circumstances, allow yourselves to be misled as to the situation. Stand firm, and do not lose courage. We have no hesitancy in saying that our cause will triumph."

Yours Fraternally, P. M. ARTHUR,
F. P. SARGENT.

At the time this was written negotiations were pending with President Perkins which possibly lent some strength to Messrs. Arthur and Sargent's assurance. This meeting was brought about by Mr. Geo. E. Detwiler and Judge Parker, who thought that if a meeting could be arranged between the belligerent parties that some understanding might be reached. The meeting finally took place in President Perkins' room in the Grand Pacific hotel. There were two of the board of directors present, Mr. Detwiler and Messrs. Arthur and Sargent. A long discussion of the points at issue was had, and the grand officers appealed to Mr. Perkins to grant the requests of the men, but to no purpose. The only proposition from Mr. Perkins was, "If you will declare the strike off, I will take back seventy-five per cent of the men, and the balance I will re-employ as soon as possible." To this Mr. Arthur replied: "Mr. Perkins, before I will go to the men and ask them to declare the strike off on such terms, I will sever my right arm from my body."[1] This left them as far apart as ever. This meeting, of such grave importance to the participants, as illustrated by the press,[2] was serious, malicious, and comical. The earnest effort to secure peace

TRIANGULAR POWWOW OF THE CHIEFS.

between labor and capital was illustrated in the triangular powwow, the three interested leaders, Messrs. Perkins, Powderly and Arthur, smoking the pipe of

[1] A participant. [2] Chicago News.

peace, while the Burlington scabs were smashing the property, and the traveling public were going on foot rather than take the chances behind such men. The meeting caused the circulation of stories of a settlement, which did not please the management, and Mr. Stone sent the following to all superintendents and master mechanics: "The reports which I understand have been sent out to our old engineers and others to the effect that the company intends to yield the position it has taken is positively without foundation." Press Agent Morton lost nothing of his importance as these things were transpiring. While he passed round the cigars, he fairly beamed with information. To a running fire of questions, he summed up the situation in this way; "The situation, so far as to the relations between the strikers and the railroad, is unchanged. The conference last night was not sought by the company, and nothing was accomplished by it. We don't consider that any terms of compromise were offered or suggested. We consider it a great misfortune that our old engineers have been induced to give up their places, and it is with painful reluctance that we see their places being rapidly filled by strangers." [1]

There is plenty of evidence that only a small percentage of the strangers were Knights of Labor. But men came, and in astonishing numbers. Mr. Arthur said: "From all statistics in my possession there cannot be three hundred competent engineers in the country out of employment."

[1] Chicago News.

CHAPTER XLI.

RULE OR RUIN.

Messrs. Arthur and Sargent, and the strikers along the line who had been brought up under Burlington rules, could not believe that the Burlington officials would grab at anything in the shape of a man to fill their places, regardless of character or fitness. But they were soon made to realize that such was a fact. The Chicago *Daily News* had the following cut and comment:

"A long line of men—labor-looking people, stood in line waiting an opportunity to go before G. W. Rhodes, superintendent of motive power, and A. Forsyth, master mechanic, who were detailed to examine applicants as to their competency. After entering Superintendent Howland's room they gave their names, and then were sent with a card to the examining-room. A stationary engineer was soon made aware of the fact that he could not run a

SAMPLE APPLICANTS FOR WORK.

locomotive. And, too, the engineer who used to jangle a bell on a State street grip car was hastily informed that he was not wanted."

There must have been some of the stationary engineers, and street car bell janglers, that were sharp enough to fool the examiners if it was necessary to fool them, for it is certain they got many of that kind, and men who had their character and their watches—to use a slang phrase—in soak.

" A number of the engineers examined and accepted by the Burlington company had no watches. An engineer without a watch is like a ship without a sail; a fork without a knife. The company gave these men watches. Half a dozen of them took their time-pieces to pawn-shops, and before the sun set had painted the town a purple hue.

"The first train to leave the city went out at 12:01 o'clock. W. H. Chapin, an imported engineer, was placed in charge of the lever, and a young man who answered to the name of Rankin and claimed to have hailed from Iowa, piled in the fuel. There was an impression abroad that Chapin was a Reading man, but he denied the charge. A funny thing happened just before the train started which afforded considerable amusement for the crowd. The new engineer was somewhat abashed at the conspicuousness of the position which he occupied, and seemed to be unable to tell one end of the engine from another. He oiled the headlight and smokestack instead of the piston, and grabbed the fireman's arm instead of the lever. Finally, having familiarized himself with the various parts of the machine, he was about to pull out when the fireman suddenly exclaimed: 'Say, pard, you've forgot your ticker.' "

" By Jove, I haven't got one," was the reply.

" You blamed fool, you can't run an engine without a watch, kin you? "

" I kin run it, but I can't run it on time."

" Guess you fellers must a been workin down south where they hev lots o' time, piped in a striking engineer who had been enjoying his discomfiture."

" Shet your trap," shouted the fireman, and the police stepped in to prevent bloodshed, while a gateman presented the eastern man with a ticker."

" About four o'clock Superintendent Howland was seen meandering down the track closely followed by a lot of seedy-looking individuals who were at once recognized as importations."

" Where did you get your men? Superintendent Howland was asked."

" From all over. I've got fifty to-day, and more are coming all the time. We will have all of our trains by to-morrow. We are going to win this fight."

" Considerable difficulty was experienced in selecting a fit man from the squad, but one was finally found and placed in charge of engine 206 and it drove out for Aurora at 4:45. Another train was sent out at 5:15, and the last one left the depot at 6:30."

" The incoming trains did not seem to materialize. The bulletin-board announced in big letters that several of the trains were on time, but the bulletin prevaricated. The depot master said that certain engines would steam in at certain times, but the depot master was talking over his left shoulder. The 6:20 train was not right on hand, and eleven hours later a tall man in a wolfskin overcoat solemnly affirmed that he had watched for that train since daylight."

"Some experiences of the company with its new engineers were amusing to the strikers but essentially exasperating to the officials of the road. A train started from Galesburg with a new man, who said he knew his engine as well as if he had made it. His engine pawed and snorted like a race-horse at the starting stretch. It wanted to get away at the minute scratch and skim along the track like a bird. He got the word; the engineer 'gave her sand.' Away she sped for five miles. Then she balked; did not like her new rider. The injector belonged to the Brotherhood and the engineer did not. Before he knew what was up the injector had pumped the boiler full of cold water. The stop-cocks froze up and so did the engineer's gayety. He sadly walked to the nearest station and telegraphed for an engine to pull him back. His engine was dead."

"Four engines were reported to be 'burned out,' or dead, between Chicago and Galesburg. Two were said to be burned out on the Kansas City branch. A 'burned-out engine' may cost $50 or $1,000 for repairs, according to the size of the burn."[1]

As an illustration of the danger to property and life daily occurring, we take this one instance from the Chicago *Herald* of March 2, 1888: "The 12:01 train which left the city on Wednesday came very near meeting with a serious accident, about 4:30 o'clock in the afternoon, 108 miles west of this city. The engineer of the locomotive was J. W. Chapman, an eastern

[1] Chicago News.

man, it is claimed, of considerable experience. With him was General Superintendent Besler, who acted as pilot along the road. The train was the heaviest that had left this city since the strike was inaugurated, and consisted of three coaches, two sleepers, two postal, and an express and baggage cars. The point mentioned is about four miles west of Princeton, and three miles east of Wyanet. At this part of the road there is a bridge across a creek, the trestle upon which it is erected being ninety-six feet high. Up to near the bridge and east of it the road is double-tracked, but there is only a single track across the bridge. In order, however to prevent collisions, the road has laid automatic switches at each approach, so that if trains come in opposite directions, the one at the east approach will be thrown from the main track and on to a short spur, which at this point, runs a short distance into a dense piece of woods. When the train was approaching this bridge, it was running at the rate of forty-five miles an hour. Suddenly the locomotive gave a lurch and the clerks in the postal cars were thrown on their faces by the jar caused by the rapid and sudden turning from the main line on the spur. The bank of the creek is very high, and a calamity was threatened by the train being thrown over the precipice, as the cars rocked heavily from side to side. General Superintendent Besler seized the lever, whistled down brakes and reversed the engine. There was no train coming in an opposite direction at the time, but it was by only a miracle that a fearful calamity was averted. The postal clerks insist that the accident was due to the incompetency of the engineer, who had no business to run at such fearful speed when approaching the bridge, and had he been running at the ordinary rate of speed—twenty miles an hour—the train would not have left the track."[1]

"At Council Bluffs, Iowa, a petition signed by all the mail clerks on the Iowa division of the Burlington will be sent to Washington to-morrow, asking F. E. Nash, general superintendent of railway mail service, to have the government compel the road to put competent engineers on the mail trains."[1]

Yet, regardless of all risk to patrons, employes and property, Press Agent Morton said: "The Iowa divisional superintendent telegraphs that twenty freight trains are running there to-day, and a few freights are running on most of the other divisions. Two freight trains loaded with coal left Streator this morning for local points. Everything along the system is quiet, and the company's property is well protected."

"How much will the strike cost the Burlington company?"

"The company doesn't know and doesn't care."[2]

Neither did they care what kind of men they employed, and as hundreds of men presented themselves, Messrs. Arthur and Sargent concluded that some other steps must be taken beyond an effort to keep these men away. Thousands of dollars had been paid out all along the line in this effort, and the more men they induced to leave the more came to find work, or to sell themselves to the strikers. The situation looked serious and perplexing. Other companies were evidently helping the Burlington. The men who came to take

[1] Chicago Tribune. [2] Chicago News.

the strikers' places said they came on passes furnished by the Burlington agents. Burlington tickets were said to have been honored by other roads, because of the Burlington's inability to transport the passengers after selling the tickets; and direct charges were made that the Burlington freight business was being handled by other roads. The grievance committees from the various systems centering in Chicago, were asking for advice about transfers, and they were told by Messrs. Arthur and Sargent, "Do not handle Burlington cars."

The order created much uneasiness among general managers of other roads. It brought many of them to the Grand Pacific to consult with the Brotherhood leaders. There were so many parties seeking advice as to duties, that it was deemed best to call in the grievance committees, and on March 2, 1888, the following order was issued to the chairman of the general grievance committee of the Brotherhood of Locomotive Engineers and Firemen on the railroads centering in Chicago.

To chairman General Grievance Committee, B. of L. E. and F.—Dear Sir and Brother: You are hereby authorized and ordered to come to the city of Chicago at once and report at the headquarters. There are many important matters to consider in connection with the Chicago, Burlington and Quincy strike, and your immediate presence is imperative. Be prepared to convene your committee from here at a moment's notice. Fraternally,

P. M. Arthur, G. C. E.
F. P. Sargent, G. C. F.

This order was sent to the chairman of the committees on the following roads:

Chicago & Alton; Chicago, Rock Island & Pacific; Missouri Pacific; Wabash; Burlington, Cedar Rapids & Northern; Union Pacific; Wisconsin Central; Chicago, Milwaukee & St. Paul; Baltimore & Ohio; Chicago, Burlington & Northern; Louisville, New Albany & Chicago; Illinois Central; New York, Chicago & St. Louis; Chicago, Burlington & Quincy; Atchison, Topeka & Santa Fe; Chicago & North-Western; Minnesota & North-Western; Chicago & Eastern Illinois; Chicago & Atlantic; St. Paul, Minneapolis & Manitoba; and Chicago & Grand Trunk.

In the meantime large union meetings were held throughout the country. At New York city strong resolutions were passed against other railroads assisting the Burlington, and also strongly approving of the strike and offering financial support. At St. Paul, two hundred and fifty members of divisions 150 and 369, Brotherhood of Locomotive Engineers, passed resolutions in hearty sympathy with the strike, and guaranteed their financial assistance, and ordered one thousand dollars sent to Chicago. At LaFayette, Indiana, the following resolution was adopted and sent to P. M. Arthur, Grand Chief Engineer: "Our sympathies are with you and the enginemen of the Burlington. Fight it out to the bitter end. We send you one thousand dollars." In Indianapolis, March 4, at a meeting of Division No. 11, representing the engineers employed on the sixteen railroads centering there, the strike on the Burlington was approved, and a telegram sent to Chief Arthur urging the strikers to stand firm, that the members of that division were ready to meet any demands that might be made upon them. From all over the country came assurances of loyalty to the Brotherhoods and liberality in furnishing money that was astonishing. There were many instances of members tendering their whole month's salary, and many men, who were not members of either organization, gave their money freely, vacating their places as readily as the members. It was the prevailing opinion among laboring men, that the Burlington had been chosen as the battle field between capital and labor, and that companies other than the Burlington were equally interested in the outcome. And almost a unit was secured of the responsible, thinking laborers, in working for a common cause regardless of personal pique. With this vast army, loyal to the common interests of labor, sending heart-cheering words and money, good fellowship and good wishes, the way seemed clear, and the time auspicious, for a test of whether labor, numbering thousands, should have a voice equal to one in fixing the price of its product. Under these circumstances the committees which had been called by the order of March 2, by the grand officers, arrived in Chicago on March 5, 1888, and held the most important meeting of the year. They held within their grasp greater possibilities than any other. They had the power and voted to use it, which no other meeting within my knowledge had.

This meeting was held in secret session, or was so intended by the participants. But there must have been a black-sheep among them, moved by some other motive than the good of the order, who gave to the Chicago *Tribune* a verbatim report of the resolutions passed which were as follows: "Resolved: That the chairman of each system here represented, go home, convene his local committee, call on the officers and notify them that the engineers and firemen will not handle Burlington cars or traffic of any kind." "Also that the men are to be instructed by the chairman of the grievance committee of each road, that if a Burlington car, or any freight, shall be put upon them they will refuse to handle it, and if they are compelled by the company to do so, they will still refuse, and if they are discharged, then the engineers and firemen on the system will strike." Messrs. Arthur and Sargent were asked if they would sanction a strike under such circumstances and the answer was, "In war times we must adopt war measures. We will give our sanction."

Here was a power that was almost unlimited, but it was a negative force, so far as the officers were concerned and was not available, only so far as the men themselves would vote to adopt the measures suggested by their chairman. These measures might be sanctioned, but could not be ordered by the grand officers, so that upon the union of sentiment depended all this power. When the resolution to boycott Burlington cars was adopted, the seed of discord was sown. In war, there is a vast difference between supporting the line of battle and being in the line of battle itself. It was so in the Burlington fight; it was found there is a vast difference between passing resolutions to sustain the Burlington strikers, and voting themselves into a position that might plunge them into a strike themselves.

These committeemen left for their homes to follow out the instructions contained in the resolutions. Upon one road there was found a minority, who, when put to the test, were found on the safe side. They went to the general manager and told him they would handle Burlington cars. This general manager had said that he would not try to handle Burlington cars as long as the other roads did not. In taking this action, and notifying the managers what they would do if they compelled the enginemen to handle Burlington business, they only wished to go to that extent that the doors of their respective roads would be closed against Burlington business. This could not be done without taking the chances of finding some general manager who would demand that the men choose between handling any business offered them, and quitting. It was a critical test, yet it was the only means by which they could expect to succeed in boycotting the Burlington. It left the general managers to decide whether they would have a strike or not. If the men on all the lines had shown a positive determination not to handle Burlington cars, and if there had been no weakness shown at any point, it is reasonable to suppose that none of the managers would have made the demand which would have closed their road by a strike. The grand officers, and other leaders of the Brotherhoods, believed this move would have a powerful influence on the Burlington, and they were willing to await developments, believing the men, without an exception, would prove loyal. From this move nearly every road in the whole

WRECK AT MEAGHER STREET AND STEWART AVENUE, CHICAGO.

circle of the Burlington's connecting lines was closed. While the leaders of the strike are waiting for developments, let us look at the situation along the line of the Burlington.

The Burlington officials were giving the public to understand that they were getting all the men they wanted, and that the quality was equal to the old men, but from certain letters received at the strikers' headquarters it would appear that the Burlington company was not having things all its own way securing engineers. The following letter sent by Master Mechanic R. W. Colville, of Galesburg, Ill., to one of its former engineers, discharged five years ago for alleged incompetency, is self-explanatory. The name is purposely suppressed, but the engineer's present address is Racine, Wis.:

Dear Sir: You are, of course, aware ere this of the situation on the 'Q' system, brought about by the demands of the engineers' and firemen's brotherhoods. Are you willing to come back to Galesburg at once and aid the company during this temporary trouble by service as a locomotive engineer? I will give you my positive assurance that if you do come, all of the past will be overlooked by the company, and your action in rendering assistance at this time will be remembered by the management. Furthermore, your position here after the end of this trouble will be a permanant one, and one which will give you no cause or reason to regret leaving your present one. Please wire me at once on receipt of this if you will come, and if so, come by the first train by any route by which you can get here the quickest, and whatever expense you incur will be made good to you."

Engines were being burned, the company's property destroyed, and the public greatly inconvenienced.

"No. 4, the fast mail, due in Chicago at 6:53 A. M. arrived at the Union depot at 11:03. At Naperville at 8:10 o'clock, this train passed No. 8, a through train, which should have arrived in this city at 6:20 A. M. This train was helpless, because the engineer, a new and incompetent man, had burned out his fire-box and was unable to make steam. The passengers, and their baggage, were transferred to the fast mail, and brought into the city."[1]

"At Ottumwa, Iowa, the company put several brakemen on passsenger engines."

At Quincy, Ill., March 1, "The first freight sent out since the strike began, went out this afternoon on the Carthage branch to Burlington, with Follet, a submarine diver, as engineer. Passenger trains on the St. Louis, Keokuk & Northwestern had been abandoned, because the Wabash engineers refused to take the trains over the Wabash to St. Peters, the Burlington having no track from St. Peters to St. Louis. The St. Louis bridge engineers refused to transfer Burlington cars."

A telegram to the Chicago *News* from Omaha, Nebraska, March 1, said: "A Burlington official said to-day: 'The road, by working steadily, has now secured a man for every engine, and to-morrow even the switch engines will be running."

The same report said: "Not a pound of freight has been moved by the Burlington and Missouri river road since the strike began. Passenger trains are beginning to arrive more frequently, although most of them are from one to three hours behind hand. Twenty-eight Pinkerton men arrived and went west from here last night. All were armed with Winchester rifles."

"Creston, Iowa, March 2. The situation shows a turn to-day favoring the Brotherhoods, so far as the west Iowa division is concerned. State Commissioner Peter A. Day, has held an investigation here to-day at the direction of Governor Larabee, examining engineers regarding their fitness. Nine acting engineers were on the witness stand, and nearly all testified that they were inexperienced, and did not consider themselves competent engineers. Some acknowledged they were now running engines for the first time, and were pulling passenger trains."[1]

Lincoln, Nebraska, March 2. Pinkerton men were added to the military display at the Burlington grounds to-day, and from the fact that not a disturbance of any kind had occurred or any arrest been made, or any interference whatever offered by the striking engineers, the citizens look with no favor on the latest importation."[1]

"Denver, March 2. One of the two men who had been secured by the Burlington road to handle its engines, has come to grief. He has been conducting a photograph outfit on wheels. This probably inspired him with the idea that he could run an engine. He took a train out yesterday morning, but when he reached Brush station the engine was so badly burned that it was unfit for further service."[1]

"Kansas City, Missouri, March 2. Engine 75,

1 Associated Press report.

in charge of Engineer Grange, was burned out near Harlem this morning." [1]

"Brookfield, Missouri, March 2. The usual day passenger trains have gone through, carrying passengers and express and mail, though somewhat out of time. The efforts of the strikers are mainly put forth to induce the men who come to take their places, to quit. In this they have partially succeeded, buying off some, and scaring off others, but careful surveillance is kept by the officials, and thus far no train has been delayed here. Last evening one freight was sent west. None went out to-day. The public confidence in the ability of the company to master the situation is somewhat strengthened by the movements of trains, but the resumption of business is far from an accomplished fact. The inexperienced character of the new men is shown in the disabling of several engines, and inability to make time. There was a rumor of acts of petty lawlessness by which it was sought to endanger travel, but none have occurred here, and it is the constant assertion of the resident strikers that they will not countenance or allow any act of trespass upon company property."

"Lincoln, Nebraska, March 4. Sixty new engineers arrived in the night from the east, and have been put to work here and distributed among the different divisions in the state. The company expresses itself as able now to handle all business, but the trains do not depart in numbers sufficient to warrant the statement. No through business of any character is attempted, but the company has a force of engineers who are yet untried, though in numbers sufficient to handle local

[1] Chicago News.

business. Travel is very light, and the other roads centering here are reaping a harvest. The Brotherhoods have been diligently at work on the new men making converts. A number of them were in the Brotherhood's hall and announced their intention of returning home. They said they were promised $4 a day to come, but they found that the company would put them on their graded rates which only pay $2.25 a day. The same class of work they declared paid $3.10 a day on eastern roads. A Reading Knight of Labor, engineer, made a speech in the hall, and said that their coming west was a mistake. He thought the railroads were using both the Brotherhoods and the Knights of Labor to destroy each other."

"Hastings, Nebraska, March 4. Practically, there is no change here since the beginning of the strike. Two mail trains run irregularly each way on the main line every twenty-four hours, and fragments of freight trains, carrying coal principally, are occasionally sent out to supply the demands along the branch lines where no other service is had. Fuel is becoming scarce on the Burlington lines in this state. The Burlington is losing its hold on the mercantile trade of the city which is being transferred to its competitors."

"Clinton, Iowa, March 4. A Burlington freight train pulled into the yard yesterday. It was the first since the strike. On the engine were two strangers, who were at once beset by the Brotherhood men who begged them to leave the engine. At length the engineer asked for $80 for himself and his fireman, which was handed him. He then said he would pull his engine back to the Mendota end of his division and leave the employ of the company. He pulled out for the roundhouse and had not gone but a short distance when the fireman jumped off the engine and went back to the Brotherhood men, who greeted him with a cheer. He was given some money and then he went back east." [1]

Denver, Colorado, March 6. In addition to the single passenger train, in and out to day, the Burlington sent two freight trains east, and one freight train is expected to arrive. Freight is being received for local points, but shippers invariably send by other routes anything destined for common points. The mayor has taken offense at the presence of deputy sheriffs who are doing police duty about the Burlington yards. He declares that the city police are equal to all demands. The strikers are conducting themselves in the same orderly manner as they have done from the outset." [1]

The Burlington had great appearance of success in manning their engines; they had gathered a large number of engineers such as they were, and they were putting the best face possible on their side of the story. They were indifferent as to the cost or the destruction of property; the road was lined with deputy sheriffs and Pinkerton detectives, evidently without consent or pre-arrangement of local authorities. While their facilities were improving, their business was going to other companies; their losses and increased expenses were enormous. Even the great military display did not deter the strikers from soliciting their new men. The company built places for the new men for dining and sleeping, and commanded

[1] Chicago News.

them to stay within their walls, yet many of them would violate this rule—their appetite demanded it. In Brookfield, even a prohibition hotel keeper was seen wending his way on Sunday with a basket filled with the sparkling "elixir," so necessary to the wants of these men. On all sides the road was closed to through traffic. The railroad commissioners of Iowa had investigated the character of engineers employed in Iowa, and had pronounced them incompetent.

CHAPTER XLII.

THE STRIKE, IN CONGRESS AND IN COURT.

In Congress March 5, 1888, representative White, of Indiana, had offered the following:

"Whereas: There has been inaugurated a great strike on the Chicago, Burlington & Quincy railroad, which, if not speedily checked, will end in wide spread disaster and suffering, not only to those immediately engaged in it, but to others who are not directly connected therewith, yet nevertheless, are greatly affected by the prolongation of said strike; Resolved: That a special committee of five be appointed by the speaker, to proceed at once to Chicago and there investigate the conditions, and that they be empowered and requested to act as mediators between the Burlington and Chief Arthur, and bring about a settlement of the pending trouble and difference which will be amicable and agreeable to both parties, so that the strike will terminate. Referred to committee on commerce."

The Burlington had, before the strike, reduced rates for freight below reason, to compel other lines to do their bidding. Reductions in the freight tariff began to occur for other reasons. On March 2, Chairman Midgeley was notified of a tariff reduction on packing house products from Missouri river points to Chicago, to ten cents per one hundred pounds, to hold its business. Yet Press Agent Morton said, when asked about the situation, "We are running forty-seven passenger trains and one hundred and one freight trains on the Iowa division, and on the Illinois division we are running more trains than in Iowa. All around we are doing quite well. Everything is lovely and the goose hangs high."[1]

It will not be questioned that the Burlington's news dispenser was equal to his task. While he is giving such a charming picture of the situation, the Chicago *Tribune* of the same date, March 7, had a review of affairs, of a contrasted hue:

"The boycott on the Burlington is almost complete, so far as the western roads are concerned. At all junctions along the line of the Burlington may be found long rows of cars, delivered by the company to roads that will not move them from the place where they have been left by the non-brotherhood crews. The Chicago & North-Western had hundreds of cars lying in its various yards consigned to points on the Burlington, while the Burlington has hundreds of cars that the Chicago & North-Western will not accept and forward to points of destination. The same is true of the Chicago, Milwaukee & St. Paul; the Chicago & Alton; the Chicago, Rock Island & Pacific; the Santa Fe; the Eastern Illinois; the Illinois Central; and the Wabash. The officials of the Alton, Rock Island, Northwestern, Wabash, and other roads, admit that they had agreed to refuse to handle Burlington traffic. They said they could not afford to do otherwise, as the loss to them from stoppage of their business would be immense. One of them said he could not see why his road should allow itself to become involved in the

[1] Chicago Tribune, March 6, 1888.

strike, simply to help out the Burlington. When the western roads lately tried to restore rates to a paying basis, the Burlington objected. It paid no consideration to the desires of its competitors then, and there is no reason why the latter should show any consideration to the Burlington now. 'Self-preservation,' he said, 'was the first duty of his road, and he meant to act upon that principal.'"

While it was evidently the desire of all the other managers to keep out of the fight, the Burlington management was bound to bring them into it. They have never been very considerate ot any one's interest but their own. A writer in the Aurora *Daily Express* says: "When the Burlington gets on the defensive, and is weak in the knees, it piously turns to the law. When the Burlington has any scheme to carry out in utter defiance of law, then, the law be ——"

They were hemmed in on all sides at this time, and at once instituted legal proceedings to compel compliance with the inter-state commerce law. They chose the Wabash, as that was in the hands of the United States court under General McNulta. Assistant General Passenger Agent Wakely said: "The fight between the Burlington and the strikers is over. We have won the battle and can now take a rest and look on, while Chief Arthur and his hosts tackle the other fellows. We have stood the brunt of the shock, and set the pace for our competitors to follow. I see that some of them hesitate about showing fight, and seem to lack that amount of sand necessary for a good sol dier. I am of the opinion that the strikers are playing a bold game of bluff, and that they will stop all of this foolishness when the railroad companies take the decided stand they must assume sooner or later."[1] The smile of assurance that accompanied this declaration would no doubt have faded, had he been able to see further into the future. The Burlington had an opportunity to make the declaration that "the strike was off," many times before it really was, and continued to feel the power of the "bluff" many months.

The Grand Pacific hotel, of Chicago, is the official centerof all roads entering Chicago, and in the building was located the strikers' headquarters. Messrs. Arthur and Sargent were both there and also Messrs. Hoge and Murphy, the chairmen of the engineer's and firemen's committee. In the immense rotunda could be seen the greatest activity. Men were hurrying through the crowd, type writers with nimble fingers were weaving the thread of information, or instruction, and the electric current was kept busy with messages, in and out. It had the appearance of a great national caucus. The strikers' headquarters were no less active. Men representing roads in all parts of the country, came for advice, eager to lend a helping hand; proffers of money, votes of confidence, and gratuitous advice came on wings.

While the Burlington had only their own road to watch, Arthur and Sargent must watch and direct all roads, and at this time, March 6, nothing but united, unselfish devotion to the cause of the two Brotherhoods could be expected to win the battle. The Burlington were finding substitutes. So the boycott had been decided on as the most powerful weapon, but to use this successfully the most absolute loyalty was

[1] Chicago Tribune.

necessary. Realizing this, every indication of a break far or near, in the solidity of the line of boycott which surrounded the Burlington, brought with it an unpleasant realization that the chief and grand master of the two Brotherhoods lacked the power to order and compel. They must depend for obedience upon that slender thread in human nature—honor.

With this feeling uppermost in their minds, the following telegram was received from Kansas City, nearly 500 miles away: "Grand Chief P. M. Arthur: Complications may arise at any time, making the counsel and presence of Grand Organizer S. M. Stevens necessary. Answer quick. J. C. Murray."

This request was complied with, and Mr Stevens assigned to duty. Shortly another one was received addressed to the Grand Chief: "Kansas City, Missouri: Roads centering here are violating pledges not to handle Burlington business. The men feel that the time has come to act.' J. C. M

The fear of hasty action added to other combinations, made the situation anything but pleasant at headquarters, and Kansas City being the terminal point of some twenty-five thousand miles of railroad, they would naturally experience much anxiety. This was naturally increased by the receipt of another telegram from Kansas City, Missouri, March 6, at 3:00 P. M., addressed to Messrs. Arthur and Sargent: "All the roads centering here have broken agreement with our committee of engineers and firemen. Are waiting your answer. Local Committee."

To this the grand chief answered: "Send your committee here at once."

Union meetings were being held in Kansas City, composed of men from the Union Pacific; Fort Scott & Gulf; Atchison Topeka & Santa Fe; Chicago, Rock Island & Pacific; Southern Kansas; Wabash; Western & Missouri Pacific and others. Many of the chairmen of these lines were there, yet it was hard to tell what might happen, and from that time on the excitement among the men, who visited headquarters, ran high.

Beside these complications, the grand officers had been warned by their legal counsel, Mr. Alexander Sullivan, of the conspiracy law of Illinois. Under that law it was supposed that the liberty of the leaders would be endangered if they should give instructions for any combined action.

This law reads as follows:

"If any two or more persons conspire or agree together, or the officers or executive committee of any society or corporation shall issue or utter any circulars or edict, as to the action of, or instructions to its members, or any other persons, society, organization, or corporation, for the purpose of establishing a so-called boycott, or black list, or shall post or distribute any written or printed notice with malicious intent to wrongfully or wickedly injure the person, character, business, employment or property of another, or to obtain money or other property by false pretenses, or to do any illegal act injurious to the public trade, health, morals, policy, or administration of public justice, or to prevent competition in the letting of any contract by the state, or the authorities of any county, city, town or village, or to induce any person not to enter into such competition, or to commit felony, they shall be deemed guilty of a conspiracy, and every such offender, whether as individual, or as officer, of any society or organization, and every person convicted of conspiracy at common law, shall be imprisoned in the penitentiary not exceeding five years, or fined not exceeding $2,000, or both.

"If two or more persons conspire to overthrow the existing order of society, by force or violence, or to bring about local revolutions by force, or to destroy, or resist, or overcome the local authorities, all such persons shall be guilty of conspiracy, and be punished accordingly notwithstanding the time and place for bringing about such revolution or overthrowing of public order, or the destruction, or overcoming of such authority, had not been definitely agreed upon by such conspirators, but was left to the exigencies of the time, or the judgment of co-conspirators, or some one or more of them.

"Hereafter, it shall not be necessary in order to establish a conspiracy, as aforesaid, to prove that the parties charged ever came together and entered into any agreement, combination or arrangement, to accomplish a criminal or unlawful purpose, but it shall be sufficient if it appears that the parties charged were actually pursuing, in concert, the unlawful purpose, whether acting separately or together, at the same or different times, by the same or different means, providing that the acts of each were knowingly tending to the same unlawful result." [1]

Under the restrictions of this law no instructions could be given from their present headquarters within

[1] Statutes of Illinois.

the state of Illinois, and to obviate this difficulty, it was necessary to call the men in and have an understanding of what course they desired to pursue within their own states. Immediately following this came the problem of the Chicago, Burlington & Northern, astonishing the incredulous public. The picture of loyalty and unselfishness manifest in this move by these men was a new and startling vision of the power of organizations and their readiness to use it in behalf of their fellow man with orderly methods.

THE INCREDULOUS.

CHAPTER XLIII.

BURLINGTON & NORTHERN STRIKE.

The Chicago, Burlington & Northern railroad was built in 1886 in the interest of the Burlington road. This road connects with the Burlington system proper at Oregon, Ill., and runs to St. Paul, a distance of 232 miles. It was, however, managed as a separate holding, but as a feeder for the Burlington. The men employed upon it felt that they were jeopardizing the interests of their striking Burlington brothers, by handling business directly in the interest of the Burlington road. They were urged to stop this traffic. In this effort the committee called on the officers, on Sunday, March 4, and demanded that it be stopped or they would strike at seven o'clock the following evening. But it is evident that there was a want of agreement among the men as to the necessity of such a step, and they afterwards informed the officers that they would remain at work. But the next day, the meeting in Chicago of all the chairmen of grievance committees having passed the resolution to boycott, they made an effort again with more unanimity. The engineers and firemen located at La Crosse, on the Chicago, Burlington & Northern road, presented their ultimatum in the following letter:

La Crosse, Wis., March 6, 1888.

To General Superintendent Barr,

Chicago, Burlington & Northern railroad.

"DEAR SIR:

The engineers and firemen of your railroad company respectfully request that after 10 o'clock A. M., Wednesday, March 7, you do not ask them to handle any business, either passenger or freight, or any consignment in the interest of the Chicago, Burlington & Quincy railroad. Such a step will not be consistent with the present good will which exists between your company and its engineers and firemen." An answer was expected to this by seven o'clock the next morning.[1]

On receiving this document, Mr. Barr immediately transmitted it to General Manager Harris, of the Chicago, Burlington & Northern, who answered at once, saying: "It is useless to propose that the Chicago, Burlington & Northern road surrender the control of its affairs, or that it be subjected to the dictation of its employes. If any of the engineers or firemen do not like the company's method of doing business, give them their time checks, and post such notices as you may deem proper for the direction of the employes." [1]

A strike was not what these men wanted. Their pay was satisfactory and they only wished to boycott the Burlington, but when they hesitated the second time, pressure was brought to bear on them from the leaders in Chicago, and at 10:00 A. M., on the 8th, the engines were abandoned, except those which were on the road. These were run to the end of their divisions, as had been done a week before on the Burlington. In this move there was an evident lack of generalship. It is known that the enginemen in

[1] Chicago Tribune.

the vicinity of this line in their eagerness to cripple the Burlington had clamored for this movement, yet the leaders should have been ready with definite plans educed from mature deliberation as to the importance of this line to the Burlington.

This road belonged in part to the Burlington and had no outlet to the south except the Burlington, while the north end was hedged in by the boycott, so that they could not have had much business at best. The Burlington was its recruiting ground for men to take their places and when the old men stepped down the new stepped up. It was a grand spectacle of loyalty; no doubt the leaders believed it was necessary, and all were ready with all the power they possessed, and by any sacrifice, to help the cause. But the result was more disastrous than beneficial, because every step of this kind, which did not carry with it success, weakened hundreds of other men whose loyalty and co-operation were essential to success. General Manager Harris had stated his position; that the only result of a demand to boycott would be that the men would lose their places. A boycott to the Chicago, Burlington & Northern meant the suspension of business entirely, and there was consequently no choice for Mr. Harris.

The wisdom of making the demand, in view of that road's surroundings, is at this distance very doubtful and can only be measured by the result. Every failure of success, in whatever method or direction made, was far-reaching in its effect. When we remember that there was no power to compel, but every man was his own master, and that each voted to do, or not to do, we can appreciate the damage done by the weakening influence it exercised on those already weak, and the effect upon other lines in producing that lack of harmony so essential to success.

The movement in the direction of a general boycott called forth unpleasant criticism in the newspapers, and caused the following circular letter to be sent out from the strikers' headquarters.

"To the public: Owing to the reports that are being circulated in regard to the attitude of the locomotive engineers in the present strike, and there being a tendency on the part of the press to endorse the stand taken by the railroad company, we deem it necessary in our own behalf to state that the two organizations which are engaged in the present trouble are composed of conservative men, and they are ready and willing now, and have ever been, to meet the officers of the Burlington railroad and arbitrate the questions in dispute. The Brotherhoods are not only willing to do this through their executive officers, but are also willing to place the whole matter in the hands of three railroad managers and abide by their decision.

"Now, in all candor, we would ask any honest, thinking citizen, whether the organizations mentioned can do more and maintain their constitutional privileges? If this trouble shall continue, and the public at large shall suffer on account of the same, the blame must rest where it belongs, and that is upon the parties who refuse to arbitrate."

(Signed) The Brotherhoods.

In an interview with a *Tribune* reporter, Mr. Arthur said: " We will meet Mr. Perkins or Mr. Stone half way," and when asked what he would consider a fair arbitration committee, said, "Any three general managers of the roads running out of Chicago. I mention railroad men because they understand the situation better than any one else, and I agree, on behalf of the Brotherhood, to abide by the decision of such an arbitration committee."[1]

On this subject Mr. Paul Morton, for the Burlington said: "There is considerable talk about arbitration, but it all comes from men outside of our employ, who evidently desire to go to work again. These men can return to work when they accede to our terms."[1] The extent of the strike, the feeling and activity displayed by the strikers and all those in sympathy, portended insurmountable difficulties to railroads and to commerce, and they called forth many articles on arbitration. The Aurora *Daily Express* said: "The present condition of things cannot last long in this country. The public, through whose consent such corporations are organized and permitted to exist, have rights which must be respected. The railroads should be, by law, compelled to arbitrate when honest differences arise between them and their employes. This can be done quietly and without a suspension of business. The great body of working men in this country, thanks to the best government under the sun, are very intelligent and law abiding, and would accept such decision. The railroad companies, if they want the candid judgment of the public, must learn to respect the rights of the people, and to obey the law. These are things to which they pay very little attention where they affect their interests unfavorably."[1]

[1] Chicago Tribune.

The Creston *Advertiser* believes that "In the main the principles for which the Brotherhoods are striving are just and equitable, and hopes that by concessions or compromise on conditions of less importance, they gain the abolishment of the classification system, which is the cause of so many evils and so much injustice in the service, and that the mileage system may be established as the most equitable manner of compensation. If the mileage asked for is too high, surely there should be no trouble in coming to a compromise basis by arbitration. The side that refuses to submit to this means of settlement for the benefit of the public, should be visited by the merited condemnation of the people."

The strike and kindred topics were fruitful and frequent subjects of discussion in all the leading periodicals of the country, but the Burlington, regardless of any interest or of public opinion, bent upon gratifying their own magnified official powers and rights, worked under the motto: "Rule or ruin;" and, to drive other roads into the fight, went into court. Mr. Morton's assistant, Mr. Wakely, said: "The Burlington will at once institute legal proceedings to force other roads to receive and forward freight. It is claimed upon good authority that several of the roads now hesitating about handling Burlington freight, are only waiting for an order from the court compelling them to do so. Such an order would give them an excuse which the strikers could hardly afford to ignore. In the event of a general strike following this enforced acceptance of the Burlington freight by the competing roads, that company would have far the best of it. A general strike would completely paralyze the through freight traffic, but this would cut little figure with the Burlington. It is now in a position to handle an immense amount of business and is waiting for that business. A general strike would mass upon this road the entire local freight of six states.

"It would be impossible for any of the great roads, like the Chicago, Milwaukee & St. Paul, Rock Island & Pacific, or the Wabash, to fill all the places of their engineers for weeks, perhaps for months to come. During all this time the Burlington would be in clo- er, and would regain all that it had lost. This is why the Burlington officials, from President Perkins down, smile, when told that a general strike is possible."

Mr. Paul Morton was asked: "In case of a general strike being ordered, would any influence brought to bear upon their road by these companies crippled by such a strike, have the effect of forcing you to concede to the demands of the strikers, or cause you to accept a compromise?" He replied; "No, Sir: most emphatically, no."[1]

[1] Chicago Tribune.

WRECK IN CHICAGO YARD.—FAST MAIL.

CHAPTER XLIV.

THE BURLINGTON IN COURT.

To enforce the policy which the Burlington had adopted towards other roads, action was brought against the Wabash, St. Louis & Pacific, in Judge Gresham's court to which General John NcNulta as receiver of the Wabash, owes his authority. "Intervening petitions were filed in the names of Charles H. Beers, the lumberman, et al., and D. E. Richardson the grain man, who has an elevator at the intersection of the Burlington tracks and Western avenue. Specific incidents are mentioned in each, but the relief sought by both is identical. Judge Gresham was asked to require Receiver McNulta to handle the freight of the Burlington, and if it be found that his failure to do so thus far has been the result of an improper influence by Chief Arthur of the Brotherhood of Engineers, that he be ordered to show cause why he should not be punished for contempt of court, in interfering with the management and operation of the railroad in the control of the United States court. General Manager Stone made the allegations on behalf of the petitioners through Mr. Wirt Dexter, solicitor of the Burlington company. Then follows a long recitation of the complaint. The fifth paragraph of the petition says, that "the refusal of the agent was due to the direct orders of the receiver, and that when the receiver was called upon for a reason for his action, he said it was because his men had threatened to strike if asked to haul Burlington cars. This refusal of the receiver to handle Burlington freight is described as an unusual discrimination, and Chief Arthur as the head of the Brotherhood, is alleged to have brought about the receiver's action by duress. Under the prevailing circumstances it is alleged that the Wabash road is deprived of a large source of revenue, and its employes made liable to fine and imprisonment for wanton and malicious discrimination against the property of the petitioners. Judge Gresham looked over the papers and thereupon made an order as follows: 'Come now the Chicago, Burlington & Quincy railroad company, and D. E. Richardson by their solicitors, and present their petition to the court, praying for an order of the court, requiring the receiver of the court appointed herein, and his agents, officers, and employes, to perform his duties as a public carrier, as respects traffic with such petitioner, and also for an order, restraining the association commonly called the Brotherhood of Locomotive Engineers, and its officers, and agents, and especially one P. M. Arthur, its chief executive officer, as charged in said petition, from, in any way, giving any orders to the engineers in the employ of the receiver for them to refuse to haul loaded cars coming to, or going from, the railroad in charge of said receiver in usual business interchange with the said petition's corporation, and also praying for an order to punish the said Arthur for contempt of court, in unlawfully interfering with the administration of the property in the custody of the court in this cause.'[1] The case was set for March 9, at 2 P. M.

[1] Chicago Tribune.

This action was in reality an action against the Brotherhood, but not being a chartered institution, it could not be held accountable only as individuals. The action against the Wabash was for the restraining of the association, commonly called the Brotherhood of Locomotive Engineers, its officers and agents, and especially one P. M. Arthur. When the time set for trial came, Judge Gresham's court room was crowded long before the designated time, by railroad presidents, lawyers, engineers, firemen, and others anxious to hear what was to be done on this double-barreled application of the Burlington to compel the receiver of the Wabash to handle Burlington cars, and punish Chief Arthur for alleged orders to engineers not to handle them. The only way the Burlington could get an effective legal fulcrum against the strikers, was to get into court on some railroad case. Other managers were watching the case closely to see what bearing it would have on their interests. The sentiment of a large number of those present, including lawyers, seemed to be in favor of the strikers. At 2 o'clock Judge Gresham entered the court room, followed by the attorneys, and after taking his seat said:

"The motion which was to be argued this afternoon, will be postponed until Monday at 2 o'clock P. M."

The suddenness and brevity of the announcement took every one by surprise, and for several moments no one realized that the case which had been put off was the matter of the great Burlington strike.

The crowd remained in the hall for an hour or more discussing the situation, and it was noticeable that the adherents of the Burlington road were few.

The complaints were filed under the national interstate commerce law and the United States court could hardly fail to sustain it. Judge Gresham, in his decision on Monday, said: " Although the property of the Wabash company is in the custody of the court, it is operated by the receiver as a common carrier. His rights and duties are those of a carrier. He is bound to afford to all railroad companies whose lines connect with his road, equal facilities for the exchange of traffic. It is his duty to receive from, and deliver to other connecting roads both loaded and empty cars. He cannot discriminate against one road by maintaining a policy of non-intercourse with it. More need not be said on this question as the receiver has wisely rescinded the instructions which discriminate against the petitioner, and he has no purpose or desire to deny the petitioner any of his legal rights. Although the petitioner has accomplished his chief purpose in invoking the aid of the court, it is urged by the counsel that persons belonging to the Brotherhood of Locomotive Engineers, and especially one P. M. Arthur, its chief officer, have interfered with the receiver, and his subordinates, in the management of the Wabash property, and that they should be punished for their illegal and contumacious conduct. The receiver and his counsel make no such complaint, on the contrary, the receiver declares that there has been no such interference with him.

"For the present it is sufficient to say that the court will protect the property of the Wabash company, in its custody. The employes of the receiver cannot be obliged to remain in the service against their will, but neither they, nor others, will be permitted to interfere with or disturb the receiver or his subordinates in the possession and operation of the property in his custody. Lawless interference with the receiver and his employes in the discharge of their duty will not be tolerated."

"It is proper to state, however, in justice to the Wabash engineers, that they do not desire to maintain an attitude of defiance to the law, and that they are willing to aid the receiver in the lawful and successful administration of his trust. The receiver's answer renders it unnecessary for the court to do more than direct that the petition remain on file for future action should there be occasion."[1] The Burlington company was not well satisfied with the scope of this decision. They wanted to get some one into jail or into other trouble. The Burlington's solicitor, Wirt Dexter, said: "Its all right. The Wabash has resumed traffic with us. The court has placed the petition on file which leaves it open for us to come in again in case of any future trouble."

Alexander Sullivan, for the Brotherhood, said: "Its the only decision the court could have rendered. The court's declaration against lawless interference or intervention is in harmony with the doctrines of the Brotherhood, and will meet with their approval. There had been no such interference and there would be none by the Brotherhood. The court properly lays down the doctrine that no man can be compelled to work for less wages than he is willing to accept. It is on a line with the Illinois statute, and, what is greater, the constitutional amendment abolishing slavery."[1]

[1] Chicago Tribune.

This line of action was followed up closely by the Burlington, and, in a similar case against the Belt Line, of Chicago, it made the charges more specific against the enginemen, charging "that the Brotherhood of Locomotive Engineers, or their officers, have secretly resolved to carry out a boycott against complainant for the illegal purpose of injuring the Burlington's business. It charges them with unlawful conspiracy, and asks for an injunction against the unknown members of the Brotherhood whose names are to be inserted when discovered."

The Burlington was feeling somewhat elated over this new move which they expected would do so much for them. Many of the officials of other roads thought that if a decision was rendered by Judge Gresham, favoring the Burlington, the engineers would not dare ignore its condition on any other road and that the strike would be ended in a week. But it will be seen that these officers, as well as those of the Burlington, were greatly mistaken. General Manager Stone was made to realize that coercion would not work with all men, and that some of the others managers thought they had interests that should not be subordinated to the Burlington.

The Chicago, Rock Island and Pacific, having refused to take Burlington traffic, Mr. Stone, in order to get a basis for legal proceedings against that road wrote the following letter:

Chicago, March 8, 1888.

Mr. E. St. John, General Manager Chicago, Rock Island & Pacific railroad.

DEAR SIR·

I enclose copy of telegram which has been received here from Rock Island, saying that both the Chicago, Rock Island & Pacific, and the Peoria and Rock Island roads decline to do business with us. I cannot suppose that this is by any authority from headquarters, and I write to ask you to tell me the facts, and the reasons if there are any, for the alleged refusal. If the Chicago, Burlington & Quincy has done anything to justify such an attitude of non-intercourse, I shall be glad to know what it is.[1]

Yours Truly,

H. B. STONE."

The answer to this from Mr. St. John, must have made Mr. Stone feel in some doubt about the sweeping success anticipated in their appeal to the court— to save us if you kill all the rest. Mr. St. John had, on the 6th inst., made answer to a like communication in the following:

Chicago, March 6, 1888.

H. B. Stone, General Manager, Chicago, Burlington Quincy railroad company.

DEAR SIR:

"I have your favor of March 6, and must state in reply, that I am surprised that your company in the present condition of things, should insist or even suggest, that the Rock Island, or any of its adjuncts, should receive freight from, or deliver freight to your company until a better condition of things exists. To do so would jeopardize our entire interest, and this at this moment we are not willing to do. Our

[1] Chicago Tribune.

position is not different from that occupied by other Chicago lines, and you should have, I think, no feeling concerning such action on your part, which is only one of self protection. You may be assured that the Rock Island is always glad to aid the Chicago, Burlington & Quincy when it can do so without getting itself into serious trouble. Our past action is proof of this as you well know. We believe it to be equally in your interest as well as ours, that the position we and others assume, should, for the present at least, be maintained."

Respectfully,

E. ST. JOHN, General Manager.

On receipt of Mr. Stone's second letter of the 8th, Mr. St. John, in his answer says: "That there may be no misunderstanding as to the position of the Chicago, Rock Island & Pacific company in regard to exchange of traffic with the Chicago, Burlington & Quincy railroad company, I desire to add to my hastily written note of the 6th inst., the following:

"This company is willing to perform all duties imposed upon it by law as common carriers, and will do so when able. It will not refuse to perform such duties to all because it is rendered, by circumstances for which it is not responsible, unable to perform them as to one. It will not suspend the operation as to its entire line, and inflict incalculable injury upon the communities dependent upon itfor transportation, because circumstances render it impossible for it to exchange traffic with another railroad company. The engineers and firemen positively refuse to handle freight received from, or delivered to your road. We have done nothing to induce this resolution. To discharge them would not enable us to exchange with you, while it would render it impossible to carry for anybody else."

"We occupy no attitude of non-intercourse, but do refuse to injure all of our patrons because we cannot help you. I cannot see how bringing about a general suspension of the operations of railways in the west, can aid you in your present struggle, while I can see that it would work great injury to the country. We are not willing to attempt the impossible, with the knowledge that the attempt will injure many and benefit none."[1] Respectfully Yours,

E. St. John.

For once, Mr. Morton, the Burlington's news dispenser, was obliged to hold himself in. Upon being respectfully touched by the pencil of a reporter, "Comment upon such a document is unnecessary," said Mr. Morton, "and it is hardly right for me to express an opinion upon the sentiments contained in that letter. I will say that under no circumstances would such a letter have emanated from this office." But their harrowed feelings found great solace in the restraining order of one Judge Dundy, of Nebraska, on March 9.

The Chicago, Burlington and Quincy railroad by its solicitors, C. G. Green and T. M. Marquette, counsel, filed in the United States court, and immediately had submitted to Judge Dundy, a bill in equity against the Union Pacific, its officers and employes, praying for an injunction restraining them from refusing to handle the traffic of the Burlington on the Un-

[1] Chicago Tribune.

ion Pacific lines, also restraining the engineers of the Union Pacific from striking, or confederating to organize a strike, to force the Burlington to accede to the demands of the strikers, and from discharging the men now employed. In Judge Dundy they found a man who came very near doing what they wanted him to do. We extract from Judge Dundy's restraining order the following passages:

"That you each and everyone of you, do absolutely desist and refrain from striking, combining, or confederating, for the purpose of organizing or assisting a strike, and from doing any other act or thing, and from refusing to perform any other act or thing in carrying out your unlawful, unjust and wicked purpose, through your unlawful, unjust and wicked combination, connivance, and conspiracy, either as individuals or as members of the Brotherhood of Locomotive Engineers."[1]

The Burlington officials mixed this morsel of good cheer with their utter contempt for managers who had refused to jeopardize their own interest to help the Burlington. Yet regardless of this order, "the Union Pacific; Atchison, Topeka & Santa Fe; Denver & Rio Crande and Midland railroads were not handling Burlington business, and it was intimated that they did not intend to."[1] The strikers and the Union Pacific enginemen were somewhat concerned about this order, but the Union Pacific men said the court could not force them to touch the Burlington cars, and if it was demanded they would quit.

The Union Pacific men employed General Cowin as their legal adviser, and at the trial in behalf of his

[1] Chicago Daily News.

WRECK AT DE KOVEN STREET, CHICAGO.—HOUSE FRONT BROKEN IN,

clients, the engineers, General Cowin contended "that the bill was filed against them by the Burlington and Missouri railroad, as a part and parcel of a plan to compel them to work in direct opposition to their wishes for the purpose of aiding them, the complainants, in their fight with the Brotherhood of Locomotive Engineers. As a naked proposition of law, he submitted as a question of common sense, that there is no law to compel men to work when they desire to quit, and that alone seems to be the object of the bill."

Then said the court, "If that be the sole object, this case has no business here. I shall never order a man to work against his will by injunction."

During General Cowin's argument, the word strike was used several times as it had been in the bill, which provoked the following comment from the court: "This word strike is of modern origin; the question is regarding its legal definition and on that this case may turn. If it means, and it can be shown that its meaning in this case is, a project to kick up the devil generally, derail cars and ditch trains, then this court can order a writ of injunction to restrain the injury contemplated as a measure of contemplative justice, and the charge of conspiracy is well taken. If, on the other hand, the word in this case is synonymous with an intention of quitting work, and quietly walking out, I don't see how this court is going to restrain this action."[1]

J. M. Thurston, for the Union Pacific road, averred in part, "that the greatest rivalry had always existed between the two roads. Much of their revenue was

1 Chicago Tribune.

derived from the same sources, and the Burlington road had never lost an opportunity in competition, to further its interest at the expense of the Union Pacific; that the Union Pacific recognized its obligations under the law, and had ordered its men to handle the traffic of the Burlington, and when the men refused such orders, they were taken suddenly ill with an epidemic which, for want of a better name, was known as the "Q colic," and refused to obey the orders. If the company persist in the demand under the law and the men quit the great corporation, the Union Pacific would have to cease operations because of its inability to supply their places."[2] The Burlington contended, "that where the common action of a body of men tended to produce the same result by the same common means, controlled by the same power, and the object was to damage and injure any single individual, or corporation, it was the duty of the court to restrain such action."[1]

Judge Dundy gave as his decision that "the engineers on the Union Pacific have the right to quit work when they please, but they have not the right to enter into a conspiracy, and by concerted action suddenly leave the Union Pacific road without engineers, when the purpose of the conspiracy is to prevent the Union Pacific road from exchanging freight with the Burlington as by inter-state commerce law it is required to do. Against such action the court will enjoin. Neither have the engineers the right to refuse to pull Burlington cars, and such refusal would subject them to imprisonment. The Union Pacific is the creation of congress. It bears the national birth

[1] Chicago Daily News.

marks upon it. Congress has distinctly enacted that its officers, agents and operatives, must at all times exchange with, and handle freight of certain intersecting lines, among them the Burlington & Missouri, and has made refusal a misdemeanor, punishable by a fine of not less than $1,000, and imprisonment not less than six months on conviction."

Regardless of this decision, which appeared to be so full of danger to the liberties of the Union Pacific men, under the guidance of their chairman, G. W. Vroman they continued to have "Q" colic and were the last in the whole circle of the boycott to get well, and the Burlington officials were made to realize that the "bold bluff game" would not down by the decision of Judge Dundy.

To add to all these combinations and difficulties that beset the leaders of the strike in Chicago, there came —in addition to a great multitude from all parts of the country, who were eager to learn something, or advise or assist as the case might be—a faction who organized themselves into an advisory board, something not warranted by the laws of the engineers and evidently not desired by the grand officers. However it is reasonable to suppose they were actuated by the best of motives, yet with mature deliberation these men must have seen that an advisory board, whether legally constituted or not, must have some influence, presumed or real, with other men, and unless they were guided in their every act by the grand officers, whom their name implied that they represented, they must do much harm. The newspapers said some of them were there under the pay of the companies for whom

[1] Chicago Tribune.

they worked.[1]

From the best information obtainable this board held meetings and adopted plans for their own guidance, exercised an influence over the grand officers, meeting with them and doing divers things. They were not, like the staff of a general, responsible to him, and subject to his final decision, but as individuals, representing fractional interests, in the interest of one road instead of the whole. In forming this body these men laid themselves liable to grave suspicion of looking after their own interest, instead of the common good. However good their intentions might have been, it is certain the influence exercised by them as a whole, was harmful.

No man can serve faithfully one interest, and be paid by another. He may honestly think his interest and the common interest of the engineers and firemen are identical with the company whom they serve. This is the right principal in peace, but not in war, and much of the lack of harmony among all, emanated from a lack of harmony of opinion among the advisory board, as they termed it. Many things were laid at their door, perhaps unjustly, yet their assumed position made them a target for charges made later, of a grave nature.

The Burlington management issued the following bulletin order to conductors: "As we are going to open up our business, and will discontinue the running of pilots, we will expect you or one of your brakemen to show the new engineer the road when necessary." This obliged the brakemen to pilot and assist the new men. The grand officers of the strikers, having been

[1] Chicago Tribune.

assured of Mr. Wilkinson's good will, that gentleman was invited to headquarters, to which he immediately responded, and after consultation he was requested to go over the road and instruct all concerned that no member of the brakemen's order would be allowed to do anything but his legitimate business and to do no piloting. He visited all the terminal points on the Burlington system, and did all he could to prevent any special services being rendered to the company outside of their regular duties. The Burlington had manned every engine with a pilot to keep their new men out of trouble, but it was expensive, and they thought to do away with it by having the conductor or brakeman ride on the engine and still keep them out of trouble. The Burlington officials evidently expected much from the conductors in piloting, and compeling the brakemen to do the same. They no doubt, based their assurance upon an understanding with Messrs. Belknap and Cross, employes of the Burlington, who issued a circular March 10, which was sanctioned by the chief officer of that order, Grand Chief Conductor, C. S. Wheaton. An extract from the circular reads as follows:

"The railroad officials commenced Sunday afternoon, February 26, to clean up the line, and Sunday night saw all freights abandoned as fast as engineers and firemen refused to go out. Loyal employes stepped on their engines, and the result was that passenger trains continued to run from that day to this. Conductors and brakemen, with scarcely an exception along the whole line, tendered their services in any capacity where they could be most useful. They ran engines, fired engines, acted as pilots, and performed police dnty. All, whether members of any society or not, seemed to vie with each other in showing their loyalty in this time of trouble, and tendering their services in any capacity where needed. This full expression of loyalty on the part of the trainmen was far beyond the most sanguine expectation of any of our officers. While they counted on some remaining firm, they were not prepared to see the loyalty so universal, and as train after train was taken from its starting to destination in safety and nearly on time, by faithful men, they could not find words to express their approval of our acts, and we are satisfied that they will express their feelings in a very substantial way when the proper time comes." There is much more to this circular, but this extract embodies the essence of it. This brought a reply from the Brakemen's *Journal*, which places the circular in its right light:

"The above statement is a lie out of a whole cloth, so far as it pertains to the brakemen, and no one knows it better than Messrs. Belknap, Cross and Wheaton. The brakemen preserved a strict neutrality, and took no part in this strike. They performed their usual duties promptly and faithfully, but did not take the place of the strikers, as stated in the circular.

"The action of the brakemen on the Burlington is endorsed by our Brotherhood everywhere, by the Locomotive Brotherhoods, and by the Burlington officials. They adopted a manly course and behaved like men, and not like the fawning sycophants who, lost to all sense of manhood and honor, tried to curry favor by offering their services in any capacity, mauy of them giving up good positions on other roads thousands of miles away, to come and defeat the engineers and firemen on the Burlington."

The pilots were mostly conductors who knew the road, and smash-ups had been few owing to this precaution. But the engines had suffered. Many of their engines had been very badly burned, although the officials denied that such was the fact. I am personally knowing to a case where the flue sheet was pulled away from the crown sheet until your hand would go into the space. It was stated on good authority, that a large number suffered from this cause; but the Burlington seemed to care nothing for cost. They were not, however, opening up their interchange of business, as they had hoped would be the case. From the legal proceedings, nearly all the lines held their doors closed against the Burlington.

Meetings were being held in Kansas City, attended by men from all roads centering there, watching the situation. At East St. Louis, March 11, Division 49 held a meeting attended by some 200, and it was decided not to handle Burlington cars. The Missouri and Pacific men had the "colic" at the sight of a Burlington car as bad as did the men of the Union Pacific. In fact, at any time from March 1 to March 15, from all indications of the temper of the enginemen throughout the country, almost every western road could have been stopped at the word of command. Had the leaders of the brotherhoods adopted the same course as that chosen by the Burlington, i. e., "rule or ruin," and had similarly violated their own laws, and been equally indifferent to public weal or woe, there would have been one of the greatest strikes in the annals of history. The strike on the Burlington system, as it was conducted, would have been but a drop in the wave of business disaster.

But instead of crowding the issue, destroying property, and violating their own laws, as it was so freely charged they would do, they followed a conservative policy that prevented general disaster, preserved their self respect and forestalled defeat. When the grievance men came to Chicago and passed resolutions to boycott, in order to carry out the conditions, they must go home to their respective roads, call their committee together, vote to sustain or not sustain its conditions; if sustained by the home vote, they must wait on the home officers, and ask them to comply with the boycott and so prevent trouble. This considerate method was carried out in every case.

If the strikers had been indifferent to the public good, and had used such means as were at their command on March 6, it is reasonable to say that they could have stopped every connecting line west and south of the Burlington, and a majority of those running east. But they commenced the strike by leaving the Burlington engines at terminal points, in good order; they persuaded, hired, and bought away the new men. It had failed to keep the Burlington from finally, in some manner, manning their engines. The next best means, and the least injurious to the public, was the boycott. The power of the boycott was killed, so far as compelling a settlement was concerned, by conservatism in the use of that power. The resort to a boycott can be successful only when it is entered upon with unanimity, and pursued vigorously and regardless of consequences. There was evidently a lack of harmony in the opinion of the men as to the necessities of the situation. Thomas Jefferson said: "Every difference of opinion is not a difference of principle." They were united in defending their principles, but differed as to the means. One policy should have been adopted and adhered to with the firmness of the signers of the declaration of independence. Said one of the members, "We must all hang together in this business." "Yes," said Benjamin Franklin, "we must all hang together or most assuredly we will all hang singly."

The decision of Judge Gresham on March 12 had opened the Wabash to the Burlington. The judge said: "The Wabash engineers do not desire to maintain an attitude of defiance to the law, that they are willing to aid the receiver in the lawful and successful administration of his trust." In war, a break in the line could be closed up, but in this case it must stand so long as the men themselves would not form the line. This had two results: first, a tendency to weaken others, who by this time had time to weigh in the balance their own interests with the common interest, and with many, self-interest is found to outweigh the other, and such as these held up the decision of Judge Gresham, and withdrew active support. Second, the vivid impression of the conspiracy law and the specified effort to find some means by which the grand officers could be held accountable under legal process, caused them to transfer the active control of the strike to the local committees, the direct result of which was the strike of the Atchison, Topeka & Santa Fe, on March 15.

A committee of engineers and firemen of the Atchison, Topeka & Santa Fe had waited on the managers of that road on March 8 and 9. The object was to solicit them not to handle Burlington freight, assuring them that the best of feeling existed between the company and the employes, but that they wished to assist their friends, the strikers on the Burlington, and that they should refuse to handle Burlington business after Sunday morning, March 11. It was not their intention to strike, but each man would act for himself. "The officers assured the grievance committee that they could not expect that the company would act in violation of the laws of the United States, that they would lay their notice before the board of directors for their consideration, pending which it was presumed that no action would be taken by the engineers. The officers of the road said further that from that time on, in no instance was any engineer, against his wishes, asked to handle any train containing Chicago, Burlington & Quincy cars."[1] While the engineers and firemen, on the contrary, claimed they were trying to aid the Burlington.

There seemed to be a combination of circumstances at Kansas City that caused feeling to run high, and the moderation so prevalent elsewhere was wanting at this point. The Burlington owns the ground and yard surrounding the Union depot, where the trains of nearly all the roads centering at Kansas City come in and go out of one depot. This brought together men from the Union Pacific; Missouri Pacific; Atchison,

[1] Chicago Daily News.

Topeka & Santa Fe; Wabash; Fort Scott & Gulf; Chicago, Rock Island & Pacific, and many other lines of less importance, to meet with the strikers.

The direct connection of freight traffic of all these roads with the Burlington yard kept the men busy watching all the outlets. Every encroachment upon the boycott was magnified by one after another of the men congregated there, who were not committee men, and consequently not held responsible for the influence they exercised. It was unavoidable that the mature deliberation, so necessary to unity of action, became impossible; besides, the Fort Scott & Gulf and the Atchison, Topeka & Santa Fe were both Boston interests, and holders of stock in these roads were stockholders in the Burlington, which created an antipathy against them, the men believing—from the known pecuniary interest of these roads—that they were making special effort to help out the Burlington. The Union Pacific is another Boston interest, but a Burlington car made thirty engineers suddenly sick on the morning of the fourteenth at Omaha. At Council Bluffs the "colic" was raging, because there were Burlington cars in the trains as made up. Judge Dundy's restraining order had no terror for them. The heat of the battle seemed for the time to be transferred from Chicago to the south and west.

An Associated Press reporter went over the Burlington line from Chicago to Kansas City, visiting Aurora, Mendota, Galesburg, Burlington, Chariton, Creston and Kansas City. The object being to ascertain the true state of affairs on the Burlington system. Not only were the meetings of the brotherhood men visited by him, but at each point the railroad officials were seen. As nearly as one could judge from the evidence of both sides, "the Burlington system was doing from 40 to 50 per cent of the business which it did before the strike. At every point mentioned passenger trains were from one to six hours late. In regard to the freight business each division superintendent that was seen frankly stated that the road was doing much less business than before the strike. They said that there were no cattle carried over the road, except where the company had bought the cattle in the pens. Freight trains, where they were formerly made up of about thirty cars, were then composed of from nine to twenty. In some instances engines drawing way cars were sent out and counted as trains. While they did not express themselves in sympathy with the strikers, they did say they wished that the old hands were back at the throttle."[1]

The brotherhood men were making strenuous efforts to decrease even this small showing. The progress of the Burlington, added to the court proceedings, made many fear for the future of the brotherhoods, if the battle was lost. The railroad officials no doubt hoped, and the brotherhoods feared, that failure would be a Waterloo to these institutions, that a retrograde movement would be demanded by other companies. This feeling created a radical sentiment, especially among the western men.

It was charged that freight was being transferred at Kansas City, from Burlington cars into Atchison, Topeka & Santa Fe cars, by teams drawing it some distance. This was taken for bad faith on the part of

1 Associated Press report.

the company, and no doubt caused the following:

Kansas City, Mo., March 15, 1888.

"J. F. GODDARD, general manager, Atchison, Topeka & Santa Fe.

Topeka, Kansas,:

Engineers and firemen of the Santa Fe system will quit at 4 o'clock P. M.

J. CONROE, Chairman."[1]

On receipt of this, Manager Goddard sent the following:

J. CONROE, chairman grievance committee, Atchison, Topeka & Santa Fe Railway.

Kansas City:

At 3:50 this afternoon I received your telegram, notifying me that the engineers and firemen whom you represent would quit at 4 o'clock to-day. As we have faithfully kept every written and verbal agreement made with your organization, your action is a surprise, and I would be glad to know on what it is taken. Also, do you intend that it shall cover passenger train service as well as freight?[1]

Mr. Conroe sent to Grand Chief Arthur a telegram stating, "Engineers and firemen are satisfied that the Santa Fe did not remain neutral, and sav they were justified in this move." Answer

J. CONROE.

No one expected this move, and the strike of the engineers and firemen on the Atchison, Topeka & Santa Fe road was the exciting topic at the strikers' headquarters. From all the reports received it was ascertained that this strike carried out about 1,300

[1] Associated Press report.

engineers and a corresponding number of firemen. The Santa Fe men appeared to be determined to stand out, although no specific cause of grievance could be discovered. Chief Arthur was completely taken by surprise at the announcement of the strike, and sent a telegram to the chairman, Mr. Conroe, to come to Chicago immediately.

Mr. Arthur was inclined to think that some subordinate officer had attempted to compel the men to handle Burlington freight and had thus precipitated a strike which he had been most anxious to avoid. And he said that if the men have struck without cause they have done wrong.

Interviews with a number of the striking engineers of the Santa Fe road, developed the fact that they had examined the list of stockholders on the Chicago, Burlington & Quincy, and the Atchison, Topeka & Santa Fe, and found that a considerable number of the Santa Fe stockholders are also largely interested in the Burlington. The Fort Scott & Gulf stockholders were also interested in the Burlington. The enginemen had no grievance with the Santa Fe, but they would rest until the Burlington road should come to terms with its employes.

Much having been said by the press about the men giving the Santa Fe only thirty minutes notice, one of the old engineers said: "Now, that's all wrong. Our committee had been urging the company every day, since we found that they were smuggling Burlington freight into the cars, to stop it. The committee called on Mr. Goddard no less than three times and told him the company was handling Burlington freight and that the men would not stand it. He gave us no satisfaction. The Santa Fe has not acted fairly with us."[1]

The extent of the Santa Fe road and its branches is nearly 7000 miles, on which were employed seven hundred engineers and a like number of firemen, and 2,800 trainmen. It is said there was standing along the line 1,200 cars of merchandise. Many officials who had been watching this great sympathy strike at Chicago, were transferred to Kansas City, with nothing to do but watch developments. The grievance committeemen from all the roads were there, and everything had the appearance of a general strike of all southwestern roads. The men of the Fort Scott and Gulf had contemplated going out on the same day, or soon after the Santa Fe, but the men on that line were apparently not a unit. Without the sanction of their grand officers, the chairman of that system had gone to Chicago to see the grand chief and enter his complaints, and this prevented any extension of the strike.

Although the Santa Fe strike was ill advised, it was one of the most astonishing exhibitions of good will towards their fellow men that the world has ever seen, when we remember that they take no obligation that compels obedience to command, and that a strike of this kind could not be inaugurated only by the individual consent of each one, and in this case they were spread out over 7,000 miles of territory, and as one met the other and told the news, their places were instantly vacated, all alike, actuated by the same sentiment. It is our brother in trouble; let us do whatever

[1] Chicago Daily News.

we can to help him out of it. What a picture of unselfish devotion! and what a comparison between these men who forgot self in their anxiety for their brothers, and that mass of selfishness, incompetency and drunkenness, that had within the last two weeks been poured into the vacancies of the Burlington.

"On the morning of the 16th of March, at Kansas City, not a wheel was turning except a few switch engines. The engineers and firemen persisted in saying they had received no orders to strike; they were simply tired and wanted rest. The Union depot presented a regular castle garden appearance, as though hundreds of emigrants had been brought in whose destination was somewhere on the Santa Fe. Two hundred of them were crowded into the emigrant room, and there were new accessions hourly." [1]

At 11:20 A. M., the foreman of the Santa Fe roundhouse, at Argentine, backed an engine up to the Union depot and coupled on to train No. 3, which was the through California express. Ben Horton, who had been an engineer on the Santa Fe road for ten years, mounted the engine. He was not a Brotherhood man, having been expelled from that organization during the strike of 1877. He afterwards applied for re-admission, but was rejected.

"A sensation was created in the crowd that surrounded the engine, by the appearance of Horton's wife, who pushed her way through and was assisted to a seat by her husband, when she declared her intention of acting as fireman on the trip. She covered her clothing with a rubber ulster while a fireman's cap set jauntily on her black hair." [2] Before starting, the

[1] Kansas City Journal. [1] Associated Press report.

THE HOUSE ON DEKOVEN STREET AFTER THE WRECKED CARS WERE TAKEN AWAY.

enginemen made an effort to induce Horton not to go, offering him money, but the wife, the would-be fireman, is said to have been armed with a revolver, and compelled her liege lord to stay at his post. This woman who went out as fireman was formerly Hattie Reed, of Kewanee, Ill. During the strike of 1877 she acted as fireman for her husband from Galesburg to Burlington. The news gatherers gave her considerable notoriety, but the reader will probably make his own estimate of this exception to the timidity of the gentler sex.

Callers were kept busy hunting the city over for engineers and firemen, but they kept out of the way. The Kansas City Journal said:

"Two weeks ago a traveling printer was dropped from the *Journal* sub-list. To-night he showed up at the office with two revolvers strapped on his person, and with an engineer's book, etc., showing him to be a full fledged Burlington engineer. His experience is two years in a machine shop. He was loaned to the Santa Fe and goes out to-night for one week's work. He has had two accidents." This young man is one of those 'competent men'' of whom Officer A. C. Dawes, of the Kansas City, St, Joseph & Council Bluffs road said: "In no instance has there been a high grade engineer displaced to make room for a low grade," yet this man or boy, was pulling passenger trains on that road when Mr. Dawes gave this information to the public. "The Santa Fe did not seem anxious to make use of such material, and preferred to wait before adding the evils which follow the employment of scabs to those which already beset them.

'The general superintendent received many applications for situations as engineers, but no new men were engaged.' "[1]

The situation was hourly becoming more complicated; the lack of concerted action was apparent. Leaders were wanting who could command a view of the whole situation, with power to guide, and formulate plans for the action of this great army of enginemen. They were like a ship at sea without a rudder. The laws of the Brotherhoods had not been made with powers centered in the leaders. They could only advise and consent, and with the grand officers located within the scope of the Illinois conspiracy law, that advice must be of a peaceful nature. The Santa Fe was out. The Fort Scott & Gulf was on the balance, and were to have followed the Santa Fe at four o'clock the same day, but the chairmen of the grievance committee of that system requested that positive action be deferred. The general manager expected it to go at any moment.

At Marshalltown, Iowa, the Central Iowa enginemen notified Receiver Dudley that they would not handle Burlington cars. "The receiver said that his duty under the law was plain, and that he should insist on its enforcement. He therefore declined to allow any cars delivered to him to be set out of trains, and at 5 o'clock he ordered the machine shops closed, and all employes in the shops, roundhouses, offices, and all along the road, laid off, except enough to look after the passenger service."[2] This virtually tied up the Central of Iowa. Like notices were sent to the railroad officials at Jeffersonville, Indiana, and to Chatta-

[1] Kansas City Journal. [2] Chicago Tribune.

nooga, Tenn.; at the same time the Ohio and Mississipi was making an effort to have the Burlington business boycotted.

While these efforts were being made by separate systems guided by their own feelings, the Fort Scott road, situated by the side of the Santa Fe, "made no secret of the fact that it handled all the freight sent to it by the Burlington." [1] In an interview with Vice-President C. W. Smith of the Santa Fe, "he admitted that several of the stockholders of the Burlington, including Malcom B. Forbes, and President Perkins of the Burlington, were large holders of the stock in the Santa Fe, but he did not consider that fact sufficient grounds for a strike on the Santa Fe." Yet that knowledge was without doubt what actuated the Santa Fe men in pursuing the radical course they did. It was a combined action of individuals, each actuated by one sentiment, to help their brothers of the Burlington. Mr. Conroe, chairman of the grievance committee, was called to Topeka by Governor Martin where he met with the Governor and railroad commissioners of the state of Kansas. "Governor Martin asked Mr. Conroe to state the case of the engineers. He said they had no grievance against the Santa Fe, but the Burlington men could not hope to win so long as the Santa Fe hauled Burlington freight, which he claimed the road had been doing." [2]

At the request of the Governor, Mr. Conroe and the board of commissioners, held a conference with general manager Goddard, of the Santa Fe, in the hope that an understanding might be reached but the conference resulted in nothing. Mr. Conroe denied

[1] Chicago Journal. [2] Kansas Clty Journal.

having ordered the strike and said it was the individual action of the men. They had considered the matter carefully at their lodges and had decided to strike, therefore neither he nor Mr. Arthur could order it off, until the strikers gained their point. He was not antagonizing Mr. Arthur but things were in such shape that he could not comply with Mr. Arthur's directions. Governor Martin, speaking of Mr. Conroe, said: "My interview with him leads me to believe that he is a conservative, level headed, intelligent man. He talks sensibly upon the situation, and believes he is acting with the best interests of the men he represents. I would take him to be a man well informed upon general business affairs, and not a man who desires to gain notoriety as an agitator."[1]

Mr. Conroe and the Santa Fe men held their ground manfully. It was purely a sympathy strike and their position was a trying one. Manager Goddard had issued a circular letter on the 17th, covering the ground of complaint and stated that the company had decided to retain the services of all the old men, and would give them until the next Thursday to resume work. The fairness and generosity of this proposition to men who had no personal feeling against the officers, and the failure of the Fort Scott men to carry out their part of the presumed program, caused the men to feel that the strike was ill advised. Much has been said against Grand Chief Arthur for requesting the Santa Fe men to return to work, yet it was the only wise course to pursue. The men could not have maintained their position, standing alone as they were. There must have been a break, and Mr. Conroe's

[1] Kansas City Journal.

official notice, issued at 6 P. M., 18th of March, was timely and judicious.

Kansas City, March 18, 1888.

To the engineers and firemen of the Santa Fe system:

"I am advised by our grand chief to request of you to return to your respective positions at once. Further that I am to repair to Chicago and adjust all misunderstandings."[1]

I. CONROE,

Chairman, General Grievance Committee.

Mr. George Royal, a prominent member of the Brotherhood, was sent to Kansas City by Grand Chief Arthur to assist in bringing about this result which ended the strike on the Santa Fe. This strike was a mistake. Had they adopted the Union Pacific plan, and had taken the "Q colic," it is not likely that they would have been discharged, and yet the doors would have been closed against the Burlington, and the chief object would have been attained. Its redeeming qualities were that there was no viciousness, no disorder, no hatred of the Santa Fe officials, but an unselfish devotion to their brothers on the Burlington that outweighed all other considerations—misconceived, but grand in good fellowship.

The Santa Fe strike was over and the Kansas City lines began to open to the Burlington business. This caused the greatest dissatisfaction in the south and west, where the men were all loyal and willing to boycott, regardless of consequences to themselves, but they only saw a portion of the field. They could maintain their ground without sacrificing many of their

[1] Kansas City Journal.

positions, but the situation was not as propitious elsewhere.

We find the Central Iowa road still in trouble. The engineers out on this road only numbered sixty-five, and a like number of firemen, but this number suspended operations for nine hundred other employes, and the receiver on the 19th, issued the following notice: "All engineers and firemen who fail to report for duty at 8:00 A. M., Tuesday, March 20, ready and willing to haul any and all cars that may be put on trains, will be discharged from the service."[1] The machine shops, car shops, roundhouses, and part of the general offices had been closed in pursuance of his previous order. It was not easy to dissuade men who had taken a voluntary stand in the process of the boycott, but on the 20th this strike was brought to a close through a five hour conference between Receiver Dudley, a member of the court, and six representatives of the Brotherhood. The Burlington, Cedar Rapids, & Northern was pushed into line by a decision in Judge Love's court, under the inter-state law, and the strike was again closed on the Burlington, and the attention again turned towards Chicago.

[1] Chicago Daily News.

CHAPTER XLV.

ANOTHER CLOUD RISING.

Owing to the many and grave complications that were continually arising, that were absolutely beyond the control of the grand officers, located, as they were, within the limits of the conspiracy law of Illinois, it is evident they lost faith in the power to compel a settlement upon the original conditions asked, and at their suggestion Chairmen Hoge and Murphy made another effort, on March 10. They left their pride behind and waited upon President Perkins and General Manager Stone, when it was proposed that the men be allowed to go back to work on the old terms, with the question of increase to be decided upon by amicable agreement thereafter, but they did not arrive at any satisfactory conclusion. The Burlington officials declined to negotiate with them upon any terms but absolute surrender.

When the embargo was raised on the Santa Fe there was great indignation expressed by members of the Brotherhood, against the grand officers, for being instrumental in accomplishing it. Thomas Jefferson said, "When right, I shall often be thought wrong by those whose positions will not command a view of the whole ground;" so in this case, could all have seen the situation as it really was the strike would not have lasted another day, but they could not, and the Burlington strikers along the line were holding their ground as tenaciously as on the first day. Letters were being received from all over the country encouraging them to stand firm. Every local point along the line had a correspondence committee, and more than fifty letters were received and as many sent out. It was a mode of feeling the pulse of all the men along the line, and the social and encouraging nature of the letters kept up the animation and good feeling, and furnished the panacea that kept away ennui and disgust.

Laboring men of all creeds, seeing the two most powerful organizations extant roughly handled by centralized capital, began to see the danger to themselves, and buried much of the feeling that was so patent at the beginning of the strike, which had been engendered mostly by the engineers' policy of "no entangling alliances." Amalgamation among diversified labor brings as many difficulties as do entangling alliances among nations. But an alliance which contemplates federated good fellowship, has become essential to the welfare of labor, and the strike so far had brought vividly to the minds of laboring men generally, the necessity of some concerted action that would equalize their power, and make them able to successfully maintain their right, endangered by corporate power. The following is the result of this feeling, adopted by the Union Pacific employes:

ARTICLES OF FEDERATION.

BETWEEN THE BROTHERHOOD OF LOCOMOTIVE ENGINEERS, BROTHERHOOD OF LOCOMOTIVE FIREMEN, AND THE KNIGHTS OF LABOR, EMPLOYES OF THE UNION PACIFIC RAILWAY.

The Brotherhood of Locomotive Engineers, the

Brotherhood of Locomotive Firemen employed by the Union Pacific Railway, and the Knights of Labor employes on the Union Pacific Railway, of the organization known as District Assembly No. 82, do mutually agree to the following Articles of Federation, to govern our relations to the Union Pacific Railway Company and ourselves:

First.—Each organization shall retain fully its individuality and govern fully its own internal affairs as heretofore; each to have its Executive or Grievance Committee settle all disputes between themselves and the Union Pacific Railway Company if possible.

Second.—There shall be a Federation Board consisting of representatives of each Executive or Grievance Committee of each organization, on the basis of equal representation to the Brotherhoods and the Knights of Labor.

Third.—In case of the Executive or Grievance Committee of either organization failing to effect a settlement satisfactory to them, they shall comply with the laws of their organization regarding grievances and strikes, and if their action in the matter receives the endorsement of their organization, said grievance shall be submitted to the Federal Board for final action.

Fourth.—Should the Federal Boards agree on the justness of the alleged grievance they shall at once proceed to adjust the same.

Fifth.—The Federal Board failing to satisfactorily adjust the difficulty they shall take final action thereon, and if thought best may submit the same back to their various organizations.

Sixth.—The organizations represented in this agreement mutually agree to do all in their power to build up and strengthen each other by influencing all persons to become members of the organizations representing their trade or calling.

Seventh.—An expelled member of either organization shall be ineligible to membership in any of the other organizations unless by the consent of the organization from which he was expelled.

Eighth.—Any local misunderstanding between the organizations represented in this agreement shall be adjusted by a joint committee representing each of the local organizations.

Ninth.—Any differences arising between members of either of the organizations regarding alleged encroachments on each others rights, either party to the alleged difference can call through the local committee of his organization, for a conference of the joint local committee to settle the same.

Tenth.—Any difficulty that may arise affecting the members of either organization in their just rights as employes of the Union Pacific Railway Company, shall be considered as comprising all matters to be submitted to the Federated Boards. Just rights to be understood as meaning the questions of wages, hours of labor or mileage, the unjust discharge or discrimination against members, rules or regulations of the Company affecting the duties, interests or liabilities of an individual member or of all employes, or any division, trade or calling.

We, the undersigned members of a committee representing the organizations herein mentioned, mutually agree to these articles of federation, for our organizations on the Union Pacific Railway system, subject to the approval of the Chiefs of our several organizations.

This was signed by eighteen representative men of the K. of L., B. of L. E., and B. of L. F.

In an interview with a reporter, Mr. Powderly said: "Any differences which might have been between the Brotherhood and myself are at an end. I have no fight with any labor organization. I would rather take a blow from a labor organization than give one. Last Saturday I signed articles of agreement between members of the Brotherhoods of Engineers and Firemen, and Knights of Labor, employed on the Union Pacific railroad. They will work together, and anything concerning their interests on the road will be carefully considered by both sides, and all troubles will be settled without strikes if possible."[1]

The same disposition had begun to manifest itself among the switchmen. They, as a class, never had any love for a scab, and it must have been a trying ordeal for them to work with them as long as they did. An effort had been made at the beginning of the strike to secure the co-operation of the switchmen and brakemen. "Grand Master Wilkinson, and Grand Secretary and Treasurer Oshea of the brakemen, and Grand Master Monoghan had expressed sympathy and a wish that they could enter the contest, but the past policy of the engineers of "going it alone" prevented any coalition. But after the boycott had practically failed, another effort was made and Grand Masters Monoghan and Wilkinson expressed a willingness to make an effort. All they required was a pledge from Grand Chief Arthur that in case of trouble with the

[1] Chicago Tribune.

switchmen, or brakemen, that the engineers would stand by them. Mr. Arthur could not do this, but promised to use his influence to bring about co-operation at the convention. This effort, like its predecessor, failed from the same cause—lack of fraternal feeling between the engineers and the other orders. Later on, however, a better feeling was brought about at a meeting of the switchmen attended by chairman Hoge and other committeemen. It is reasonable to suppose that some pledges were made at that meeting which changed the attitude of the switchmen. At a meeting held at Turner Hall, composed of engineers, firemen and switchmen, plans were matured for future action. Paul Morton had said on March 20: "It's three strikes and out. Next Saturday we shall start our fast trains No. 1 and 15, and then our road will be in exactly the same circumstances that it was before the men struck." On Friday, March 23, appeared the following:

"The Great Strike Is Over."—"The Burlington road continues to run. It has surmounted its difficulties. Its trains are running on time. The management of the road remains in the hands of its officers. The public need have no fear. The responsibility for its care and comfort is fully assumed by the company. The Burlington takes the lead. It was in advance of all other lines in establishing dining-car service on its through trains. It was in advance of all other lines in giving the people of the West their fast mail service. It was in advance of all other lines in reducing the time of passenger trains between Chicago and Missouri River points from 20½ to 15½ hours. It has been progressive in the past. It will lead in the future. If you admire an institution that has the courage of its convictions give it your patronage. Commencing Sunday, March 25th, 'the Burlington's Number One' fast train will leave Chicago daily at one o'clock P. M."

These trains had been discontinued since the inception of the strike, and they were still destined to disappoint those who wished quick transit over the Burlington, as well as the officials who so loudly proclaimed the strike was off. They were evidently not prepared for the storm already brewing. The withdrawal of the Burlington switchmen the next day, March 24, caused the Burlington to announce, "Owing to further complications we will not be able to start the fast trains as advertised." Business was again stopped. The Burlington was obliged to inform its connecting roads that they could not receive business from them.

The switchmen were notified that they must return to work on Monday, 26th,—Monday was blue Monday for the Burlington; it recalled the first days of the engineers' strike. No attempt was made in the morning to handle freight, the company ostensibly hoping that wiser counsels would prevail and that the switchmen would return to work before being locked out. The limit given by the company, one o'clock, passed without a sign from the men. The key was turned in the lock, and the company began to hustle around for new men to fill the places of those left vacant,"[1]

Then commenced the scraping up of whatever kind of man could be found no examination was needed.

[1] Chicago Daily News.

Seven, such as they were, were found, and "seven freight conductors came to the front, to do by the switchmen as many of them had done by the enginemen. The conductors seemed to be extremely obedient to their laws, as non-combatants." "Three freight trains were finally made up and dispatched to the west." This was a great falling off from the previous week's business of from fifteen to twenty-five freight trains daily, and, as a consequence, goods waiting shipment were piled up in great quantities. The company declined to receive more freight for points which could be reached by other lines, and confined its efforts to reaching points covered only by its own system. It also refused perishable freight to and from the points on its own lines.

The switchmen followed suit all along the line of the Burlington where there was any large force employed. "The calling out of all the switchmen in Chicago was talked about; the walk out of the Burlington was slowly but surely spreading. The men at Plattsmouth, Lincoln and East St. Louis went out with Chicago on the 24. Aurora, Ill., followed, with Council Bluffs, Iowa; Omaha, Nebraska; and Galesburg, Ill., following, on the 25th and 26th, and St. Joseph, Missouri, April 1, leaving the Burlington with scarcely any men with which to do business.

The Burlington officials believed it was Mr. Monoghan's plan to have all switchmen go out and that he would carry it out to the letter. But they said they would fight this new trouble, cost what it might. President Perkins received an endorsement of his conduct of the business affairs of the Burlington company, from the directors in Boston; on March 27, in the following resolutions: "The board of directors unanimously approve of the President's course during the late strike, and consider that it is their duty to offer a steady resistance, regardless of consequences, to any attempt to take the management of the road from the hands of its owners.

J. M. FORBES, Chairman.

When directors, after their experience and immense loss, are as indifferent to cost and consequences as this indicates, the result of the action of the switchmen at that late day must, of necessity, have but one end—the loss of place. Had the brakemen and switchmen joined issue with the engineers and firemen in the start, the Burlington would have been confronted with almost an impossibility. A knowledge of the road bed, its ups and downs, and peculiarities, are as essential as the knowledge of the locomotive, and to have all green men, must have caused even the Burlington officials, with all their indifference, to be more considerate at least, of the capital they represented.

There is a lesson in the conduct of the Burlington strike, that with a little wisdom, might be used to greatly benefit railroad labor in the future. The Burlington officials, with vast resources at their command, Pinkerton detectives and police, and the experience of a month, were well equipped for this strike. The scabs already with them, knowing that the switchmen's strike implied their abhorrence of them, rendered all assistance possible in finding others of their kind to come to the Burlington, and at "five o'clock, Tuesday afternoon, forty-five switchmen had been engaged, and information received that many more were on their way to Chicago from the Reading road. The Burlington had only hired one hundred and thirty so far, and if it needed more there were still four hundred idle switchmen in the Reading region ready to respond at any time."[1] Had Reading men been as plentiful from 1861 to 1865 as they were in 1888, the forces of 'Lee,' instead of surrendering to the silent captain, would have lowered their colors to a Reading mob, and Appomattox would not have found a place in history."[2]

The Burlington officials expected trouble with the switchmen; they seldom do things by halves, and a characteristic episode in a switchmen's strike occurred Tuesday afternoon at the Stewart avenue station. General Superintendent Besler, Assistant Passenger Agent Wakely, Train Master Pope, Pay Master Sturges, Master Mechanic Smith, Superintendent Upham, of the Illinois lines, and many other officials, took a trip down in the yards to see how the strike was progressing. They also made preparations to quarter and feed the new switchmen and Pinkerton men. The entire party, and a number of reporters, were standing around the Stewart avenue station waiting for the west bound train for Western avenue. A dozen or more of the striking engineers and switchmen stood a short distance away. From the earnest conversation and gestures, it was evident that the officials were recognized.

A heavy loaded freight train of forty-five cars came down the track just ahead of the passenger train.

[1] Chicago Daily News. [2] Letter of S. M. Stevens.

WRECK IN CHICAGO YARDS.

The foot board in front of the engine was guarded by four armed Pinkerton men; there were Pinkerton men in the cab, upon the tender; they clung to the brake wheels of the freight cars, in fact the train was well protected. Superintendent Besler's face wore a satisfied smile as the long train of cars rattled over the switches at an eight mile gait. The group of railroad men had vanished or separated. The half dozen policemen were lost in the contemplation of the small army of Pinkerton men.

As the last few cars were passing the station, the rear car faltered a moment and fell behind. The pin had been pulled. Superintendent Besler's smile froze upon his face, and he made a remark not mentioned here. Train Master Pope confirmed his statement. A chorus of yells and laughter arose from the railroad men and the crowd of loafers. There was a wild frantic rush of Pinkerton men, policemen and railroad officials for the daring man who had pulled the pin; he had vanished into the air. The train was checked about three quarters of a mile west, and slowly and sadly backed up.

The action of the switchmen of the Burlington was as individuals. At Creston twenty of the thirty-one went out. At Quincy seventeen of the twenty-two, leaving five, the master of the Union there remaining at Galesburg; two remained with the company. "At Lincoln twelve switchmen quit on Monday. Seven claimed to have quit to attend as delegates a meeting of the striking firemen; two gave sickness as an excuse, while three admitted they were on a strike. At St. Joseph, Mo., a switchman was killed by one of the scabs and they quit. The fever was contagious, and rumors that the Burlington would be boycotted by enginemen and switchmen of other roads was heard on every hand. Chicago was kept in a condition of excited expectation, while the feeling among railroad officials in regard to the attitude of their employes was one of great nervousness. They had little to say but agreed that they had no assurance that their men would not walk out at any time.

There was an atmosphere of decided uncertainity about the Lake shore yards at Forty-third street on Thursday afternoon. Everyone expected trouble for the reason that there was a belief that a train of Burlington cars was to be delivered to the Lake shore road. A veteran policeman on duty shook his head gloomily at the prospect, and said that never before had he seen so many idle men ready to take a hand in anything that might come along as there were then in the district

From the inception of the Burlington strike, a flood of all sorts of men flocked into Chicago, from men driven by necessity to the lowest bum element, such as always follow in the wake of excitement, and the opportunity for this element was offered in the Milwaukee & St. Paul yards when a Burlington engine was sent to the Milwaukee yards at Western avenue and Kinzie street to transfer a train of cars just turned out of the manufactory. A mob of about two hundred "made an attack on the engine and drove from the cab the Pinkerton officers stationed there to protect the scabs. The officers, though well armed, refrained from firing on the crowd, and for their leniency, were rewarded by having their revolvers taken away from them and used to beat them over the head. Superintendent Besler, of the Burlington, was attacked and seriously beaten. The mob was dispersed by the arrival of a platoon of city police, and a switchman who had attacked Mr. Besler was taken to the station. This was a signal for the St. Paul switchmen to quit work. They went in a body to the station and when bail was refused they went out on a strike, being joined by the switch engineers and firemen. Later in the day the man was admitted to the bail and all was quiet in the yard, but the outlook was far from being peaceful."

On March 29, Grand Chief Arthur left Chicago for his home in Cleveland. This gave rise to all sorts of comments from the press, and much condemnation from members of the Brotherhood. "In railroad circles it was agreed that the departure of Mr. Arthur meant one of three things: that he had to go to Cleveland owing to the expiration of his lease of the house in which his family lived, or it was as the radicals hinted, the beginning of his retirement; or to get out of the jurisdiction of the courts in the west. The air was filled with all sorts of rumors. Mr. Arthur was conservative and believed in orderly methods. He was in a position to survey the whole situation and had made up his mind that the Burlington men were defeated, and had told them so, but they would not have it that way. It is said, "One who doubts is already defeated," and it is presumed he thought he had accomplished all he could by remaining. "The advisory committee of the Brotherhood, consisting of A. G. Dunn, W. B. Husky, A. W. Logan, and W. R. Hanby, adopted resolutions expressing their confidence in Mr. Arthur and their implicit faith in his judgment, and indorsed his action throughout. This left the headquarters of the Burlington strike with Messrs. Hoge and Murphy; Grand Master Sargent remaining as an advisor.

"On Saturday, at the headquarters ot the striking switchmen at Fourteenth and Jefferson streets, the room was filled with striking engineers, firemen, and switchmen, all day, and the prevailing sentiment was opposed to the violence of the day before. They said it was not their purpose to interfere in any manner with the company, and they would not countenance any act of violence by their men. But the yard men were full of strike all over the city. Committees were there from the Fort Wayne, Pan Handle, and North-Western, and announced their intention of emphatically refusing to handle Burlington cars, and to quit work if the companies required them to do so."

The Burlington having obtained a sufficient number of switchmen to begin business again, determined to push the issue, and to call upon the Pittsburg and Fort Wayne, the Lake shore and Michigan southern, the Rock Island, the Illinois Central, and Alton roads for assistance to raise the blockade in its yards. There seemed to be an understanding on nearly all the roads that they would strike before they would handle Burlington freight. The Burlington directors in Boston had made up their minds to wreck the property of the Burlington and bankrupt themselves, rather than yield, and the situation had anything but a pleasant aspect. Burlington cars had been standing in the yards for days and that company was now bound to push the other companies into a fight or into court, under the inter-state commerce law. There seemed to be no escape for the other companies, the Rock Island being the only one to take a positive stand against the Burlington.

The St. Paul strike was confined to the Chicago yards; the officials, having gathered up men along the line, on Saturday had eight switch engines at work, manned by conductors, machinists and railroad police who had been engineers or firemen. "About nine o'clock A. M., the first switch engine was brought out. Two St. Paul special police officers were on each end, and two more took care of the cab. It steamed slowly down to the coal bins and got coal. The new hand was not very brisk at the throttle and called out many comments from the strikers, but no attempt was made to interfere. They coupled on to a few cars and steamed away at a funeral pace."[1]

Fifty men who were regular freight and passenger conductors on the Council Bluffs division, arrived at the roundhouse in the morning. They were brought by the St. Paul people to fill the places of the striking engineers, firemen and switchmen, and all seemed anxious to pull the throttle or throw a switch. Jerry Doherty, one of the leaders of the switch engineers, went to the roundhouse and talked with the men and gained their sympathy, and they declared they had never scabbed a day in their lives, and never would. Doherty was ordered away by one of the blue coats, but Mr. Doherty told him he wanted to get his time

[1] Chicago Journal.

check, and he was allowed to remain. The new men were not so anxious to do switching as they had been. The climax came when one of their number came up and said, "Come ahead, boys! They want us down in the middle of the yards." "They don't get us down there," was the reply that came from the call. The men finally agreed to go down and see what was wanted of them, and on the way a captain was appointed, and the men fell into line with a Council Bluff's conductor at the head. They had only gone down the track about two hundred feet, when one of them suggested that if the St. Paul officials wanted them they would have to come down and make their proposals. The men all agreed and marched back to the roundhouse. Up to noon the officials had not come to negotiate with them. They said they would act as conductors or engineers, but would not throw switches. One hundred more were on the way from other divisions of the road and would arrive at 2:15 P. M., the officials saying by Monday everything would be running."[1]

The readiness with which men all along the roads in trouble, came to the rescue of the officials, and broke down all efforts of the yard men, must, as Mr. Powderly said, have been a gratifying spectacle to the officials. The Burlington, in following out its plan of pushing the issue with other companies, on Saturday, "at 10:15 A. M., took a train to the Pittsburg and Fort Wayne road. Soon after this a crew of the Fort Wayne switch engines was ordered to take charge of it. The crew refused to handle the train and was immediately discharged. Six crews, one after another,

[1] Chicago Mail.

were ordered to take theBurlington train, but each refused to obey the order and was in turn discharged. Fniding that the company was in earnest, the remaining crews in the yard ran their engines intc the roundhouse and quit work. One hundred and seventy-five men were employed in the Fort Wayne yard. Soon after a crew was found and the objectional train moved without opposition from the strikers.

An attempt was made by the strikers to draw the passenger engineers and firemen into the strike. The first crew leaving at 2:20 P. M. would not join them. At 3:30 however a crew refused to take the train out, but another crew was immediately found, and the train left after a delay of about fifteen minutes. this exception there was no disposition shown by the passenger men to strike." "A train was also taken to the Lake Shore and Michigan Southern, Saturday afternoon. The cars were received, but were immediately run upon a side track, and the yard men refused to haul them out."

"At one o'clock, Sunday morning, the switchmen on the Atchison, Topeka & Santa Fe went out in a body. They were followed by the Chicago & Alton switchmen on Sunday evening at six o'clock P. M., when they quit work and housed their engines." [1]

Meetings were held Sunday evening in Chicago, and a majority of the switchmen were in favor of the boycott. "The switchmen employed in the Milwaukee & St. Paul yards at Milwaukee, held a meeting in the evening and formulated a demand that no Burlington cars be handled. If not complied with they would quit at 11:00 A. M. on Monday. The boycott fever among

[1] Chicago Tribune.

the switchmen also reached Kansas City, and the officials of roads running into that city were notified not to handle Burlington cars."[1] It looked as though there would be no limit to the extent of this movement.

"A mixed train of twenty cars from the Sixteenth street yards of the Burlington, arrived at the Michigan Central yards at Randolph street at 10:30 A. M., Monday, and was delivered without trouble to that company. It was followed around by a large crowd of idlers who expected to see fun, but they were disappointed, for there was not the slightest interference offered the train at any point along the route between the two yards. As soon as the train approached the Michigan Central yards the engineers on the Illinois Central road opened their whistles and made a most unearthly noise, but this was the only demonstration. The train was placed on a side track, and no attempt was made to take it out."[2]

All this excitement had brought an opportunity for the hoodlum element, and on several occasions they had created disturbances which cast serious reflection upon the Burlington strikers, on the supposition that they were bringing this state of things about. Grand Master Monoghan, of the switchmen's union, was much incensed that such things should happen, to cast reflections upon the orders whose members were engaged in it, but such things always follow exciting demonstrations and probably always will. The grievance committeemen of the engineers and firemen expressed much feeling to have the orderly non-interference of a month overbalanced in a day

[1] Chicago Tribune. [2] Chicago Journal.

The officials of the Michigan Central gave the men notice and had limited the time for them to decide whether they would handle Burlington cars or not, and at a meeting Sunday night the men voted to go out at 7 o'clock Monday morning.

In the morning the forty engineers, firemen, and switchmen in the yards of the Michigan Central, at the foot of Lake street, with the exception of two non-brotherhood engineers, refused to handle the Burlington cars sent in the day previous. The men went to work at seven o'clock as usual, but upon a notice being sent them a half hour later that "Q" cars must be handled they all quit with the exception of the two non-brotherhood men, and in ten minutes the entire business of the yards was suspended. The next work the strikers started in to accomplish was to subdue the two engineers who had declined to be counted in as strikers. There was a disposition on the part of several switchmen to exercise their pugilistic powers on these two, but the better sentiment prevailed, and the striking forces marched away to hold a conference at Randolph street and Michigan avenue.

In the meantime the company was not idle and in response to Superintendent Brown's dispatches seventy-five engineers, firemen and brakemen from Jackson and Detroit, Mich., came in at once. There were various and conflicting rumors regarding the attitude of these men toward the company, but Superintendent Brown said that if the old men did not return to work in an hour the new men would take their places. This was emphatically denied by the Michigan trainmen who said they had come to Chicago without knowing what disposition was to be made of them.

At any rate both sides seemed desirous of avoiding trouble, and at 9 o'clock Superintendent Brown sent a message to the strikers to the effect that the Detroit and Jackson men were desirous of holding a joint meeting, to arrive, if possible, at some definite conclusion. Before the communication was sent, however, Miles McHugh, the leader of the party from Michigan, told Mr. Brown that his delegation was not in Chicago for the purpose of taking the places of any of the strikers, and that they were as much opposed to handling "Q" freight as the regular men were. These preliminaries over, however, the conference was entered into, and for three hours both sides were behind closed doors in the superintendent's office. While this meeting was in progress, word was re-received from Kensington, where the south branch yards of the company are situated, that the five engines there had ceased transferring freight, and that the twenty-four men there, five engineers and firemen and fourteen yardmen, had gone out as soon as the news of the strike at the north end of the line was received.

At nine o'clock Freight Agent Nichols issued the following, which was sent to all the roads:

"Until further advised we cannot receive any more freight or cars from you. Will let you know as soon as we are ready to receive again.

F. P. NICHOLS, Freight Agent."

The strikers, after a conference of several hours' duration, decided at one o'clock to go back to work.

This ended one strike, but the day was an eventful one.

"General Manager Miller, of the St. Paul road, issued orders to reduce the forces on that line, and to lay off every employe whose services were not absolutely necessary to carry on the business of the road. This affected nearly 7,000 men, and in addition to this, an order was issued to reduce the salary of every man in the employ of the company, including the general manager. Such an order was unexpected and caused great consternation among the employes."[1]

Judge Gresham issued an order to Milton Knox and William Briggs, two Belt Line engineers, restraining them from refusing to promptly haul Burlington cars. A case was brought against the Rock Island road by the Burlington in Judge Gresham's court. The Rock Island, however, had its switches locked and spiked against Burlington business. The union and non-union switchmen of the Lake Shore road were at outs, because of a threat by one of the union men. The switchmen were out, or ready to go out, at the slightest provocation, on nearly all the roads entering Chicago. The Michigan Central strike had been only of a few hours duration, and amid all this confusion and turmoil, it was discovered that some one, or more men, had issued a circular and sent it to the train men out along the road in the following: "We advise you to handle all cars regardless of who makes up the trains in the yards." It was openly charged that this emanated from the advisory board of engineers, but whether so or not, it was like a bomb shell in the camp. The Milwaukee had got tired of waiting, and

[1] Chicago Daily News.

had concluded to discharge the old men and take on new, and the Pittsburg, Fort Wayne and Chicago men were not much better off. Men who had evidently helped by their promises and encouragement to get the switchmen out, when it came their turn to make a sacrifice were found wanting.

The fruit of discord, "demoralization," began to be apparent. It was evident to the leaders that something must be done or this single handed, headless contest, would sacrifice the positions of half the good men in Chicago. Grand Master Sargent and Grand Master Monoghan, and the two chairmen of the Burlington strikers, Messrs. Hoge and Murphy, held a conference and resolved to make an effort to put a stop to this if possible, and get the men all back to work. This was no trifle, as many of them were in an ugly mood. But it was election day and the Burlington concluded it would not be politic to force the issue as the police were nearly all on duty at the polls, and business was wofully stagnated by the strike, so that a majority of the men could attend the meeting which was held in Turner hall, in the afternoon. The two Grand Masters, bent upon sparing no effort to bring order out of chaos, attended this meeting, accompanied by General Manager Jeffery, the manager of all managers, who had the most influence with the laboring men. Stirring addresses from these three men brought the desired result, and the men were ready to go back to work, but all was not yet done; they must have the consent of the officials of these roads before they could go back. This work was immediately taken up. General Manager Jeffery,

Chairman Hoge, and C. Naylor, master of Lodge 244, of Chicago, waited on General Manager McCray, of the Pittsburg, Fort Wayne & Chicago, and finally secured consent for the men to go to work in the morning. All cars were to be handled, and the same relations were to exist as before the strike. The Michigan Central men were already back. But the Milwaukee road was in a bad condition; the road had suffered considerable loss. General Manager Miller had tried hard to keep the road out of trouble, and he felt that he had been badly treated. He was in no humor to be approached with a proposition to the affect that the men would go to work if he should reinstate them all to their former positions. These gentlemen finally succeeded. The men went to work at seven o'clock, April 4, and the boycott in Chicago was raised, and the strike confined to the Burlington.

The St. Paul employes who had been ordered suspended, were also ordered back at their old wages, and the wheels of traffic were again set in motion. The raising of the boycott caused much feeling among those who could not see the difficulties of the situation. The effort was made by the switchmen with honest and good intentions, but they were too late to be useful to those in whose interest they were made, and Grand Masters Sargent and Monoghan are deserving, not of condemnation, but great praise, for putting a stop to this futile effort, saving the men's places, and ending the opportunity it offered to criminals and desperadoes with no interest in the strife or its results, "who regarded human life as a cheap offering on the altar of discord." In the midst of all the difficulties which beset men of labor, there appeared in the Chicago *Mail*, of April 2, a long circular letter which the *Mail* said, " was intended for railroad managers only, but in view of the complications in railroad circles, the *Mail* deemed it proper to make public: "

"The advance sheets from the report of the grand secretary of the Order of Railway Conductors have been sent out to the managers of the various railroads."

"By way of preface the grand secretary says: I am directed by the executive committee of the Order of Railway Conductors to send advance sheets of a portion of my ninth annual report to the general officers of the principal railways in the United States, in order that the position of our association in regard to labor troubles and strikers in general, and the strikes of engineers in particular, shall be fully understood by them. In taking this position we make no claim to a philanthropic feeling toward, or love for, railway companies. The conductors feel, and with good reason in many cases, that they do not receive justice from the companies, that the loyalty toward their employers in times of trouble in the past has not been appreciated; but they recognize the fact that to assist the engineers or any other class of employes in procuring more than justice is to assist in placing it beyond the power of railway officers to give to the conductor the recognition and remuneration that they believe he is entitled to."

"The love of the engineer for the conductor so loudly professed has been plainly illustrated on more than one occasion within the last few years. Reflect upon the treatment accorded your representatives at Chicago, when by the direction of the grand division, a communication was addressed to them on the matter of license. To this respectful communication not the slightest reply has ever been made. They come to you holding out the right hand of friendship, but in their left hand they held the dagger to stab you at the first opportunity."

"It has been asserted in the *Railway Conductor's Monthly* that a large majority of the conductors of the United States are capable of successfully running locomotives and the assertion is made here, without fear of successful contradiction, that if it were not for the unreasonable prejudice existing in regard to taking another's place and the false sympathy in regard to 'taking the bread out of a brother's mouth' the place of every member of the Brotherhood of Locomotive Engineers in the country could be suceessfully filled within thirty days, and the engineers as a class would be more intelligent men than they are at present."

"It is time for the conductors to teach railway officers what the engineers themselves already well know and are anxious to conceal—that nine-tenths of the conductors of the United States are capable and trustworthy engineers. The conductors on the Chicago, Burlington & Quincy have already demonstrated this, and they are ready to do it on other roads. I hope sincerely that the time is close at hand when they will not only be ready but willing to do so all over the United States."

We only give extracts of this document, which is too long to admit of space in this work. All the evidence goes to show that the animus contained in this did not emanate from the conductors' order, but from the individual, the Grand Chief Conductor. It is true he was sustained at the convention held in Toronto, Canada, but there are always men at the conventions that follow the leader rather than their own convictions. Strong speeches were made in opposition to the Grand Chief Conductor's position. Delegate Ransom said among other things. "These organizations have advanced the interests of the laboring man. The Grand Chief Conductor has said that where his report was written all was turmoil and unquiet, and it was written in an atmosphere different from what he found in Canada, admitting that had he been in peaceful Canada that the objectional portion of the report would never have been written. I beg the members to decide upon the subject matter of the report, and to consider the grand chief upon the same basis that he would place any other member, when he had so considerately stepped down from the chair to defend himself, thereby admitting that his course needs defense; do not permit the fact that it is the report of the grand officer to deter you from condemning any language calculated to array this body against any other organization whatever; and do not take any action calculated to cause trouble where there is now peace and harmony." [1]

The report was sustained, but the harm of it did not remain within the walls of the convention. When printed it created immense feeling among labor organizations, and secured open condemnation from some of the divisions of the conductors' order. It brought dis-

[1] B. of L. E. Journal, June, 1888.

ACROSS THE TRACK IN WOOD STREET YARD, CHICAGO.

cord where before had been harmony; incisive remarks made by those actuated by passion, as was Chief Wheaton, widened the breach. The seed sown was reaped in the formation of a new order of conductors called the Conductors' Brotherhood, and its growth has been astonishing.

The real cause of the feeling on the part of Messrs. Wheaton and Daniels, was their effort to have passed a license law. Circulars had been sent to all divisions of the Brotherhood, asking their support, but the conditions contained in the bill were such that they did not consider it to their interest to do so. The same was presented to the engineers' convention at Chicago, where Mr. Wheaton claims he did not receive the respect he deserved. There are twenty-eight sections in this bill. The first section prohibits any railroad company employing any but licensed conductors and engineers. Sections two to nine inclusive, relate to an army of examiners, who, under this bill, would become United States officers.

SEC. 10. Every railway conductor, and every locomotive engineer, who receives a license hereunder, shall, before entering upon the discharge of his duties, make and subscribe an oath before one of the examiners herein provided for, that he will faithfully and honestly, according to his best skill, judgment and ability, perform all the duties required of him by law.

SEC. 11. Every railway conductor and every locomotive engineer who shall receive a license as herein provided for, when employed upon any railway, shall keep such license, and shall upon request of any passenger upon his railway train, exhibit such license. And for every neglect to comply with this provision by any such railway conductor or locomotive engineer, he shall be subject to a fine of one hundred dollars, or to the revocation of his license.

Sections twelve to twenty-one relate to examiners.

SEC. 22. If any licensed officer shall, to the hindrance of commerce, wrongfully or unreasonably refuse to serve in his official capacity on any railway, as authorized by the terms of his certificate of license, or shall fail to deliver to the applicant for such service, at the time of such refusal, if the same shall be demanded, a statement in writing, assigning good and sufficient reasons therefor, his license shall be revoked, upon the same proceedings as are provided in other cases of revocation of such license.

Sections twenty-three to twenty-eight, inclusive, fix salaries of examiners, etc. The whole bill looks more like an effort to make room for office, than to benefit the railroad employes. It only adds complications to those that already beset railroad men and offers nothing to better their condition. It was so peculiarly useless and unfitting in its application, that it called out the following from the fertile brain of Bill Nye, in the St. Louis *Post Dispatch*, of which we give extracts: "Some anxiety is being shown on the part of the people relative to the condition of a certain bill, introduced in congress, January 10 of the present year.

Conductors, under the provisions of this bill, are required to submit to a rigid examination under the eye of the chief examiner, appointed by the president, and who shall receive $3,500 per year, and mileage at the rate of 10 cents per mile, together with reasonable traveling expenses. The chief examiner will delegate his power as an examiner to twenty supervising examiners, retaining only the bitter anguish and enervating toil incident to the life of one who looks out at the car window all day and patiently accumulates mileage."

"The chief examiner, and supervising examiner shall constitute a national board of examiners, who shall meet at Washington, D. C., every little while, to think it over and then go away. The national board of examiners shall divide our unhappy country into twenty districts, each of which shall be cheered by the presence of two districts examiners, and they shall be men of good moral character, who can ask difficult questions and be willing to work on a salary. They shall receive a salary of $2,000 a year, mileage, stationery, and press notices. The duties of district examiners as prescribed are optional, but the salary is compulsory. Assistant district examiners may be appointed at a salary of $1,500, and clerks, when necessary, may be employed to do the work at $1,200 per year."

"The chief examiner, supervising examiner, district examiners and assistant district examiner, shall be at all times guarded by a cloud of mileage by day and a pillar of salary by night."

"The board may revoke the license of any conductor at any time upon the commission of certain acts, and he will then be arrested under the provisions of the United States statutes, if he undertakes to run a train, even though the railroad may desire to retain him. This gives the conductor the chance to work for the railway companies and the United States of America, providing he behaves himself, and at one salary. In other words, he buys a license for the privilege of doubling his responsibilities without increase of pay. Upon passing a satisfactory examination the conductor will be permitted and required to wear a large tin badge, bearing the remark "Conductor" upon it, also the number of his license, the number of the district in which the license was issued, the number of his residence, his post office address, and any other information desired by a morbidly curious public. He may also be required to wear a muzzle during dog days. Conductors on receiving their license will be required to subscribe to an oath in substance as follows:"

"The schedule of examination has not yet been fixed, but it must be so prepared that it shall cover the physical and mental conditions of the applicant, and will no doubt run something as follows:"

"State your age, weight, height, sex, complexion, where born, and who, if any one besides yourself was present at the time."

"I, A. B., having been duly sworn, upon my oath, do remark, set forth and state, that I am——years of age, that I reside in the county and state aforesaid, that, feeling the loneliness of a man who is employed by a railroad, and the isolation of one who is responsible only to the President, board of directors, receiver, general superintendent, general traffic manager, general passenger and ticket agent, claim agent, road master, and division superintendent, I desire to be thrown in contact with the United States Goverment, and to become responsible to the civil and military authorities, in order that I may be duly examined and overhauled by congress; I also do further swear, and set forth, that I will be a good, fathful conductor to the best of my ability, and that I will wear such badges as my health will permit, providing my bosom is wide enough, and that I will report promptly to Washington every day, what is said on my train that might be of political interest, and that I will assist in defraying campaign expenses, be kind and courteous at all times to chief examiner, district examiner, acting examiners, assistant examiners or breath testers, who may be en-route, and that I will love, honor and obey them as long as we both shall live. (Signed) A. B. I only ask, on behalf of several anxious friends, what has become of this bill, and whether it is, or is not now a law, and if not, why not. Bill Nye."

The hits of Nye upon the conditions asked for in this bill are forcible, and under his ridicule there is reason. No class of laboring men should quarrel because some individual was not supported in an effort to pass a law, in order to furnish official places. State license has enough politics in it, but would be a benefit to both engineers and conductors, and add safety to the public, but a license recognizing your knowledge and ability need not imply the abrogation of individual liberty. The Burlington strikers had a heavy load to carry—all their own troubles, and the slurs of every one who had a grudge against any individual who belonged to the 30,000 who composed the Brotherhood—but they stood their ground; and as the strike had been confined to the Burlington road, let us look along the line.

CHAPTER XLVI.

RAILWAY AND WAREHOUSE COMMISSIONERS.

"A complaint signed by fifty-two citizens and business firms of Aurora had been filed with the Railroad and Warehouse Commission in which the complainants say: 'We are informed and belive that numerous engineers and firemen now in the employ of the Chicago, Burlington & Quincy Company, and engaged in running trains through this city, are unfit and incompetent to perform the duties of their respective positions, and that thereby the lives and property of people patronizing said railroad are daily endangered. We therefore respectfully request that you will immediately cause an examination to be made into the truthfulness of the above matter, and take such action as may be by law required.' Among the signatures are those of Charles Wilson, John J. Davis, D. C. Pease, Titus, Marshall & Co., H. Knapp, Andrew Welch, J. M. Kennedy, C. Abel, Hall and Ballard, and James Shaw."[1]

The first case before the commissioners was that of W. H. Pierce, which has been given on page 181.

The next was Hosea DeWitt. "Hecter H. Hall testified he had known him eight years, that he was an habitual drunkard, and that his (De Witt's) wife had been to all saloons, forbidding them to sell him anything."[1] The evidence of his habits was corroborated by Stewart H. Haddock and John B. Clark.

[1] Chicago World.

De Witt was discharged from the Burlington for having a collision prior to the strike. The next case was G. Gray, of Streator, who had been discharged for a collision in the yard at Streator, by the Burlington before the strike. The testimony also showed him a drunkard. Witnesses, John Bexon, Nicholas Plain. "Next came George Rogers, who had been discharged from the Milwaukee, Lake Shore & Western, for general unreliability and drinking. Witness, Cornelius Sullivan." "Next, Harry Smith, discharged from the Marynet, Houghton & Ontonagon railroad for drunkenness." Then the next case was that of Zeb Sammis, alluded to on page 184.

George W. Wheatley, on behalf of the complainants, was examined by Mr. Sullivan, as follows:

Q. What is your name? A. George W. Wheatley.

Where do you reside, Mr. Wheatley? Beardstown, Illinois.

What is your occupation? Engineer.

Locomotive engineer? Locomotive engineer, sir.

How long have you been a locomotive engineer? Fifteen years.

In what companies' employ have you been? I have been the last eight years—seven years—with the C B. & Q.

When did you last see Frank Hamilton? I saw Hamilton last Saturday morning.

Where was he? At Beardstown, on engine 341, if I am not mistaken.

On what road? C., B. & Q., St. Louis division.

Is that a passenger or freight train? Freight train.

When did you last see Frank Horn, and where? I haven't seen him in a couple of months, I guess it is, until lately.

Do you know what his occupation now is? He is running an engine.

Where? On the C., B. & Q., from Rock Island to Sterling, without he has been taken off in the last week.

Do you know Joseph Roach's occupation? Yes, sir.

What is it? He has been running an engine. They took him off there, and put him in the shop to learn to oil around.

When? A week ago.

For what company had he been running an engine up to a week ago? Running an engine for the C., B. & Q.

In what place has he been placed? The C., B. & Q. shop.

Do you know J. Lobstein? Yes, sir.

What has he been doing? He is in the shop learning the trade, and, with the other fellow, learning to oil an engine around in the different parts, and so forth.

Do you know Harry Zimmerman? Yes, sir.

Before Lobstein was put in that shop to get that information, what was he doing? He was running an engine.

Between what points? Between Beardstown and Rock Island, and Beardstown and St. Louis, or East St. Louis.

On the Burlington & Quincy? Yes, sir.

On passenger or freight? Freight.

You said you knew Zimmerman? Yes, sir.

What was he doing ? He was running an engine.

Between what points ? He ran a switch engine in the yard.

In what place ? At Beardstown, and he is on the road now running an engine.

Between what points ? Between the Rock Island and different points, change around from Beardstown to Rock Island and St. Louis—East St. Louis.

Passenger or freight ? Freight.

Do you know William Patterson ? Yes, sir.

What has been his position recently ? He is running a switch engine at Beardstown.

At Beardstown ? Yes, sir.

For the C., B. & Q. ? Yes, sir.

Were any of those men occupied as engineers prior to the 27th of February ? No, sir

Is Frank Hamilton a locomotive engineer ? No, sir.

What was his position prior to that time ? Conductor.

On what road ? C., B. & Q.

How long have you known him ? Since 1881.

Did you ever know him to run an engine ? No, sir.

How long have you known Frank Horn ? Since about 1882, I guess. Somewhere along there.

What was his position from the time you first knew him, beginning from 1882 up to the 27th of February ? He first started in as brakeman for freight, and then went braking on a passenger, and then baggageman.

Braking first on freight, and then passenger, and then a baggageman ? Yes, sir.

Was he running as baggageman up to the 27th of February ? He was running a passenger train as conductor. He was made a freight conductor and from that to a passenger.

Then he was a passenger conductor at this time, the 27th of February? Yes, sir.

Had he ever run an engine before that time? No, sir.

What was Joseph Roach's occupation prior to the 27th of February? He was a freight conductor.

Braking prior to that? Yes, sir.

When did he come on the C., B. & Q.? About three years ago.

Since the time you first formed his acquaintance in 1876 or 1878 up to the 27th of February, was he ever employed as an engineer? No, sir.

Was he ever employed as a fireman? No, sir.

How long have you known Lobstein? I have known him about four or five years.

What was Roach's employment immediately before he was put on the engine? Conductor of freight.

What was Lobstein's occupation prior to the 27th of February? Freight conductor.

For the C., B. & Q. road? Yes, sir.

Had he any experience as a locomotive engineer? No, sir.

Do you know any other occupation that he ever followed but that of conductor? He was brakeman.

Braking prior to that? Yes, sir.

Was he ever a fireman? No, sir.

How long have you known Harry Zimmerman? I have known him about the same length of time; four or five years.

What was his occupation prior to the 27th of February, this year? He was freight brakeman and passenger brakeman and running baggage on the train, and then he was put on running as a freight conductor.

Conducting a freight train? Yes, sir.

During all that time was he ever employed as a locomotive engineer or fireman? No, sir.

How long have you known William Patterson? I have known him since along in 1870 I believe it was.

What has been his occupation during that time? He had been braking on the Wabash when I first knew him.

And after that? After that he came on to what used to be called the old Rock Island & St. Louis railroad, and broke there awhile, and then there was a lapse of a year that I dropped sight of him. When I came back since 1881 he was on the C., B. & Q.

In what capacity has he been on the C., B. & Q.? Switching. Run a train a while as switchman and then run a train on the road.

In what capacity did he run a train? Conductor.

Freight or passenger? Freight.

Did he ever serve during that time as an engineer or fireman? No, sir.

Evidence corroborated by W. A. Ennison, engineer in employ of the C., B. & Q. railway, who testified on cross-examination:

John E. Dooley, a clerk in the mail postoffice car, related that he was in the collision near Naperville, February 27; that he was injured in the shoulder and side, and laid up three weeks; that W. F. Stinson, a postoffice clerk, and a railroad clerk named Clark, living at Princeton, and a man named Durkee, a mail clerk in the same car, were all seriously injured.

Fred Geyer, foreman of the Burlington locomotive department at Aurora, testified that he was in charge of engine 403 on the 27th of February, that was wrecked near Naperville; that there were three men on the engine besides himself, and that a young man by the name of Foster opened the throttle and snatched the brake out of his hand, and that he (Foster) was trying to help him; that he himself was injured, and that the fireman Parsons was a new man, and not a good fireman.

When did you ever run an engine before on a main track? I never did.

Never in your life? No, sir.

Was this a passenger train? A passenger engine.

How many passengers were attached to it? If I remember right there was ten or eleven.

Where was your run—from what place? From Aurora to Chicago.

Commissioner Marsh: There is the air guage, is there not? A. There is an air guage.

Let me ask you, is it the duty of an engineer to watch the air guage as well as watch his steam guage? I should think he ought to.

Why didn't you do it? Well, I don't really know why I didn't. The time is so short.

Was it because you were not accustomed to running an engine? Well, that may have been the case.

If you had been accustomed to running an engine—a locomotive—do you think you would have noticed that air guage? I would have been more apt to.

When you reversed your engine and was approaching your train? I would have been more apt to if I had the practice every day.

J. A. Murray, locomotive engineer of thirteen years' service, residing at Rock Island, testified that Frank Hamilton, Frank Horn, Joseph Roach, J. Lobstein, Harry Zimmerman, and William Patterson, running engines on the C., B. & Q railroad, were brakemen, conductors, and baggagemen, respectively; that he was acquainted with them all for eight to ten years, and that they were inexperienced as engineers or firemen.

Frank Hamilton, witness on behalf of the C., B. & Q. railroad company, testified: Q. Give your full name? A. Frank Hamilton.

What is your business? Formerly conductor until the 10th of last month; now I am running an engine.

Conductor on the C., B. & Q.? Yes, sir: St. Louis division.

How long have you been a railroad man? For the C., B. & Q. company, running a train since November, 1880, with the exception of five months, up until the 10th of last month.

Have you been examined as to the manipulation of an engine? To a certain extent.

By whom? Mr. Wallace.

Is Mr. Wallace here? Mr. Wallace is here.

Cross-examination by Mr. Sullivan:

Q. You never got any technical instruction as to the running of an engine in your life, did you? A. Explain that word, please.

You never got any instruction in the shop from those who manufacture engines and are familiar with their detail? No, sir.

You don't understand the meaning of the word technical yourself? I do, yes, sir.

Why do you want me to explain it? Because I want to understand.

Witness testified that he had been handling engines off and on ever since he had been on the road.

Q. What you mean is you jumped on, would go on when the regular engineer in charge was there? A. Yes, sir.

And the fireman in charge was there? I run the engine a certain distance.

You were allowed to handle it in their presence just as many others are allowed? Yes, sir.

Do you mean to tell this commission on your oath that in that way you acquired sufficient knowledge to make you a competent engineer? That is the way from what I understand, to learn to be an engineer. The way they all get to be engineers.

Where were you examined? The principal place was in the building where the general officers are.

How long after that was it before you were put in charge of an engine since you got this instruction? I took an engine on the 10th of last month, and I run up to yesterday.

When was your examination? To-day.

You were examined to-day? Yes, sir.

Was this the first examination that took place? This is the first.

You were not examined before you were put in charge of an engine? No, sir.

As an engineer or fireman? I did not.

Did you ever perform the duties of an engineer or

firemen at any time in your life, before this date on any road? That is to draw pay for it?

To draw pay for it and perform its duties regularly? No, sir.

It was stated repeatedly by the officials that "no men were taken without thorough examination" and some said, "none were taken who had not had at least a year's experience as locomotive engineers."

Something had to be said to quiet the fears of the public and the Burlington officials did their full duty in doing whatever was necessary to defeat the Brotherhood. Had they followed their rules, which were in use prior to Feb. 27, they could not possibly have filled their places. The Brotherhood felt that the fight was unfair, and they secured an investigation both in Illinois and Iowa, by the railroad commissioners, to show what kind of men they were taking so that the public might know how much one side was adhering to their principles and the other violating them. The report of the railroad commissioners of Iowa was made to Governor Larrabee which induced the Governor to write the following letter:

Des Moines, Iowa, March 10, 1888.

C. E. Perkins, President C., B. & Q. R. R.

"Frequent complaints have of late been made to me concerning the interruption, caused by the strike of the engineers and firemen on your road, as well as the danger arising from the employment of incompetent substitutes for such employes. The inconvenience and disappointment which the present state of affairs causes to the traveling public, and the loss which commerce, in divers ways sustains, are such that further delay, in adjustment of the difficulties existing between the management of the C., B. & Q. road and its striking employes, would be a manifest injustice to the people of our state. In the territory controlled by your road, traffic is deranged and travel inconvenienced to such an extent as to demand a speedy solution of the difficulty. I therefore appeal to you in behalf of the people of Iowa, to make every effort possible to come to an understanding with the strikers. It appears to me that even self-interest should dictate such a course to you, and especially as your company can be held responsible for damages caused by failure to furnish reasonable facilities for the transaction of business on your lines of road; allow me to suggest, that unless you soon succeed in some way to secure a settlement, you submit the case to arbitration."[1]

Yours Respectfully,

WILLIAM LARRABEE.

The Burlington officials were not inclined to arbitration. They were going to fight it out regardless of damage or inconvenience.

[1] Creston Advertiser.

ENGINE 208 RUNNING INTO A TRAIN AT WOOD STREET, CHICAGO.

CHAPTER XLVII.

DESTRUCTION AND DISCORD.

"At Aurora, Ill., March 27, at 8:15 P. M., the whistle at the Burlington shops was blown as a fire alarm, and in a few seconds a lurid flame shot up into the sky, and it was easy to be seen that one of the large buildings of the Burlington shops was on fire. It proved to be the coach paint department structure, which was entirely destroyed inside of an hour. The firemen worked hard and did noble service in preventing the blaze from spreading to the surrounding buildings, many of which were afire a dozen times or more. The demolished shop was only built a year or so before, was 90 x 330 feet, and one half of it had been partitioned off for hotel purposes by the company for the accommodation of the new engineers recently employed."

"Berths were provided for 216 men, and more than half that number were in the building, when the fire started. They were forced to jump from their beds and get out the best they could. A new pay car just completed at a cost of $4,000, and six coaches, were destroyed, as were the tools of the men. The loss was fully $50,000. The fire was caused by the explosion of a kerosene lamp. According to the report of one of the night watchmen, when the lamp exploded in the varnish room, used as lamp room, it was at once discovered by night watchman John Lowe, and special policeman Quackenbush, who in attempting to wipe out the fire with a pair of overalls scattered it so much that the room was all ablaze in a few seconds. The inflammable goods which were stored there caused a conflagration that was absolutely uncontrollable, and only prompt action confined the destruction to the building in which the fire originated."[1] In speaking of this fire, Mr. Morton said: "We have not the least doubt that this thing was the work of the Aurora strikers. Perhaps they wanted to damage the company, but I think their main object was to burn out the new men who were housed there."[2] This was enough from which to manufacture a specific charge that the strikers burned the paint shop. It being impossible to give the same notoriety to the facts, as had been given to the first report, that charge is still in the minds of many, and is still doing injustice to those men, as I heard the charge repeated in July, 1889. "A committee was appointed by the mayor of Aurora to investigate the cause and they found that the evidence all proved that the fire started in the corner of the room where the lamps were trimmed; that there was no evidence that a combustible was, or could have been, thrown into that part of the building; that there was no evidence of assaults or riotous conduct during the fire, and that the fire was undoubtedly of an accidental origin. R. W. Gates. John F. Thorwarth, committee."

In the excitement of the time it was natural to charge everything to the strikers, and such charges were easier made and believed than the truth was, when found out.

1 Aurora (Ill.) Express. 2 Chicago Tribune.

The Burlington had built a temporary boarding house in Chicago for the new men. Mr. Morton said: "We have found it necessary to put up temporary barracks for these men and place them under protection."[1] But we would rather mistrust that the real difficulty was shown in the following:

A THREE CORNERED FIGHT.

THE NEW SWITCHMEN, the PINKERTON FORCES, AND THE CITY POLICE DO NOT PULL TOGETHER.

"There is at present a great deal of ill feeling among the non-union switchmen, the city police, and the Pinkerton men at the Western avenue yards of the 'Q' road. The feud arose some time ago when the Pinkerton men showed signs of dissatisfaction when they were put in too close contact with the new switchmen, who were classed as being 'a set of tramps' by the tony deputies. As soon as the switchmen found out that their company was not desired by the Pinkertons, they immediately took the part of aggressors and seemed anxious that a crisis should be reached. The deputies learned that the switchmen were not in a very healthy sanitary condition and did not associate with them at all. Even on the trips over the road the deputies would try to keep a couple of car-lengths away from those occupied by the switchmen. At meal times a Pinkerton man and a 'Q' switchman can never be found sitting at the same table. When all the seats are taken, except one near the deputies, a switchman will never take it, but wait until some other seat is vacated so that he will not sit near one of his guardians."

"The matter reached a most bitter state when the

1 Chicago Tribune.

city police became involved in it. They not only refused to associate with the deputies but with the switchmen also. They set up a general protest when they learned that the switchmen were infested by a tribe of vermin, which proved to be very irritating after a few day's sojourn in camp."[1]

It is possible boarding houses might not want such company. The crowding process of the Burlington officials under the inter-state commerce law created much feeling between the Burlington officials and those of other roads. A case was brought against the Chicago, Rock Island & Pacific, to compel them to handle Burlington cars. "The Rock Island's attorney, Robert Lincoln, made answer charging the Burlington with cutting rates to compel the formation of a trust in violation of the inter-state law.

"Attorney Withrow said they could also prove the Burlington refused concessions to its men allowed by other roads, merely to bring about a general strike, and put competing roads in a mood to submit to the Burlington. If we have made any wrong charges, he said, it is the power of this company to put us in confusion before the whole world by going before a master. The Burlington makes a pet aversion of the Brotherhood of Engineers. Now we may get indignant as much as we please at the so called despotism of these organizations, but we have been living under the despotism of coal combinations and cotton combinations, and the like; now this combination of the engineers is a legal one. They have the right to quit work. After six weeks scouring, if the Burlington can't get competent engineers, what prospect is there for us, or for

[1] Chicago Mail, April 3, 1888.

another road, if we provoke a quarrel with our men? Continuing, he said, the Burlington had so much of the Boston flavor about it, that it fancied all other roads were run for its convenience, and it would not do what it wanted others to do. The Rock Island was solvent and might better pay for the cars than stop its whole system and injure thousands of people." [1]

"At the conclusion Judge Gresham said, even if the allegations made by the Rock Island were true, it did not relieve that road from its duty as a common carrier. Again, he did not think the Rock Island had refused to do its duty. The 'Q' did not need protection from this, its strongest competitor. As there was no danger of injury accruing to the 'Q' road, no injunction would be issued just now. The future developments, he said, might alter this.

The unpleasantness of the strike penetrated high quarters. Everybody was in a mental state to make strong statements. With the boycott raised, the case was dropped by mutual consent. The strike was off on all other lines, and the Burlington had given notice there would be no more pilots. Business was expected to be good on the Burlington, as the gates were once more opened. The men employed by the Burlington were charged with incompetency by the Brotherhood, which was strenuously denied by the Burlington. There is an old saying that the workman is known by his chips. We have already recorded several mishaps. We shall try to give only important ones, so that the readers may judge for themselves, whether incompetent labor is profitable in railroad service. We have said before that wrecks were avoided in a very great measure by

[1] Report of Chicago Times.

the presence of pilots, who were old trainmen, and many engines were kept from being burned by the same assistance, but engines were burned and plenty of them. More grates were burned in one week, than before the strike in one year. On the Hannibal & St. Joseph division, first week, engine No. 20 was run through the roundhouse at Kansas City, knocking down wall and landing in the street. Engine 29, burned very badly; flues had to be reset. Engine 66 on passenger train, after going five miles, could go no farther; could not work injector; master mechanic took switch engine and went after him to show him how. In March, engine 67, had injector pipes frozen up, bursted, engine towed back to Brookfield, dead. Engine 39, passenger train No. 3, Engineer Reed, Conductor Fitzgerald, was lost to dispatcher between Round Grove and Macon. After a long time waiting engine came into Macon without train, could just get on to side track, another engine was sent for and the 39 remained on siding for a week before it was taken away. Query. What could have been the matter with it ?

Engine 34. Cooked at Utica, Mo.; engine was tried after thirty to forty days' work was put on boiler, but could not use engine and had it to be sent to general shops.

Engine 54. Engineer Jones smashed up tank while doubling New Cambria Hill, by running into train.

Engine 78, light engine, Engineer Phillips, Pilot Gahagan, ran into hind end of No. 11 standing at station at Meadville, Mo., smashing front end of engine and disabling way car.

Engine 33. Engineer Sharritt, Conductor Flaharty,

ran into Rock Island train No 17, at Prairie Tank, Mo., losing front end head light and stack, besides damage to Rock Island train. No one discharged.

March 27, at 12:45 A. M., Charles Poole, a switchman, was killed in Brookfield yard, Farley engineer. Poole was jerked off car and run over. Coroner was not notified, and body was shipped to his relations in Illinois without inquest. Poole lived fifty-two hours; was nursed by Martin Culleton.

April—Engine 34, Engineer Simpson, Conductor Garrity, ran into rear of train No. 9, breaking up front end of engine, and causing such damage as naturally accompanies such accidents.

Engine 37, Engineer Wood, Conductor Birdsall, engine broke down at Breckenridge. Wood, in trying to disconnect, cut off bolt heads in strap and tried to drive the bolts down through. Every engineer will appreciate his difficulties in this effort with a tapered bolt, but he did not propose to be behind the times, so he took a chisel and drove under strap and pried it up, and straightened it to get it off.

Engines 1 and 48 collided in Brookfield yard; loss, two cylinders. Engine 43 was run into turn table pit at Winthrop, Mo. Engine 65, off switch at Cameron, lost pilot. Engine 67 lost pilot in yard at St. Joseph, Mo. Engine 61 broke spring hanger at Osborn, delayed train two hours and twenty minutes. If we add to this, a large list of grates burned, eccentrics cut, guides cut, brasses burned out, incompetent disconnecting and blocking of guides, that did more damage than the original break, you may form some idea of what was being done in the way of expense. I mention the Hannibal & St. Joseph because of my own knowledge and belief that every allegation is true. I have left out many minor accidents, and all that appear of a natural occurrence, and not chargeable to incompetency.

April—Engine 27, Engineer Clift, Conductor Wilder, passenger train No. 2, came into yard at Brookfield, ran past the station, engineer and fireman both very drunk. Hostler was sent to take care of engine.

Collision two and one-half miles east of Brookfield, between engines 55, Engineer Woodlief, and engine 69, Engineer Toppin, Conductor Baily. Toppin and Baily had orders to meet No. 13 at Brookfield, a train pulled in which they took for No. 13 and they pulled out and made a meeting point for themselves. They were laid off, I think, thirty days; with the old men it would have been thirty years. The report along the line shows:

At Monroe, Thursday, April 5, engines 22 and 49 engaged in a bumping match, and both will be in the shops many days. In both these wrecks the competent men jumped and saved their lives.

At Bristol, Friday, April 6, engine 175 ran into a local freight and demolished fourteen box cars.

Galesburg reports a little $2,000 collision between engines 55 and 162."[1]

The following is from a paper printed in New Cambria, Mo., where the accident happened April 4.

LAST NIGHT'S WRECK.

TWO MEN SERIOUSLY, IF NOT FATALLY, INJURED.

A disastrous wreck occurred at this place at 12 o'clock last night. The first section of freight train No. 10 was standing on the main track waiting for

[1] St. Joseph Gazette.

orders when the second section ran into them. The engine completely telescoped the caboose of the first train, and smashed up twelve freight cars. A stock-man by the name of Robt. C. Auld, from Pinkney, Mich., was in the caboose asleep. His hands, face and parts of his body were badly scalded by the escaping steam, and he barely escaped being burned to death as the wreck took fire immediately. Engineer Markham, who was pulling the second section with engine 20, stood at his post and escaped uninjured. His fireman, E. S. Robbins, of Denver, Colorado, jumped and was struck in the back by a box car. He is seriously, but it is thought not fatally injured. The two injured men are being cared for at the Wallace house, by Dr. T. H. Hughes. Brakeman Theihoff was on the caboose but jumped off just in time to save his life. Brakeman Sevy, whose home is in Clarence, was thrown from the top of the train but escaped with only a few scratches. The caboose, an empty box car and two cars of corn were totally destroyed by fire, and the engine is a complete wreck. The wrecking train arrived from Brookfield at 2:30, and at 6 o'clock the side track was cleared so as to let the night passengers by. The signal lights on the caboose could be seen for at least three fourths of a mile, and if the engineer had called for brakes when he first saw the lights the train might easily have been stopped.

A bad accident occurred at Pacific Junction at 3 o'clock this morning (12th inst.) The Burlington & Missouri train did not stop for the Kansas City, St. Joseph & Council Bluffs crossing. Engine 353 was standing on the other side of the crossing, and was struck by the B. & M. engine between the tank and engine, and smashed the tank; engine 353 broke from her tank, as the throttle was wide open, and went "wild" down the track, without an engineer or fireman, and went into some cars in her way up to her home. The engine is a complete wreck.

CRESTON, IA., April 15.—The fast mail train on the Burlington road collided with a freight about one mile west of here early this morning, on a curve just beyond a bridge, and the engineer of the passenger train had only time to apply the air brakes before jumping. C. A. Shoot, fireman of the freight train was instantly killed and the engineer, J. M. Osborne, was slightly injured. Brakeman Henry Gibbons had a leg crushed and L. J. Miller was internally injured. Both engines were totally wrecked. Two mail cars were thrown down an embankment and burned, together with the bridge. The mail clerks were rescued uninjured.

The coroner's jury in this case rendered a verdict as follows: "Said jurors upon their oath do say, after having heard the evidence, and examined the said body: We find that the deceased came to his death on the 15th day of April A. D., 1888, by a collision about 4:30 o'clock A. M. between freight train No. 12 going east, and passenger train No. 5 going west, at a point about one and one-half miles west of Creston depot, deceased being employed as fireman on said freight train, and we further find that the collision was caused by the negligence of Conductor Seymour Armstrong, and by gross negligence and incompetency of engineer

J. M. Osborne. The negligence of conductor Armstrong consists in his falling asleep while on duty, but from the evidence we find that he had been kept on duty continuously for about fifty-four hours, which in the minds of the jury would unfit him for the responsibilities; and we further find Engineer Osborne was grossly negligent in running his engine without time, his watch having run down at 2:55 A. M., two minutes before leaving Corning station, as shown by the train record. We further find him incompetent as an engineer, from his lack of knowledge to construe the time as shown by the time card."

Jurors. { J. R. Powers,
W. N. Kelly,
A. Wilson."

The verdict fixed the blame chiefly upon the scab engineer, J. M. Osborne, who was pronounced grossly negligent and incompetent. Regarding the latter quality the following facts were brought out:

"He had run on west division since March 17, but did not yet know the names of all stations without schedule or distance between stations. Named five stations between Council Bluffs and Creston; could not say whether Cromwell was registering station or not; run through Cromwell because he was signaled to go ahead, he thought, by the operator."

He looked at his watch and time card at Cromwell, and it was 2:55 exactly. He had two hours to make Creston from Nodaway, twenty miles. He was positive of the time at Cromwell. He was more careful this trip than any that he had ever made before, because he had had such bad luck. Had only made two trips without a pilot; run an engine on Lehigh Valley about the year of Centennial and had run no locomotive since. Run stationary engine at Homer, N.Y., before. Did not know what time he was due at Cromwell. He arrived there at 2:55. He was pretty well acquainted with the road and grades on the west end.

"ST. JOE., MO., April 18.—Engineers at this point are very scarce. The Burlington is having a great many accidents. Train No. 17 and train No. 20 collided and damaged both engines badly. Eight or ten box cars were thrown in the ditch."

"BEATRICE, NEB., April 19.—Burlington business at this point is very light. Engines Nos. 4 and 33 collided in the yards this morning, and both engines are total wrecks. The engineer on 33 was running about thirty miles an hour through the yards.

"GALESBURG, ILL., April 20.—Bad wreck in yard to-night. Engine 367 and passenger engine 33 collided, and both engines are total wrecks."

"CRESTON, IA., April 20.—The following engines are burnt at this point: Engines 35, 392, 422, 248. Engine 248 was on the fast mail and played out near Pacific Transfer. A switch engine had to pull the fast mail in."

"QUINCY, ILL., April 20.—Passenger No. 1 and freight collided here; both engines total wrecks; also engine 45 came in on one side."

On the 26 a special, with Burlington officials aboard, drawn by engine 139, ran through a switch at West Quincy, and all turned over in the ditch, the occupants were badly shaken up, the fireman was badly injured.

[1] Chicago World.

There were hundreds of minor mishaps that were chargeable to incompetency. We only give the more expensive and dangerous for the sake of comparison, so the reader may judge which is the cheaper, good wages and competent labor, or incompetent labor, and the disaster that accompanies it for the sake of saying, "We run our own business and allow no dictation or arbitration." In *Harpers Weekly* of April 21, appears an article from Mr. W. D. Howells, a writer known and read from one end of the Union to the other. He writes from the standpoint of a stockholder in the C., B. & Q. railroad, takes decided grounds in favor of arbitration, and is not flattering to that management, in the last paragraph, which persists in looking upon a railroad's affairs as private affairs. His article is as follows:

"With grief that I think must be shared by a good many other holders of Chicago, Burlington & Quincy stock, I saw that stock go down from 129 to 112 under the effect of the private war waged between the railroad and its engineers and switchmen. I am told by the press that the loss was through the fault of these employes of the road, and that its officers illustrated a beneficent principle in standing firm against them and refusing their demands. The principle was that the road had a right to manage its private affairs in its own way."

"But here, I think, is an error. A railroad has, strictly speaking, no private affairs. It is a corporation which in return for certain franchises has assumed certain obligations, and before all corporate rights it has these public duties. It ought to consider these always, and from the beginning; but it is said that when early in the war the opposite faction offered to submit its claims to arbitration, the officers of the C., B. & Q. replied that there was nothing to arbitrate. If this was true, it is a great pity, and I believe a great mistake. There is no question here of the road's treatment of its employes, but if these thought themselves underpaid, and the road thought they paid them enough, it was the very moment for arbitration."

"That truly christian device for averting public war has now been successfully tried, and it seems to me it would have been well to use it in the danger of the private war which has embarassed travel and commerce on the Chicago, Burlington & Quincy, and spread loss far and wide. It is in quality of a timid capitalist that I write; and I wish to say that I have no particular affection for the Brotherhood of Engineers; it has before now shown itself short-sighted and selfish, and in its betrayal by the Knights of Labor it is said to be paying the penalty of a treason of its own. But however this may be, it is unquestionably a power lawfully organized for defense and offense, and it was the part of policy for the opposing force to recognize its strength. It was also a duty to do this in view of its obligations to the public, which neither of the belligerents in the case has considered. The road was bound to come to any tolerable accommodation with its employes, so that the public might not suffer. The quarrel, so far as it concerned the engineers, was between them and the road; but as concerned the road, it did not end there; the community was an immediate sufferer from its impolicy—the community which had a sovereign claim upon its service."

"When the strike began, I suppose that nearly every humane person said to himself, 'Well between men who want to make a better living and a corporation that wants to make more money I can have no choice.' I said something like this myself, not remembering my C., B. & Q. stock in my magnanimity. But of course when the strike came, as strikes must, to involve violence, the general sentiment changed, and many lectures have been read to the engineers on their misbehavior, but to the road none. That is my reason for attempting to read it a little one now, to remind it that it is the creature of public favor, with duties to the public which it had no right to fail in through any mistaken sense of its corporate dignity or interest. I dare say that the engineers' strike against it will end, as all strikes have hitherto ended, in disaster to the strikers. But I am sure that strikes will not always end so. It is only a question of time, and of a very little time, till the union of labor shall be so perfect that nothing can defeat it. We may say this will be a very good time or a very bad time; all the same it is coming. Then the question will come with it: Shall the railroads fulfill their public obligations by agreement with their employes, or shall the government take possession of them and operate them? It is folly to talk of the withdrawal of capital, and the consequent ruin of the country. The country belongs to the people, and they are not going to let it be ruined. Their possession of the railroad would involve much trouble and anxiety, but the railroad receiver, who is an agent of theirs, is not unknown, and his management of roads is good; so that the public may take heart of hope if the worst ever comes to the worst."

"But let us understand that it is not engineers or switchmen or brakemen who can bring it to the worst; it is only directors, and managers, and presidents who refuse to arbitrate, and who forget their public duties so far as to talk of a railroad's affairs as private affairs." W. D. HOWELLS.

Owing to the natural sympathies of the people in the cities along the line where they were best acquainted with the strikers, the company threatened to move shops away or close them up, in order to drive them into line, and compel them to furnish special police and stop any demonstration in the strikers' favor. "General Superintendent Brown, at Creston, received orders to close the machine shops and prepare to run trains through the city, if the authorities did not take immediate steps to protect the company's employes."[1]

The strikers had some of the new employes arrested for carrying concealed weapons, and the Creston *Advertiser* of April 3, said; "Superintendent Duggan has been furnishing security for thugs and bullies convicted of carrying concealed weapons. The significance of his remarks to an *Advertiser* man, that there would be blood spilled over this yet, is beginning to be more fully understood, and we are now convinced that he was better posted on the claret market than the press representative. Thanks to the vigilance of the police, his braggart employes have, as yet, failed to carry out the prophecy of their superior." This threat to boycott the cities was made all along the line. At Brookfield, Mo., a threat was made to move the shops

[1] Chicago Evening News, April 2, 1888.

to Chillicothe, Mo. This scare worked on the minds of the people so that at the municipal election, prohibitionists voted the free whiskey ticket, because the prohibition candidate was an honorary member of the Brotherhood.

Because one out of more than a hundred strikers at Brookfield had committed an unmanly and unlawful act in striking a scab with his walking stick, a law and order meeting was called "April 20, 1888, at 2 o'clock P. M., for the purpose of taking such action as is necessary to uphold the civil authorities of our city and country in the enforcement of law, and the suppression of vicious, violent idlers in our midst."[1] This wholesale condemnation of these men who had been citizens, some of them for twenty-five years, created much feeling. As it was a call for citizens, the strikers attended in a body, and were there promptly at the appointed time, and occupied the reserved seats.

An effort had been made to get as good an attendance as possible by those issuing the call; the men employed in the company's shops were invited, and a special effort was made to have the new men there to hear the good things to be said to them and the bad things said of the strikers. When they came and found the strikers present—and no one questioned their right there—it was a great drawback to their liberties of speech. It is much easier to say hard things of one absent, than present. The strikers went as listeners only, with an understanding that they should neither vote, nor talk; they were not there to disturb, or overawe anyone: they were there to find out how bad they were. The meeting was called to order, a

[1] Copy of call.

chairman elected, and a resolution read by an attorney —who was retained by the company as its legal advisor—condemning lawlessness and the strikers by implication, offering taffy to the railroad officials and a hearty welcome to the new men. After the resolution was read and passed, the strikers not voting, the chair asked if there was any further business. No speakers responding from the other side, the strikers called for a speaker, who responded in a short speech questioning the justice or propriety of calling a meeting to condemn such men as he saw before him among the strikers, who had been with the city and helped build it from its infancy. This speech pleased the strikers, and put a wet blanket on the promoters of the meeting. But the next speaker put them to route with ridicule, and a motion was made to adjourn. The new men present did not like the outcome, and after the meeting adjourned one of them, named Murray, who had been welcomed to the city by the resolution of the meeting, ran two brakemen off the streets with his revolver; complaint was made and this nice new comer was taken in by the Marshal, and put under $100 bond to appear the next morning. He appeared the next morning and was given a dose of whitewash and let go—no cause of action. The strikers, after such a wholesale condemnation by the law and order meeting, did not like this one-sided way of doing; all they asked was that the law should take its course no matter what it hit. And they sent for the assistant prosecuting attorney. He, finding the evidence abundant, caused Murray's arrest on a state warrant. The same lawyer who read the resolution of welcome at the meeting conducted the defense. Trial came, a change of venue was taken and the case was postponed two days, with the prisoner out on bail. In the meantime the new engineer got drunk, raised such a row that he had to be clubbed and put in the jail for safe keeping. Trial came again, so did the evidence, so the company's attorney wanted to avoid trial and the strikers were asked to say upon what conditions they would withdraw the prosecution, their only object being to show the one-sided legal proceedings. If the new man would make an acknowledgement, pay all cost, and agree to leave the city, they would be satisfied. They wanted law and order; the law was being perverted and used to the detriment of the strikers, and the protection of the scabs. The police judge had found nothing against this man and liberated him, but the state's attorney had found too much evidence and the prisoner was glad to choose between leaving, and working for the state. Was the meeting called for law and order or was it called in fear of a great corporation? At Aurora, Ill., April 14, 1888, at a meeting held in the city council room, resolutions were passed and committees appointed to circulate the petition on both sides of the river which the committee says under the date of April 24, "I can assure you was thoroughly done. I give you below the names of those who were 'men' enough to sign it."[1] This petition asked the mayor to put on 30 to 100 special policemen at the city's expense. To many business men, the necessity did not seem to exist, and they refused to sign it. The Burlington officials had this petition and the list of names printed for dis-

[1] Quotation from the document.

tribution to their scabs, and on a slip was written with a type writer twenty-five names of business men who would not sign the petition, and one of these was handed into each house to be boycotted so they would be sure to know it. I have both documents obtained from one of the new men. A bulldozing policy was practiced in court and out, all along the line, and the influence that controls legislatures was never more apparent than in the Burlington strike. Fear on one hand, and money where that would not do, secured power along the line, not warranted by any consideration of justice.

The aggressive policy of the Burlington was bringing organized labor nearer together each day. Meetings were being held in all parts of the country. "At New York, April 8.—Members of the Brotherhood of Locomotive Engineers and Locomotive Firemen to the number of 1,500 met at Tammany Hall J. J. Hanahan, Vice-Grand Master of the locomotive firemen, and Joseph Porter of the engineers of the C., B. & Q. system, addressed the meeting and told what they had seen and heard on a recent trip over the C., B. & Q. system from Chicago to Denver. Mr. Porter declared the losses already amounted to a million of dollars. Among other things he declared that already 157 engines had been disabled through incapability of the 'scab engineers.' Remarks were also made by leading members of eastern divisions of the Brotherhood of Engineers and Firemen. The meeting unanimously adopted these resolutions:"

"*Resolved:* First. That the action of the Chicago strikers—acts of violence excepted—are hereby endorsed and approved."

"Second. That our pledge of financial and moral support to our striking brothers of the C., B. & Q. railroad is hereby renewed and will be continued as long as necessary."

Like meetings were held in all large business centers, and similar resolutions passed. An appeal had been sent out over the Burlington system, which was signed by thousands of business men asking "the Inter-State Commerce Commission to take action on the 'Q' strike in reference to the mismanagement of the Burlington and the interference with the traffic of the country. Judge Cooley, chairman of the commission, has consented to an investigation. Mr. Alexander Sullivan, the attorney for the Brotherhood of Locomotive Engineers, was preparing the evidence to be submitted."

As a further evidence that the two Brotherhoods were not disheartened, the following is significant:

"St. Louis, Mo., April 14.—The grievance committee of the Brotherhood of Locomotive Engineers and Firemen on the St. Louis & San Francisco railroad, made a settlement this morning on the basis of three and one-half cents per mile on passenger, and four cents per mile on freight trains, with the abolishment of all classification."

"The terms of this settlement are exactly what the striking engineers and firemen on the Burlington asked for. The Brotherhood men are to be congratulated upon having won a substantial victory, and St. Louis & San Francisco management upon their display of fairness and great good sense."

"Grand Master Sargent arrived at headquarters in the Grand Pacific from St. Louis Thursday morning. In respect to the concessions made by the St. Louis & San Francisco road, he said; 'One strike has been averted; twelve hundred engineers and firemen continue to work with their condition bettered, and the 'Frisco line running out of St. Louis, over 1,446 miles of western territory, is no worse for the conference it gave a committee of employes, and the subsequent settlement which it magnanimously agreed to. The enginemen on the 'Frisco line had submitted to the officials of that road a set of resolutions almost exactly the same as were laid before the Burlington management. Within five days from the date of which the paper was received by him, General Manager Morrill expressly desired to settle with the men themselves, and for that reason there was no need of myself nor Mr. Arthur being present. His conduct is deserving of much praise."

When interviewed, Mr. Sargent said: "Don't forget to say that the same request was made that caused the strike on the 'Q.' That was the abolishing of classification and the adoption of a mileage system as a basis for wages. This point was agreed to at once."

"When Paul Morton, of the Burlington road, was asked why his company could not have settled the Burlington difficulty the same way, and thus avoided a strike, he turned to his desk and wrote the following reply:"

"I am glad to hear that the 'Frisco strike is settled peaceably. The probability is that if our men had presented modified demands before striking we would have had no trouble. Our strike is settled, too, but in another way, and it has clearly demonstrated the old adage that it takes two to make a bargain."

"There! 'That's my answer', said he, handing over the paper."

In this answer Mr. Morton forgot that the Burlington would allow no second party to the contract, and a strike resulted.

"On the 19th, J. J. Hanahan, Vice-Grand Master of the Brotherhood of Firemen, returned from a trip through the principal cities and terminal points of the east, where he held joint meetings and found a warm welcome, and on every hand the greatest enthusiasm and warm commendation of the course of the officers of the Brotherhood. The members pledged any support, financial or moral, that might be necessary, and Mr. Hanahan brought back the equivalent of $250,000 in cash. Mr. J. Porter, of Aurora, accompanied Mr. Hanahan. They were followed on the trip by Burlington detectives, and evaded them at several points, only to be overtaken again.

Mr. Morton again declares the strike off:

Chicago, Ill., April 13, 1888.

Chicago, Burlington & Quincy Railroad Co.,
Passenger Dept.

To Ticket Agents.

Gentlemen:—Commencing Saturday, April 14, the Burlington fast train will be resumed. The strike is over. Our engineers are thoroughly competent. These trains will be run on time as heretofore.

Paul Morton,
General Passenger and Ticket Agent.

CHAPTER XLVIII.

THE STRIKE NOT OFF.

Paul Morton had said the strike was off and everything was running smoothly as before the strike. But the statement of Messrs. Hoge and Murphy, the spilling of blood, and public opinion, would indicate that it was still on.

At Galesburg, Ill., on the 28th of April occurred the killing of H. B. Newell, one of the striking engineers, by gun shot wounds from a revolver in the hands of William Albert Hedburg, a Burlington scab fireman. At the coroner's inquest, as was the case always where the Burlington was interested, and contrary to common usage, lawyers employed by the company were on hand necessitating the presence of other lawyers, and at this inquest " a confab arose as to who Mr. Brown, who was conducting the examination, represented. The coroner then demanded who all the attorneys represented. Mr. Brown said that he represented the people at the request of friends; Mr. Lawrence said that he and Mr. Williams represented Mr. Hedburg; Mr. Carney said that he represented the city of Galesburg; Mr. Welch said that he was there at the request of parties interested and proposed to stay. The squire then said that there had been considerable criticism on allowing attorneys present and their asking questions. He had admitted it so that the examination might be thorough and searching. Mr. Cooke offered to withdraw, if there was any objection to his representing the State. The matter was finally smoothed over and the inquest proceeded."

The inquest lasted three days. State's Attorney Cooke remarked that the inquest seemed to have been run by the defense. The jury brought in a verdict that the shooting was done in self-defense. A warrant was immediately sworn out by a brother, A. B. Newell, charging Hedburg with murder, and the prisoner was held to the grand jury.

The Funeral of Herbert B. Newell.

"The funeral service over the remains of Herbert B. Newell was held at the house on East Main street at ten o'clock this forenoon. It was probably one of the largest funerals ever held in Galesburg. The house, yard, and walk were thronged with people. It is estimated that not less than one thousand persons were on the grounds."

"There were several fine floral offerings, perhaps the most prominent being the one representing the drive-wheel of a locomotive, with one of the spokes broken, and the initials, 'B. of L. E.' and 'Div. No. 62', worked in flowers. This emblem was very suggestive and stood at the head of the coffin. There was also a harp made largely of calla lilies and roses at the head of the coffin. At the foot there were two beautiful pillows of white flowers. In one, in immortelles, was the word 'Herb,' and in the other one 'Newell.' The services were opened by a quartette consisting of Messrs. Manning, Fleharty, Fairbank, and L. H. Jelliff, singing, 'Asleep in Jesus.' Rev. J. W. Bradshaw then read several selections from the scripcures, after which the quartette sang 'Last Good Night.' Rev. Bradshaw then, without taking any text, made a short address. The following is a synopsis of the first part of his remarks:'

"'We are gathered under the shadow of a great and shocking calamity—a calamity which has cast its gloom not upon us alone who are assembled here, but upon the whole community. One of those appalling occurrences which shock our deepest emotions, which kindle excited feeling; which tend to unsettle the judgment of the calmest and most judicious. At such a time it behooves all right-minded men and women to summon into exercise their utmost self-control; to quiet excited emotion; to suppress every trace of passionate feeling, to give calm judgment full sway; to let their words be few and cautious, and their actions most discreet. He who should act otherwise would, by so doing, make himself the enemy of the best and most sacred interests of society. Of the circumstances attending this sad occurrence, this is neither the time nor the place to speak. Not till by lapse of time excited feeling has been stilled; not till, viewing these events from a distance, we are able more accurately to perceive the true relations of things; not till, by passage of time, calm judgment is restored and truth fully brought to light, can anyone wisely speak of these sad circumstances or venture to pass judgment upon them.'"

"In closing Mr. Bradshaw spoke comforting words to the bereaved and urged the necessity of preparing for death while we still have health and opportunity."

"After Rev. Bradshaw's address the quartette sang 'Beautiful Land.' The house was then cleared and the family and relatives of deceased took their last look. The remains were then brought out and placed on the sidewalk and all given a chance to view them. The Brotherhoods marched two abreast and as they came to the coffin they clasped hands and passed each side of the remains. Over 300 thus filed past the coffin. There were visitors here from Burlington Div. No. 151, Marshalltown Div. No. 146, St. Paul Div. No. 150, Aurora Div. No. 32, and Beardstown Div. No. 127."

"The procession down Main street was a solemn, magnificent and imposing one. The streets were lined with spectators, and the utmost silence prevailed. It was shortly before 12 o'clock when the line of march reached the business center. At the front was the Galesburg Marine band, playing a beautiful funeral march very smoothly and impressively. The marshals of the line preceded them, and were Mr. Robert Barnhill and Mr. Thomas McGann. Then was seen the crimson banner of the Switchmen's lodge. There were in line some 60 of these, including the delegation from Burlington and other points. Each wore around his sleeve a piece of crape. On their hands were white gloves. The next banner was the elegant one of the B. of L. F., and of those marching behind the banner proclaiming "Benevolence, Sobriety and Industry" there could not have been less than one hundred and fifty, including the visiting brethren. Each, as were also the switchmen, was adorned with the regalia of the fraternity as well as the symbols of sorrow.

The long line of engineers came next, and they were the center of all eyes. The beautiful, brotherhood banner at their head was gracefully adorned with festoons of crape. Each wore an elegant badge of mourning. The appearance of these one hundred and thirty or forty fine looking men, the face of each wearing an expression of sadness, was impressive and touching. The sincerity of the demonstration was apparent to all. Then followed the carriage containing the crippled members of the Brotherhood. Following this were the hearse, the lovely floral wheel discernible through the rear windows, and the pall-bearers, Geo. Best, Frank Reynolds, E. Updike, A. H. Vanwormer, Geo. Stofft and G. McDowell, walking on each side of the hearse. Next were the carriages. It is estimated that the procession was a mile in length. In addition to those in the line, many sympathizing friends passed along the sidewalks on each side."

"Arriving at the grave the Brotherhood formed in a circle around it and the impressive service of laying away a brother was performed by Chief Engineer Thos. Hill, assisted by Chaplain John Saddler, after which the quartette sang a beautiful song, and the benediction was pronounced by Rev. Bradshaw." [1]

Paul Morton came out in the Associated Press dispatches, May 1, and declared the strike off on the C., B. & Q. This was the third time that Paul Morton had declared the strike off since the 27th of February.

"No doubt the Burlington officials would have been glad to have it declared off, because they were being scored most unmercifully by western newspapers.

[1] Galesburg Republican Register.

The St. Joseph, Mo., *Gazette*, of May 7th, says, "We have a few more items of interest to present for the edification of the Burlington managers and the instruction of the traveling and shipping public. The strike is over, it is said, but somehow things do not seem to get the proper hitch in their trousers."

"B. & M. engine No. 128, and K. C. engine No. 1., met on a single track a mile north of Nodaway station, thirteen miles from St. Joseph, yesterday morning. The meeting was more forcible than profitable, and the locomotives will have to be almost rebuilt before they will be of any special service to the company."

"The accident occurred in this manner: Both trains had orders to meet and pass at Nodaway, but the K. C. engineer, a new man named Jones, forgot his orders. Conductor Harrington was not attending to business and the train ran gaily by the station and into the B. & M. train. A dozen cars, about half of which were oaded, were converted into kindling wood and the engines were total wrecks. They were towed into St. Joseph in the afternoon and taken to the shops. The rainmen jumped when they saw a collision was inevitable. Some of them received severe bruises but fortunately no one, so far as can be learned, was killed. All trains were delayed three or four hours. Damage $20,000."

During the first week of May occurred the Rope Creek disaster, near Alma, Nebraska. In 1887 an immense amount of money was spent by the Burlington in replacing wooden structures with iron, and other bridge work. But in 1888 retrenchment was necessary, and the comments upon this wreck from the press of the west, could not have been very consoling in the face of a declaration that the strike was over and their men were competent. The St. Joseph Mo., *Gazette* had an article headed "B. & M. Butcheries," and illustrations were shown from photographs taken on the spot. Mr. Morton said all these stories of wrecks were fakes, and we give a few extracts. The *Gazette* says:

"That the B. & M. railroad in Nebraska is in a fearful condition; that travel over it is extremely dangerous; that those who are compelled to buy its services take their lives in their hands there is no need denying, and not an official will seek to deny. Traveling men feel a sense of perfect insecurity, and breathe with more ease when at last, after numerous unwarranted and inexcusable delays, their destination is reached. Dead engines, wrecked freight cars, damaged coaches, splintered sleepers, and generally demoralized rolling stock fill half the sidings and all the repair shops along the line. Wreck after wreck has been reported, all coupled with loss of life, maiming of limbs, and injuries to a greater or less extent. Trains meet on the iron highway, at all hours, day and night, and often fatal accidents are only averted by the interposition of providence on behalf of those who are compelled to travel over the B. & M., and therefore are not responsible. The once famous 'cannon ball' is a cannon ball no longer, except that acting in the capacity of a loaded van it is armed, thanks to incompetent men with double the death-dealing qualities of the missle from which it takes its name. It would be a greater means of destruction but for the fact that its passengers are to and from local points only. Through passengers are an unknown quantity. In spite of the vigorous and earnest, would they were honest, protests of managers, superintendents, passenger agents, and hired organs, all, or nearly all of the once handsome through business enjoyed by the road has gone; vanished like the tramp's dream of wealth; and it will not soon be regained. Imagine the famous B. & M., the once great through route to Denver, running solid day and night trains of never less than three cars each for the accommodation of never more than twenty passengers. No. 40 has made the run from Denver to St. Joseph within the last week, carrying but eight passengers, and No. 39 has done the same thing. Day coaches and smokers are well nigh deserted and the few passengers ride in the sleepers, because in case of one of the many accidents they may be enabled to at least escape with their lives."

"In sustaining this position the management has attempted to belittle any and all reports of wrecks, and this refers not only to the B. & M., but to all parts of the Burlington system. Hired organs, instead of sending representatives to scenes of accidents, have rushed them into the company's headquarters that an 'official report' might be secured! Damages amounting to thousands of dollars have been scaled down to hundreds; collisions have been averted by passengers and road men, and the incompetents now manning engines, have been excused on the plea that they do not know the road. The only thing that has prevented a succession of Chatsworth disasters, is that travel has been light and traffic has been diverted to other lines. The wrecks which have occurred are seventy per cent greater in number, since February 26, and 200 per cent greater in loss of life and property than ever occurred on the Burlington system in the same period before. And they are multiplying, not decreasing. A case in point is the recent wreck at Alma, Neb. In violation of orders the trainmen rushed on a rotten culvert at a tremendous rate of speed, and in an instant five souls had been sent into eternity. Two bodies were found two days after the accident, and two are known to be missing. Officials at once began to lie about the cause and fatalities, and every effort was made to cover the matter, that the already poor traffic might not be entirely lost. The Nebraska press was flooded with padded and untruthful accounts of the efforts of the officials to care for the wounded and find the dead. They did little or nothing; chiefly the latter; and when the coroner's juries had taken testimony every effort was made to belittle and suppress it."

"Then the company telegraphed it broadcast that every effort had been make by it to recover the missing bodies."

"Not only is every statement that the B. & M. officials or employes either assisted in the search for bodies or took any care of them when found, most maliciously false, but exactly the opposite is true, as can be established by the testimony of hundreds of the best people of both Alma and Orleans. Not only have eighteen of the best business men of Alma, composing the three coroners' juries impaneled to hold inquests on the bodies taken from the wreck, found the B. & M. company guilty of criminal negligence in connection with the Rope creek disaster; not only have two of these juries especially censured the criminal negligence of Eugene White, the section boss; not only has it been proved by the contradictory statements of this man White, but by the testimony of other witnesses as well, that White has lied in regard to important incidents of the wreck and its causes, but from the day of the wreck until the present time not one of the officers or employes of the B. & M. railroad company have ever lifted a hand to assist in the search for the missing bodies, and for this neglect the company has been censured by two juries."

"Not only has the negligence of the company and its employes, in allowing the wreck to occur, been fully established, but their utter neglect and refusal to search for bodies is known to all people. Sheriff Allen and the people of Alma are entitled to the credit for finding these missing bodies, as they have never for a moment relaxed their vigilance in the matter, and the B. & M. is entitled to nothing."

"Hardly had the last victims of the wreck been found when the employes and the hirelings of the B. & M. railroad company began to swarm in from all directions. Knowing all the circumstances of the disaster, and knowing that the first coroner's jury had found them guilty of criminal negligence, none of them ever lifted a hand to search for the bodies of the missing victims, or to render the slightest assistance to our people in doing so; but now, like buzzards to a feast, they came singly and in droves, and when Sheriff Allen, acting as coroner, had empaneled a jury to learn the cause of the accident, they were on hand ready to meddle and dictate in a matter which before had given them no concern. They had lawyers and stenographers, and bruisers, and shoulder-strikers, and witnesses to swear to whatever they were told, and were quite anxious, so long as they could not cover up the evidences of their negligence and brutality, to swear away the honest testimony that, by revealing the facts, would damage their testimony. It was not because the company cared a straw for the dead and wounded or their sorrowing relatives, but because they hoped to evade the payment of just and reasonable damages. The conductor swore to receiving slow orders for that bridge on the morning of the wreck, and yet neither he nor the engineer took the trouble to stop before going upon the bridge."

"The views of the wreck published herewith are from photographs taken by L. D. Willits, of Alma. They are kindly furnished the *Gazette*, to further its efforts to show the B.& M. managers and officials in the true, but unsavory, position which they have taken in this matter. There is also room for some hired organ which considers the strike over and objects to its ad finitum continuance to begin to tell the truth and publish a few items of news concerning the real condition of the Burlington."

A FALL IN STOCK.

"The strike hits hard in many places. The holder of stock is a sensitive plant. The

FIREMEN'S CONVENTION TRAIN.—AT THE DEPOT.—STARTING FOR ATLANTA TO ATTEND THEIR CONVENTION.

breath of a western strike makes a coupon shiver. Stocks and bonds fall before the lightest frost. But a railroad strike or war is roast jack-snipe on toast, mashed pomme de terre with apple sauce on the side, for the broker. He keeps one eye bearing on the naked facts while his judgment is on the rack. 'Buy or sell? that's the question.'"[1]

"Chicago, Ill., May 10.—The financial report of the Chicago, Burlington & Quincy road for the month of March, covering the period of the strike, was made public to-day, and, as was expected, showed a remarkable decrease in earnings, compared with March, 1887. The gross earnings were $1,211,188; operating expenses, $1,357,608, leaving a deficit for the month of $146,415."

"The foregoing telegram, published in the daily papers of the country, yesterday, needs little comment. It were time wasted to go into nice calculations, showing how far this immense sum of money would have gone in meeting the demands made upon the C., B. & Q. road by its employes—demands which were spurned without reason or argument. The stockholders are doubtless pondering this problem, and it is barely possible that even that high and mighty potentate, General Manager Stone, as well as managers of lesser degree, look ruefully upon these figures and begin to question the efficiency of pig-headedness as the ruling principle of railroad management. Whatever may be the final outcome, the great strike on the C., B. & Q. system will not prove valueless. It has served to call the attention of the public most forcibly to the fact that corporations have no conscience, and

1 Chicago News.

that sometimes the managers of American corporations have but one maxim: 'Might makes right'—a brutal maxim, the utterance of rapacity,—an echo from the depths of human selfishness. A maxim embodying a menace to the weak, its very word is freighted with malevolence."

"But if it be true that corporations are conscienceless, it is also true that stockholders have pockets, and that while all other appeals may fail, an argument which addresses itself to the instincts of Boston shopkeepers and money changers is very apt to receive most careful consideration. Under existing conditions little improvement in the business ot the C., B. & Q. can be expected. Travelers will not submit their lives to unnecessary dangers. Shippers will prefer roads unembarassed by the complications which now render the train service of the C., B. & Q. roads entirely unsatisfactory as well as unsafe. By common consent the C., B. & Q. system has been boycotted, not altogether because of its injustice to its employes, but because of its inability to discharge the duties of a common carrier. Public confidence can only be restored by manning its trains with sober and competent men. The pretense so volubly put forth that 'the strike is over,' that 'all trains are running on time,' that 'the Q. has its full complement of engineers and firemen,' etc., etc., has deceived nobody. The accidents and calamities occurring on all parts of the system tell another story. The plain and apparent fact is, that notwithstanding the great reduction in the volume of its business, the C., B. & Q. road is unable to do justice to the few patrons it retains, and that under existing circumstances it could not handle the enormous traffic it formerly enjoyed, even were public confidence restored. It has raked the slums of the nation for substitutes for the striking engineers. The lame, the halt and the blind have been drafted into its service. Drunkards, convicts, men who before the strike would never have even dreamed of applying to it for employment now have charge of its engines, and to their doubtful keeping are committed the lives and property of its patrons. To say that many, or even a majority of its engineers, are competent, is no answer to this charge. It is enough to know that many of them are incompetent, and of this abundant proof is not wanting. With all possible safeguards against accidents, travel by rail is sufficiently hazardous, and the road which willfully omits the least of these safeguards is undeserving of public patronage. The conduct of the C., B. & Q road in taking into its employment the class of men now running its engines was an act of criminal desperation. Its stubborn refusal to recognize as anything better than serfs, men who had served it faithfully for so many years, was a brutal exhibition of arrogance, and its subsequent indifference to the rights of the public and the safety of life and property, a crime."

"If the contents of the foregoing telegram do not bring the C., B. & Q. stockholders to their senses, similar ones which are sure to follow will probably do so."[1]

The Burlington directors' meeting was called to meet in Chicago on May 16, and it was deemed best by the leaders of the strike to call in all the grievance

[1] St. Joseph (Mo.) Gazette.

committeemen of the Burlington, look over the situation and make some provisions for future action. It was thought by many that at the meeting of the stockholders, the immense losses already sustained, and the depreciation of the stock, would induce the directors to modify their position and be willing to arbitrate and get the strike declared off. But the Forbes interests were there with proxies sufficient to bar out any effort to change their policy, and they voted confidence in President Perkins and the official management of the strike. This convinced Grand Chief Arthur and Grand Master Sargent that further effort to effect any settlement was useless, and concluded to advise the committee there assembled to declare the strike off—Grand Chief Arthur coming from Cleveland for that purpose. But the committee voted unanimously to continue the strike, and a vote was taken along the line and forwarded to the two chairmen, Hoge and Murphy. The vote stood 1558 to continue the strike and nineteen to declare it off. So the grand officers went to their respective headquarters as there was nothing to their mind they could do but see that the men were supported financially. The strike was as vigorously prosecuted as it was in the power of the Burlington strikers. Speakers were sent over the country, the interest kept in a lively state, and the Brotherhood men and Knights of Labor vied with each other in diverting business from the Burlington."

"Wreck and disaster followed the trail of the scabs, regardless of Mr. Morton's statement that everything was running smoothly. The fast mail train running through a Chicago & Iowa freight, at South Aurora, on May 23, and the following from the Aurora *Express*:

"A Burlington special police lost his star and club yesterday. Fred Long, who has charge of twenty-six night and twelve day special policemen in the employ of the Burlington, learned that one of the night officers was drunk in 'the cut,' yesterday. He went to investigate and found not a night man, but one of the day specials and one of the new switchmen lying side by side, drunk together."

With the good will expressed in the answer to the following, ought to be strong reminders that the strike was not off:

C., B. & Q. Railroad Company.

Mr. E. A. Barnes, Principal Webster School:

"Dear Sir: I wish to see you regarding the teachers' trip to California in July next. Kindly advise me when it will be most convenient for you to have me call, and oblige."

Respectfully Yours, Geo. R. Dunne.

Chicago, Ill., May— 1888.

Mr. George R. Dunne:

"Dear Sir: So far as I know, the sympathies of the public teachers are with the Brotherhood and decidedly against the C., B. & Q. So long as there are other routes of travel we shall never board a Q. passenger train." Respectfully, E. A. Barnes.

During the month of June laboring people throughout the west were keeping an eye on all patrons of the Burlington during the period of conventions. Appeals were made to the various political factions not to patronize the Burlington and no doubt it had a powerful influence. Immense meetings were held, and the road was placed before the public by speakers in a manner that must have been anything but pleasant for the managers. On June 11, an immense meeting was held at Lincoln, Nebraska. We give a few extracts from the speeches, as they have a direct bearing upon the subject before us, as showing the magnitude of the power with which the Brotherhoods were contending. Hon. Ex-Governor Butler said:

"Mr. CHAIRMAN, LADIES and GENTLEMEN:—I must say that I am somewhat disappointed from the fact I had no expectation of meeting so large an audience as I find here to-night, and if I fail to come up to your expectations, why, be a little charitable."

"Gentlemen, I am here to-night to talk for a few moments on the question of labor which governs the people from the Atlantic to the Pacific, and from the lakes to the gulf. This question is not confined to this continent. Go into any of the states of Europe and you will find the same quest ion being agitated there."

"There never has been on earth, never, no living man that ever honestly accumulated five millions of dollars; he never did that on earth; there never was such a thing; he doesn't need it in the first place, he can't use it, he can't appreciate it, and he never made it honestly—there never was such a thing on earth."

As an illustration he said: "Suppose that Adam had laid up a dollar a day from the day of his birth to the present time, how much do you suppose he would have been worth? $1,000,000. His overcoat would not have made Vanderbilt a vest, would it? There he had worked five thousand years. We had a class of scientists sometime since that claimed they had discovered a pre-historic man; they went on to say that he had lived five hundred thousand years before Adam; suppose they had found this man to be five hundred thousand years older than Adam, suppose he had been a Knight of Labor and had worked from that day to the present, every day, Sunday not excepted, no rainy day excepted, how much do you suppose that gentleman would have had? He would have made $182,000,000. Vanderbilt could have bought him out and had $43,000,000 to put into Lincoln street railway stock. (Laughter) How did Vanderbilt accumulate that vast wealth? He accumulated it by regulating commerce among the states. Don't you remember of reading of parties in the medieval ages taking refuge in the mountains and forming themselves into bands and tribes, and when people would be passing over the King's highway, these thieves would come out and rob the people and take all they had; they said they took what the traffic would bear; that is what Vanderbilt and his associates have been doing; they have taken the place of congress and stood on the King's highway and robbed the people from here to New York, and from New York to the old country. How shall we remedy this? Some will say, 'You can't do it.' 'Can't?' Is that possible? I think from the looks of the faces here to-night that a number of these wrongs could be rectified and I think they will be. There are three classes of men I don't like. There is the man that thinks he knows everything. I don't like the man that has the idea that everybody that differs with him don't know anything. Whenever I find a man who is truly satisfied with things as they exist, wants no change, wants no advancement, I pray God to treat him as He did good old Elijah—take him off to heaven, he is no use on earth." [1]

The Burlington having lined its road with Pinkertons, the speaker said:

"Have you seen anything like labor disturbances in this country? No. Have you seen any farmers organized for the purpose of destroying property or violating the laws? Have you seen any of the railroad men through this country proposing to destroy property in any way. I have heard nothing of it. Was it not an extraordinary speech that the governor should make the other day in Omaha when he told the militia there to be on guard—to be watchful. I will not do him injustice because I have a good deal of respect for Governor Thayer, but I thought it was a remarkable speech indeed, for them to be in readiness or something of that kind, that if these labor troubles continued they might be called into active service. What did he mean by that I wonder? Had there been any threatenings around here by laboring men that would suggest the proposition that they must be in readiness to fight. Was there anything of that kind?"

"I want to say to the governor if he has a company of militia that he let the golden opportunity slip by. There was a time that he might have used that militia not only with credit to himself, but credit to the state of Nebraska. When the news flashed across the

[1] Lincoln (Neb.) Review.

wires from Chicago that 250 thugs from the city of Chicago had taken the train with Winchester rifles, and were coming over here into the state of Nebraska to preserve peace, if Governor Thayer had wanted to give the militia exercise then was the time. He should have met those men at the Missouri river and never let them come into the state. [Long and loud applause.] But I don't want to say a harsh thing to the governor, because I have always been a personal friend of his, but whenever the governor of any state will stand idle and let the rights of the people be trampled upon by a lot of thugs from Chicago I think it is time to give that governor warning. [Applause.] I do indeed. And I will tell you one thing, had I been governor of this state those men would never have crossed the Missouri river. I understand that they are marching on the platforms of the depots in this state yet, unlawfully here, intruders, and the governor should see that they are not here. I am ashamed of it. They are nothing but thugs picked out from the slums of Chicago. They are not fit to watch a hen roost."

L. W. Rogers paid his respects to another class. He said in part:

"In the war of 1776, Great Britain proposed to rule this country and America proposed to have a right to say if a heavier burden should be imposed upon them, and who should spend their money. They think they had the right to deny that England had the power to say what taxes should be levied, and they remain passive, but if she had this right she hesitated at nothing. She asserted she had the right of dictator over the American colonies. She claims she had a right to levy and impose taxes and burdens upon the people in this country, and take that money and spend it as she chose; and in this struggle to-day England has an exact parallel in this country, and that is the C., B. & Q. railway corporation. [Applause.] There was a party of the second part. They were the patriots of the American colonies. They were the men who said, we will resist this tyranny. They were the men who said, you can rob us to a certain extent, but you cannot trample upon our manhood. They were the men who demanded justice. They were the men who said, we will resist until death, and said they were willing to die that the cause of liberty should live. They were the men who were made out of the same stuff that Patrick Henry was, who said: 'Give me liberty or give me death,' and that party has an exact parallel in this struggle to-day, and it is the C., B. & Q. strikers. And there was another party—a party of the third part—and they were called the tories. They were men who were born and bred upon the American soil. They were the men who were raised under the same influence that gave birth to freedom. They were the men who were raised by the side of these same patriots that went out to fight fearlessly for liberty, and yet these men raised under these influences turned against the country. They said, we will defend tyranny. We will arise in the defense of slavery. We will stamp down the spirit of liberty. We will destroy all good and noble principles, while such men as John Adams was saying: 'For the spirit of this declaration we mutually pledge to each other our lives, our fortunes and our sacred honors,' and that party to-day has an exact parallel in the struggle, and these are the scabs."[1]

This is only a sample of what was being done in all directions; the sympathy engendered by these meetings and the incompetency of the men employed by the Burlington produced in a great measure the following result:

The gross earnings for June show a decrease of only $186,899 compared with the previous year, but the operating expenses increased $320,047, which brings the total net decrease for the month up to one half a million dollars. The decrease in net earnings from Jan. 1 to July 1 amounts to nearly $5,000,000. With this report, it would seem unnecessary to mention any wrecks; it contains all the evidence necessary as to the Burlington's condition.

On the 5th of July was sprung the Pinkerton detective sensation, astonishing the public, and astonishing the two Brotherhoods fully as much. The two chairmen of the grievance committee were arrested; but it did not create a stampede among the strikers, a result that was very much desired and expected. Violence was contrary to their habits and their principles. They refused to believe that any of their number were guilty, and they kept on their way as though it had not happened. On the 10th the Burlington reduced their force of switchmen at Kansas City, Mo. The switchmen claimed that the company agreed to keep them all at work, if they would stay when the engineers and firemen struck until the strike was declared off. Six of them were discharged however, and they all walked out. The switchmen in the yards of the other roads, through sympathy

[1] Lincoln (Neb.) Review.

with these, again put the boycott on the Burlington. The officials of all the roads were convened in Kansas City, but by the advice of the grand master of their order, Mr. Monoghan, the strike was declared off, and scab switchmen were employed in their places.

At the suggestion of a Wabash official, two engineers of that road waited upon Mr. Stone, in an effort to get a settlement, and secured an interview, and by common consent a meeting was agreed upon when Messrs. Arthur and Sargent could be present. On July 14 these gentlemen were requested by the Brotherhood's legal advisor, Mr. Sullivan, to come to Chicago on the 16th. The meeting was appointed for that day at 2 o'clock P. M. The leading officials and their attorneys of both sides, were present. Mr. Perkins wanted the strike declared off, but the inducements were not very great. After a long conference, the following propositions were made:

1st. Mr. Perkins would take back such of the men as he wanted to fill the positions then vacant, and as he needed more engineers and firemen he would give the old men the preference, rather than hire men coming from other roads

2nd. That the order issued by General Superintendent Besler—that the switchmen could never work for the Burlington again, or to that effect—be rescinded, and they would be treated the same as the engineers and firemen."

3d. That a letter of recommendation would be given those that desired to get employment on other roads, providing they had a good record previous to engaging in the strike.

These propositions had to be submitted to the men, for they had voted the strike on, and must vote it off, the two grand officers having no power to decide the matter. With the approval of Messrs. Arthur and Sargent, the two chairmen Hoge and Murphy, were asked to go over the line, explain the situation and ask the men not to allow pride, or sentiment to prevent them from taking the course which the two grand officers were convinced was the wise one. That this was an unpleasant duty to perform, the reader can judge by the vote which stood 742 against, to 9 in favor. While the two chairmen were engaged in taking the vote, a joint meeting of the locomotive engineers, firemen, switchmen and brakemen, convened at Tootles Opera House, St. Joseph, Mo., Tuesday, July 24, to consider the Burlington strike.

"About seven hundred delegates were present, representing lodges of the United States, Canada, and Mexico. Great care was taken to keep the proceedings as quiet as possible. Mr. Frank P. McDonald, chairman of the grievance committee of the local Brotherhood, called the meeting to order. A committee was appointed to search the opera house for spies, with a lantern. Finally a pair of shoes was found on the stairway leading up into the attic, above the ceiling of the gallery. This excited suspicion, and the stage-carpenter, whose name is Moore, was asked about the shoes. He said that they belonged to him, and when asked to describe them made a mistake. A search was make for the owner of the shoes, who was found secreted in the chandelier supports, without clothes on except a honey-comb undershirt and a pair of overalls. His name was David Replogel, a short-hand writer in the employ of Lancaster, Thomas & Dawes, attorneys, at 318 Francis court."

"Replogel was found by a member of the local Brakemen's Brotherhood. He was escorted down the ladder amid the yells of the Brotherhood members, who believed that Replogel was a Pinkerton employe. Replogel stated that he had been hired by Jake W. Spencer, formerly publisher of the Evening News, but now proprietor of the Journal of Commerce, to take the proceedings of the convention in short hand for his paper. He said that he was to be paid $25 for the work, and admitted that the stage carpenter had shown him the hiding place. A large crowd gathered around him when he was brought down on the stage, and but for the interference of cooler heads, Replogel would have been roughly handled."

" He had taken lunch and a bottle of water up to his hiding place and was prepared to remain there all day."

"He was marched to police headquarters through the streets in his bare feet, undershirt and overalls; bare headed, and looked more like a chimney sweep than a stenographer."

"Great excitement prevailed while Replogel was being taken from the opera house, and cries of 'Pink-erton spy' and 'scab' were made by the delegates."

" After the excitement subsided the convention pro-ceeded to business, and elected Frank P. McDonald permanent chairman. The forenoon was spent in speech making by Frank P. Sargent of Terre Haute, Indiana, grand master of the Brotherhood of Locomotive Firemen, R. Powers, master of the local Brakemen Brotherhood, and Mr. Hitchins, general chairman of the grievance committee of the Kansas City, Fort Scott & Gulf road. M. W. Sullivan, Charles Porter' and R. Morris, all of St Joe, were elected secretaries.',

This meeting tended greatly towards harmonizing the various interests of railroad employes, it being composed of engineers, firemen, switchmen, and brakemen. It was agreed that federation was in the interest of all, and that each order should, at its coming convention, pass such laws as were necessary to put it in practical operation. This meeting heartily approved the action taken by the Burlington strikers, in refusing to accept the terms offered by that company and declare the strike off.

"Inasmuch as it was at Stone's request that the chairmen of the Q. grievance committee took their unnecessary trip over the system, they felt that it was incumbent upon them, as a matter of courtesy, to wait on Mr. Stone upon their return and announce the result of their pacific mission."

"Mr. Stone received them pleasantly, but without any overwhelming demonstration of warmth. When told that the men had rejected the proposition, Mr. Stone only said that he was sorry, and that he thought they had made a mistake."[1]

It was anticipated by the delegates comprising the St. Joseph meeting, that, at the meeting which had been called by Grand Chief Arthur, at the earnest solicitation of the western grievance committeemen, to meet at St. Louis, Mo., August 9, that it would be

[1] Chicago World.

opened to the four orders above mentioned, and that the federation should be further discussed. But that meeting was very exclusive, none but grievance committeemen being admitted. Mr Arthur stated at this meeting that he would not object to federation—each order retaining its individuality—with a board composed of members of all the orders to which problems should be submitted which the separate orders had been unable to solve. The St. Louis meeting was decidedly unproductive, and it clearly proved that conservatism was daily becoming stronger.

At the convention of the firemen, held at Atlanta, Ga., a federation law was passed, and a committee was appointed to present it to the switchmen's convention then being held in St. Louis. That body approved of a modified form, and the brakemen's convention followed without taking decided action, but left their doors open for future decision. The engineers' convention followed, at Richmond, Va., when it was thought the engineers would surely fall in line, and pass some law on federation. But the earnest believers in the benefits of such a law, were doomed to disappointment. Mr. Arthur, from some cause, had changed his mind, and the plan was defeated by a small majority. At this convention a resolution was carried, that a committee of men be appointed to settle the strike on the Burlington and declare it off, and the Grand Chief appointed A. R. Cavner, S. G. A. E., of California, chairman; A. W. Logan, Ohio; Thomas Humphry, Ohio; E. Kent, N. J.; A. L. E. May, Wis.; Thos. Holinrake, Ontario, Can.; T. P. Bellows, Miss.; A. W. Perley, Oregon: Wm. C. Hays, Minnesota.

CHAPTER XLIX.

DYNAMITE.

The Associated Press of July 5, heralded the great sensational arrest of "Thomas Broderick and James Bowles, members of the Brotherhood of Locomotive Engineers, and another man named Wilson, on a Chicago, Burlington & Quincy train this afternoon, brought to Chicago, and locked in the county jail, under bonds of $5,000 each, charged with conspiring to destroy the railroad company's property. They had a considerable quantity of dynamite in their possession when arrested."

"It is stated that the Burlington company has had a large force of detectives engaged for a long time in watching the movements of the strikers. Several so-called 'agitators,' whose movements corresponded with some of the past attempts upon the company's property, were put under special surveillance. It was discovered that dynamite was used in several unsuccessful attempts to wreck trains within the past few months. The principal suspects were not allowed to make a move, day or night, without being under the watchful eye of the officers. It was impossible at first to loeate the dynamite, but the officials of the 'Q.' assert to-night that positive information was finally received to-day that this was the day chosen for a grand attack upon the company's property. The officials are very reticent regarding their source of information, but the plot is known to them, and they admit that besides a definite plan to blow up trains upon the tracks by means of dynamite cartridges, that it included the possibility of an attack upon the depot property and magnificent office buildings here."

"The officials say that if the danger had not been so imminent they would have allowed the conspirators to go on and further criminate themselves, but the plot had reached a stage where it was necessary to take decisive steps to prevent great destruction of property, not to say loss of human life."

"Superintendent of Motive Power, G. W. Rhodes, swore out a warrant to-day, and deputy Marshal Burchard proceeded with it to Aurora, in company with detectives. Their men were located and shadowed to the 2:15 afternoon train for Chicago. Thomas Broderick and James Bowles, two ex-Brotherhood engineers of the 'Q.,' were seen to board the train in company with a man not known to the officers. A fourth man they were looking for was not identified. The strange man, who proved to be John Q. Wilson, took a double seat beside Broderick, while Bowles sat just across the aisle. The train had barely started when the officers tapped the men on the shoulders and made them prisoners. The men had taken off their coats and under the two coats lying between Broderick and Wilson upon the seat was an innocent looking package wrapped in a newspaper. When he had captured this Detective McGinty's look of triumph quickly faded as he realized the possible danger of its contents. While they were putting the bracelets on the prisoners, Broderick quickly snatched a letter from his pocket and threw it out of the window."

"McGinty sprang to the bell rope and stopped the train. Running back along the track he found the letter. It is now in the possession of District Attorney Ewing. He refuses to reveal its contents, but General Manager Stone intimated that its contents gave important information regarding the plot."

"The officers reached the city with their prisoner without incident. Broderick and Wilson being stoically indifferent to everything, while Bowles was profuse in his explanations of 'mistakes.'"

"A valise was taken from Bowles and several letters and papers. These were taken to the district attorney's office with the newspaper package, and was then, for the first time, examined and found to contain four dynamite cartridges, each about ten inches long, and an inch and a quarter square. These were fitted with a small fuse to each, and Mr. Rhodes estimated that they each contained about a pound of dynamite. In Broderick's pocket in a purse, were found several small dynamite fulminating caps."

"The prisoners were taken before United States Commissioner Hoyne on their arrival here. Bowles asked for Chairman Hoge, of the old Burlington grievance committee, and also for Attorney Sullivan. These gentlemen were sent for and while waiting Bowles talked quite freely. He claimed that he knew nothing about the dynamite, He worked on the Atchison road until March, when he was discharged for putting a fireman off his cab. During the strike he went to work on the Burlington and remained thirteen days, when his brother, a Brotherhood engineer, induced him to leave the company's employ. Since that time the Brotherhood has paid his wages and he has been traveling about. He went to Creston a few days ago, as he says, to brace the strikers up as they were becoming weak, but he claims he never counseled them to do anything wrong. He claimed not to know the men who were arrested with him."

"When Chairman Hoge, learned the full gravity of the charge, he offered Bowles but cold consolation. The district attorney arrainged the defendants under section 5,353 of the United States revised statutes, and Commissioner Hoyne held them under $5,000 bonds each for examination on the 13th inst."

"'I cannot get you any bail to-night,' said Hoge coldly to Bowles in response to the latter's fervent appeal to be kept out of jail. Then he promised that an attorney would be secured at once and that an effort would be made to get them bail to-morrow. All of the men denied positively that they knew anything about the dynamite and disclaimed ownership of the bundle found on the seat between them."

"General Manager Stone was seen by a reporter, and told substantially the same story as related above. He would not say anything more to-night regarding the nature of the information in the company's possession, but added that he believed that high officers in the Brotherhood are connected with the conspiracy to use dynamite." [1]

The Brotherhoods were as much astonished, if not more than the public. The strikers did not believe it, and voted in the face of it, to continue the strike, believing it was the work of the Pinkerton agency.

[1] Kansas City Journal.

The Pinkerton men had been strung over the length of the Burlington system, and it was in their interest to show the proficiency of that force by some startling developments. They had used up an immense amount of money without being practically useful. They must redeem their calling. The men also believed the Burlington would use whatever clue was given them, and use it to its utmost, and there was nothing in the after developments that changed that belief. Following July 5, came in quick succession, the arrests of J. A. Bauereisen, chief engineer of Div. 32, George Goding a member of both engineers and firemen's order, Alexander Smith of the firemen's order, and A. Koegal of the engineers, at Aurora. Then came the arrest of the two chairmen, Hoge and Murphy, on a charge of conspiracy, at Chicago. Then followed the arrest of George Clark and George D. Meiley, of Galesburg. A joint indictment being made against J. A. Bauereisen in each case until there were 16 charges, requiring $37,500 bail, all of which was immediately furnished. If this was not for persecution, the indications were very deceiving. All along the line was heralded the finding of dynamite, in an apparent effort to fasten disgrace upon the Brotherhoods. These stories may have originated wholly in the fervid brain of the reporter, but the public found the following food for mental bias in the newspapers:

ANOTHER PLOT AGAINST THE "Q."

NEBRASKA CITY, NEB., July 16—Officials of the Burlington road here claim to have unearthed a plot to blow up the new bridge on the Missouri river with dynamite, shipped here for that purpose, it is claimed, by striking engineers. The dynamite, it is asserted, has been located, and the parties in possession of it are under detective surveillance, and will be arrested when sufficient evidence is secured. The officers also claim that dynamite was shipped to Plattsmouth and Rulo for a similiar purpose. Startling developments are looked for."[1]

It is unnecessary to say that these startling developments never materalized, but on the other hand it produced what every aggressive move that is pushed to extremes by capital always does—solidified the very element the aggression is intended to disrupt. The following extracts from the master workman of Nebraska, is significent of this fact. He says, "I have not forgotten the sufferings of many of our own brethren at the hands of these Pinkerton freebooters. I distinctly remember, and it is within the recollection of other members of a few years ago, when a prominent Knight of Labor of Michigan was arrested and imprisoned by this same gang of mercenaries. He was arrested without cause. He was plunged into a dungeon. He was a man of clean private life and honest public record. But so skillful was the conspirator's net that the Pinkertons had woven about him—so clearly did the crime that was their doing, cling to him, that it seemed impossible to prove his innocence. Guiltless he was, but it cost the Knights of Labor $15,000 to successfully carry his case through the courts. These same miscreants under the guise of decency, have become members of the Knights of Labor Assemblies, and of the engineers, have organized conspiracies, have procured the

1 Wymore (Neb.) Democrat.

arrest of Knights without cause."

"In the city of Beatrice there are about 700 Knights of Labor in good and bad standing. Of other labor organizations there is membership enough to swell the number beyond 1,000. Suppose this number of men should absolutely refuse to buy a penny's worth of goods that was shipped over the Burlington road. Suppose that they should, as one man, boycott the merchant who ships his goods over the Burlington road! How long would that merchant be able to sustain himself in business? Indeed, how many weeks would it be before not a pound of freight arrived or departed from the B. & M. depot of Beatrice? Remember in this connection that these 1,000 men standing together, would have an influence that would lead more than double their number, or six times their number to boycott the road and the men who dared patronize it. This shows the power and resources of organized labor, and monopoly understands its capacity far better than do its members. No directions are necessary; every brother will understand for himself his duties in these premises.

"If the Brotherhoods fail, it makes doubly certain that we shall follow in their footsteps in whatever struggles of our own we may have. In a word, the hopes of corporations are in the disorganization of labor. Their wealth, and skill, and secret detective work, are all directed to that end. Knights of Labor ought to have sufficient experience from the past; and should need no warning. N. D. HUBBARD.

State Master Workman K. of L., in Nebraska.

All through the dynamite plot and trial, Pinkertonism was ever present. On the statement of John Kelley, charging them with conspiracy, Messrs. S. E. Hoge, chairman of the general grievance committee of the Brotherhood of Locomotive Engineers, and J. H. Murphy, chairman of the firemen's committee, were arrested by Inspector Bonfield, of the Chicago Detective force, on warrants sworn out by General Manager Stone, of the Burlington.

The names of John J. Kelley and John H. McGillvary were also on this list for arrest, both clerks for Hoge and Murphy. Messrs. Hoge and Murphy were taken to the police court and placed in separate cells. Frank Collier, attorney for the Burlington was there, and so was Inspector Bonfield. A moment later Alexander Sullivan entered, he being Hoge and Murphy's attorney and advisor in civil cases.

"'This case,' said Mr. Collier, 'grows out of the circular sent out to the Brotherhood lodges asking that Brotheroood men be sent on to take places on the 'Q,' and suggesting that they bring a good supply of sal soda and emery with them. The sending of these circulars is deemed prima facie evidence of a share in a concerted conspiracy, and we have a sure case against the prisoners."

"We are going to show enough to prove a clear case against them—a sure case. If you want to know anything more, ask Bonfield. He has had charge of the case all the time."

Ex-Judge Barnum was retained in the criminal case. Hoge and Murphy were arrested in the morning, and Inspector Bonfield says, "Kelley and McGillvary were arrested in the afternoon. When arrested they sent for me and I went to see them at the armory."[1] Then follows what appears to be an astonishing revelation.

"Where are these men now?"

"They are not in jail, but have gone into voluntary retirement, answered the inspector."

Inspector Bonfield gave to the public the idea that he knew nothing of Kelley prior to this arrest, but the evidence is conclusive that Kelley had furnished information to the detective agency, "and acknowledges in court that he had received pay from a friend while he was in the employ of Chairman Hoge,"[2] and there is no doubt that the arrest of the two chairmen was made on the statement of Kelley, and that Kelley furnished the detectives a copy of the sal soda and emery circular, represented to have been sent out signed by the two chairmen. Squealer Kelley, as he was called, was a switch engineer in the Chicago yards for the Burlington, and was taken into the Brotherhood of Engineers after the strike began. He had sailed under an alias, as Charles Cordell. He figured conspicuously as a 'defamer' in the case of Sophia Havelich vs. the Chicago Hansom Cab Co. This lady was injured by the carelessness of a cab driver, and Kelly was employed by the agent of the Cab Co. to rent a room of the lady's mother for the express purpose of acting as a spy. He applied for a room and was told they had none furnished. Kelley reported to the agent, and was instructed to rent the room and it would be furnished, which was done."[2] In the Chicago *Tribune* of December 22, 1888, appears the following: "Judge Altgeld waxed wroth yesterday,

[1] St. Louis Globe Democrat. [2] Court record of evidence, Dec. 19.

over the evident disposition of a witness in his court, to wriggle out of a tight box. J. J. Kelley was the name of the witness, and he has been conspicuous in the C., B. & Q. dynamite proceedings against Beaureisen at Aurora. Sophia Havelich is sueing the Chicago Hansom Cab Co. for being run over by a cab, and part of the defense is, that she has attended theaters and other places of amusement, when she claimed to have been sick. Kelley testified that he saw her go to the theater, and on cross examination by attorneys John Gibbons and Treffy, they attempted to make him admit that he was a paid spy. Kelley found that the value of his evidence would be greatly impaired if he admitted that, and he began to prevaricate, in order to free himself. Evasions were so patent, that Judge Altgeld's temper arose, and he promptly ordered him from the witness stand, and said he had a great mind to send him to jail for contempt. The jury returned a verdict for $3,500, in favor of Miss Havelich, the evidence showing that it was through the drunkenness of the driver that she was run over."[1] This specimen of human depravity who loaned himself for this despicable work against a woman, was one of the main witnesses in the dynamite case.

J. A. Bowles, who was arrested on the train on July 5, went to work on the Burlington as a scab. His brother, who is a member af the Brotherhood, hearing of it, went to Aurora and induced him to quit. He was taken to the engineers' and firemen's hall. "Bowles expressed deep contrition, shedding great tears of remorse, but shortly after he wanted to head a mob, go out and do violence to the scabs and the

1 Statement of persons present.

company."[1] He wanted to do something desperate in order to show that he was really converted. He was taken into the Brotherhood April 22. Before this, dynamite had never been thought of. Bowles testified before the examining magistrate at Aurora Juty 25, that at a regular meeting two weeks after he was initiated, and in the presence of all there assembled, that "John A. Beaureisen made a statement that the company was getting the best of them, and that there had to be something done, and advised the use of dynamite and talked it so that all could hear it. While every man present at that meeting swore that no such statement was ever made,"[2] and from my own knowledge of the men, and the Brotherhood, no such language could have been used without bringing a storm of indignation. Men of undoubted integrity were present. That the statement was a lie needs no proof. Bowles testified on page 34. Q. by Mr. Donahue. What was it that he (meaning Beaureisen) said to you? A. I made mention to him that I—oh, you are the one that began the conversation, was it after the meeting was over? A. Yes, sir. It would seem from this that Bowles instead of Beaureisen was working the dynamite plot. At the preliminary examination in Chicago, Bowles is taken with another spasm of contrition, and goes over to the side of the prosecution.

"Under cross examination by Mr. Donahue, Bowles admitted he had told both attorneys for the defense while in the county jail, that he was an innocent man; that he did not know anything of the use of dynamite, and that he had lied repeatedly to them and others as to his innocence, and about other matters. "But," he

[1] Chicago Tribune. [2] From evidence in dynamite case.

added naively, "I was not on oath then."[1]

When arrested, Bowles had a satchel with him having all the damaging evidence possible, conveniently stored in it, for his own conviction, and to compromise others. This acknowledged liar is main witness No. 2. Bowles had retained attorneys Donahue and David, but instead of consulting with them, he had consulted with the attorneys for the prosecution, and by their advice waived examination. This brought such a scathing rebuke of the court and the attorneys for the prosecution from Messrs. Donahue and David that the court ordered Mr. David removed. The prosecution asked for a continuance, and Mr. Donahue opposed it. The court said, "If the furtherance demands it, it will have to be granted."

Bowles arose from his chair and took a few steps toward the court. With his head turned toward the judge and half averted from the gaze of the spectators, with his right hand outstretched in the attitude of appeal, and in a voice that seemed to tremble in its tones, he said: "It is for the interest of justice, your honor. This will be for the good of the public. All that I will say here will only be for the sake of justice, and to prove that I am an innocent man."[1]

Alexander Smith. a fireman who was arrested as a co-conspirator with Bowles, testified that Bowles worked him into the conspiracy, and induced him to go to Eola where Bowles put the dynamite on the track. Bowles also left dynamite in the room occupied by A. Koegal, which caused Koegal's arrest as an accomplice. It seemed to be his business to rub the stuff against as many as possible in Aurora, in

[1] Chicago World.

Creston and in Galesburg. On page 117 of the court record Bowles is asked. "Are you an innocent man?" And he answered," of course I cannot be considered an innocent man, but I have been led into this by mean and unprincipled men."

The warrant upon which the men were arrested on the train, July 5, was sworn out in Chicago in the morning and the arrest was made in the afternoon; this arrest included J. A. Bowles, Thomas Broderick and J. Q. Wilson. A fourth man was with them but the Pinkerton agent said he got away.

In the preliminary trial it was developed that Wilson was not an engineer, not a Brotherhood man, and not even Wilson. His name was John Mulligan, and he was a Pinkerton detective, and not only this was the case, but it appears he has had the confidence of all the prisoners and their attorneys.

The expose was brought about by lawyer Donahue too closely pressing the cross examination of Superintendent McGinn of the Pinkerton agency, who was on the witness stand. The superintendent had the alternative of an awkward refusal to answer pertinent questions concerning Wilson, or cause the latter to show up in his true colors. McGinn chose the latter. Wilson or Mulligan obeyed a signal, went across the room to the side of the persecution.

It was developed latter, that the fourth man was also a Pinkerton man named Ray. Mulligan alias Wilson, had been in the employ of the Burlington since Feb. 29. Mulligan and Ray made the acquaintance of Broderick, they say, at Creston, Iowa, and a very peculiar feature of the detective work done by them from their own evidence, is that they were companions of Broderick, they were not shadowing him, but with him, drinking his whisky, and doing divers things of a social nature. There is no evidence given by them, that they never entered into any of these violations of law, but they went to St. Joseph, Mo., with him, to Kansas City with him, to Chicago with him, and to Aurora with him, always with clean hands, but always around when Broderick got so full of dynamite, and violations of law that he could not hold it any longer, he would have some one handy to tell it to. It hardly seems probable, that Broderick or any sensible man, would pick up a tramp cooper, and a gambler and give them all of his confidence and they do nothing, but be attentive listeners. If they did not enter into this conspiracy, how did they know that Bowles and Broderick were going to board the train at Aurora in the afternoon having dynamite in their possession and have a warrant sworn out at 8 o'clock A. M. to arrest men who were to commit a crime at 2:15 P. M.? The weight of this great trial fell upon John A. Bauereisen; his good character was proven by witness after witness to have been of the very best.

The evidence on the side of the prosecution was informer Kelley, who acted as a Pinkerton spy, while in chairman Hoge's employe, and as a liar for the Hansom Cab company. Bowles, whose testimony was impeached by his own statements, and by men who swore they would not believe him under oath. Smith testifies that Bowles worked him into the business. The two detectives and the letters Bowles

ENGINE 92, A NEW ENGINE IN THE HANDS OF J. R. KENNEDY, RUN WITHOUT WATER—EXPLODED AT PLANO, ILL., JANUARY, 1889, KILLING THE FIREMAN. ENGINEER STILL AN EMPLOYE OF THE BURLINGTON.

had conveniently stored in his satchel when arrested, which Henry L. Tolman, an expert who had made a special study of handwriting for eight years by means of the microscope, somewhat startled the prosecution when upon the stand he testified that the letters purporting to come from Bauereisen had been written by two and possibly three persons.

When the case was closed and ready for the jury, the Aurora Express of Dec. 20, located at the home of J. A. Bauereisen, with a personal acquaintance with witnesses, and the surrounding circumstances, said: "The dark clouds which have hung over the head of J. A. Bauereisen for the past six months are beginning to grow brighter, and gradually to be dispelled. There is an old saying that you can't tell what a jury will do, and although it applies to this case, it seems very probable that the jury will not convict. They may disagree, but probably will acquit the prisoner. When the prosecution were presenting such an array of black testimony against Bauereisen, it looked to some as if nothing could save him, but the defense are clearing up matters wonderfully. When it comes to a question of veracity between such men as Elwood Tucker, George Minott, Joseph Porter and others, and the self-confessed villian Bowles, none in Aurora will have any difficulty in knowing whom to believe."

In his address to the jury Mr. Mills denounced the perjury that he said had been exposed in the case.

"There has been outrageous perjury," he said; "perjury so palpable as to need no exposing; perjury so outrageous as to damn the perjurers; perjury so marvelous as to stamp the perjurers as worse than fiends and fit only for the blackest depths of infernal punishment. Akin to perjury is the motive for it, and we shall see without much of an effort the reason for the horrible perjury which has made dark, one page of the history of this court room. The vitality, the strength of this prosecution is in two men, John Alexander Bowles and Alexander Smith." Mr. Mills reviewed every statement they had uttered, contrasted the overwhelming evidence on the other, and piled to their charge perjury after perjury.

Messrs. Donahue, David and Mills, of Chicago, Alshuler of Aurora, and Irwin of Elgin, were the principal attorneys for the defense. With only the influence of an individual and his personal friends and well wishers on the side of the defense, it was an unequal contest pitted against a prosecution representing the great Burlington corporation, wanting to break the power of the Brotherhood, and the Pinkerton agency unscrupulous in practice, and whose future in such work for corporations depended upon conviction.

The eloquent Mr. Mills in closing his address said:

GENTLEMEN OF THE JURY:—You will be governed by the truthful testimony you have heard and the obligations of your oath. You will therefore, I know certainly do, as I have the assurance and hope that you will, give to this defendant the justice he demands and the vindication which is his right.

The audience, which had been held spellbound, burst into loud cheering, but were sternly called to order by the judge, who expressed his disapproval of such demonstration. The Chicago *Herald* of Dec. 22, illustrates in part this intelligent jury who were qualified

SAMPLES OF THE JURY.

to serve because they had formed no opinion upon a subject uppermost in the minds of the whole community. After fifteen hours they rendered a verdict that astonished those who were best acquainted with J. A. Bauereisen, his character and the surrounding circumstances. Bauereisen, Broderick and Goding were tried. Bauereisen was sentenced for two years, Broderick for one year, Goding a fine of $500, which was reduced to $100. The benefit of a doubt could not have been given, and while those, who were not, in the minds of the people, proven guilty, were made to suffer a penalty, those who confessed their crime, and that they tried to involved others in it, and despicable in character, Bowles, Smith, Kelly and company, go free because they could be used to weave a chain around the necks of others. J. A. Bauereisen is denied the freedom of the world and is out of the Brotherhood, but is not out of the mind of his friends, and is not looked upon as a criminal, but as a creature of circumstances, and deserves sympathy rather than condemnation.

CHAPTER L.

THE END OF THE GREAT STRIKE.

The committee of nine, named in Chapter XLVII, held their first meeting in Chicago, Dec. 27, 1888. The chairman of this committee, Mr. A. R. Cavner, in order to carry as much weight as possible with the committee he represented, called to Chicago the general grievance committee men within a given radius, to confer with them, and find how much of a unit in sentiment remained that could be used as a power to compel concessions on the part of the Burlington. The Union meetings at St. Joseph, Mo., in July, had demonstrated almost a unit on the boycott, but the Kansas City meeting was conservative, the St. Louis meeting was still more so, and the action of the convention in refusing to pass a federation law, put the possibility still farther away, and the Chicago meeting proved conclusively the impossibility of an aggressive move, the vote on the boycott standing 22 for, to 43 against. Mr. Cavner had been over the line of the Burlington, and had found the men holding their ground, and doing whatever it was possible for them to do, with their influence, to boycott the road. The Brotherhood throughout the country were doing the same, to a more or less extent, and this power was greatly felt in the west, where the Knights of Labor through their good will for the strikers, refused to ride on the Burlington, or buy goods that were shipped over it. Mr. Cavner visited each point where the men were located, and delivered an address to them, which was very encouraging. Mr. Cavner no doubt, adduced from the many promises, easily given, and the power he believed lay dormant, which would only need a little spirited discussion to bring into new life, that much might be accomplished for the strikers in this last act, by the committee appointed at the engineers' convention for the express purpose of settling the strike. But he counted without his host, and the anticipated power did not materialize. A difference in opinion is not a difference in principle. The men were all anxious to do something for the striking engineers, but ten months after the inception of the strike, was too late a day to vote to do what would, in all probability, have endangered other men's places, without any assurance that it it would benefit those in whose interest the effort was to be made. The vote upon an aggressive move should not have been taken. Men will talk, and the very influence that was anticipated from the presence of these leading committeemen was killed, with the positive knowledge of their strength in that direction, divulged by the vote, presumption was worth more than fact, as it would leave the officials in doubt, while the vote assured them that nothing could be done more than was being done by personal, sympathetic boycotting, and the desire on the part of the Burlington officials to get rid of this boycott and ill feeling, which had been engendered towards that company, was the only apparent incentive for any settlement at all.

With the strike settled by mutual agreement, a part

of the conditions on the part of the Brotherhoods must be, that, so far as it was in their power, the embargo should be raised, and the company left without hindrance, to regain its old customers if it could. The committee of nine, as a whole, were extremely conservative, and it is a very reasonable supposition that they were known to be so when appointed. This committee being all engineers, and the firemen being equally interested, Mr. Cavner requested Grand Master Sargent to appoint a committee to act with them. Mr. Sargent, feeling that he had been slighted in this matter, reluctantly appointed L. Mooney, of St. Joseph, Mo., and L. W. Dixon, of Barraboo, Wis., to represent the firemen.

An audience with the Burlington officials was solicited and granted. The ground was gone over in a lengthy discussion, and finally President Perkins was telegraphed at Boston to define the position, which was done in the following dispatch:

"Boston, Jan. 3, 1889.

To Henry B. Stone, Vice-President C., B. & Q. Railroad, Chicago.

"I am authorized and instructed by the executive committee now in session, to send you the following: The company will not follow up, black list, or in any manner attempt to proscribe those who were concerned in the strike, but on the contrary, will cheerfully give to all who have not been guilty of violence, or other improper conduct, letters of introduction, showing their record in our service, and will in all proper ways, assist them in finding employment. The first duty of the management, is to those who are in the company's employ, and we must remember and protect their interests, by promotion, and by every other means in our power. Beyond this if it should become necessary to go outside of the service for men in any capacity, it is our intention to select the best men available, and in making selections, not to exclude those who engaged in the strike of February 27, if they are the best men available, provided they have not since been guilty of violence and other improper conduct."

(Signed) C. E. Perkins.

On receipt of this document Mr. Stone was asked to define the word available, and the following is his evasive reply:

"It is important that no question should arise as to the good faith of the company, and it is our desire and intention that there should be no opportunity for such question."

"As to the meaning of the word available, I desire to say that when it becomes necessary to employ men outside of those now in our service, care must be taken to consider all of the qualifications that go to make up availability, including experience and familiarity with our surroundings and rules. In short, that the very best men are to be selected, regardless of personal relations or prejudices for or against any man or class of men."

"While men who have been guilty of improper conduct during the late strike, cannot be re-employed, and while we cannot give letters to them, no officer or employe, should continue the animosities of the conflict after it is over, or interfere to prevent the employment of such men elsewhere." Henry B. Stone.

The company also agreed they would re-employ what men they needed from the ranks of their former employes, "and all striking engineers, firemen, switchmen, and brakemen were instructed to file their applications at their respective division headquarters if they desired re-employment, on or before February, 1889. This advice was given at the request of the officials of the company." The conditions were accepted by Mr. Cavner's committee, and the strike declared off. The men along the line complied with the instructions and sent in a list of names of those who desired re-employment. The list was accepted by the company's officials, but they required that each one should make personal application, which most of them did.

A committee was appointed by the chairman of the committee of nine, consisting of A. W. Perley, and H. C. Hayes with S. W. Dixon for the firemen, who were instructed to go over the system and explain the conditions. The strikers were generally indignant, and the reception of these gentlemen was anything but a pleasant one. An undue buoyancy of mind had been engendered by what Mr. Cavner had said he expected to accomplish, and their own imagination of what the committee of nine could do, with the reality as presented by these gentlemen, was a grievous disappointment; not that they expected a surrender on the part of the Burlington, but they expected more than was given, or nothing.

They had manfully battled against all odds for eleven months; hundreds of them had refused places on other roads at the instance of Brotherhood men at large, on the ground that a battle could not be fought without an army. They had given their sacrifices unstintingly for the common cause, and the settlement embodied in Mr. Perkin's dispatch, without other written conditions, meant practically "You stop boycotting us, and we will not boycott you." The other conditions, "selecting men from the old employes as they needed men," has not been lived up to on any part of the line except the Hannibal and St. Joseph, and there the engineers are asked to go to work as firemen. The letters, with few exceptions, were simply statements, the substance of which was: "John Smith commenced work for the C., B. & Q., as a fireman January, 1880, was promoted to engineer in 1884, and quit the service on account of strike, February 27, 1888." Some of them said he gave satisfaction, while a very few were real recommendations, the best letters coming from Mr· Stone himself, but Mr. Stone's own letter giving the very best of a recomendation, has, to my knowledge, failed to secure place on the Burlington, because of the animosity of the local officials. Mr. Stone had said the animosities should not continue after the conflict was over, but it is apparently as rancorous to-day as ever, with some of the officials. Mr. Stone has lived up to his own declarations. Transportation has been furnished, good letters bearing his signature have been given to some of the old men, and favors of whatever nature that have been extended to the old men since the strike was declared off, are from the man who said "I never will concede it." But that ever present element of discord in corporation authority, unrestricted official prerogative, is a positive barrier against any good-will policy, and what few old men are left along the line should seek new fields, and leave the Burlington to enjoy its new company.

The Burlington strike, the most vigorously fought on both sides of any strike in the history of our country, causing an immense loss of wealth, the sacrifice of place, the separation of friends, and the creator of enmities, ought to have in it, a lesson that would be as lasting as the pyramids of Egypt, but until corporate autocracy is changed to autonomy, that cannot be expected. The Brotherhood lost the fight because it did not have the machinery to concentrate the power it possessed, and 'No alliances,' like the drunkard's whisky, created the vipers that sting it.

The firemen and engineers made a grand fight. I put the firemen first, because they were just as steadfast, with less at stake than the engineers. They stood together like brothers, through thick and thin to the end, and the Burlington strikers should feel no disgrace at defeat; they believed they were right when they struck, they still believe they were right. The preservation of the Brotherhoods in their present standing is due to the tenacity with which they stood their ground. Had the strike been declared off in the first week of March as was advised, the Atchison, Topeka & Santa Fe would not have asked for a loan from their enginemen, they would have taken it to have and to keep, wages would have been reduced and the Brotherhood's power to resist would have been gone. They voted to stand their ground against all advisors, and by so doing they formed the nucleus, around which, gathered and solidified the shocked vitality of the Brotherhoods and gave opportunity to realize the danger to their future and convert indifference into energetic help.

The current of good will became wonderful, money flowed like water from the National camp of the Brotherhoods, all labor came closer together, the Burlington strikers being the magnet of centralization, and at the close of the strike the Brotherhoods stood with vitality and numbers unimpaired; the strikers themselves were great losers, but there must be martyrs in any cause, and this is no exception. The younger men will find place and regain lost ground. But there are some men past the age for new fields, whose sacrifice, in the interest of their fellowmen, embodied their whole future. They must wait patiently for that last trip, over the river, and make their last report to the great master mechanic, their Redeemer, who shall estimate this sacrifice. It is hoped none of them will be permitted to make an intermediate trip, "over the hill to the poor house."

With this exception the effect of the strike to the Brotherhoods is entirely eliminated; the lesson it taught remains. How is it with their opponents, the Burlington management?

The Union Pacific, a parallel line, reports January 5, 1889. Earnings for eleven months to November 30, 1888, $26,880,398; increase, $566,504; expenses, $16,444,955; increase, $1,307,842; surplus, $10,435,-443; decrease, $741,338.

C., B. & Q. STATEMENT.

CHICAGO, ILL., January 5, 1888. For the eleven months to Nov. 30, 1888, the gross earnings and expenses were respectively $21,621,483 and $16,259,124, and for the corresponding period the year before $25,-412, 699 and $13, 885,936.

The Union Pacific keeping up all its departments is short for 1887, $731,338, while the Burlington with the greatest possible retrenchment in every department, shows a loss of $6,164,385. Following this comes the March statement of the Chicago, Burlington & Quincy. In connection with statements previously made it showed that during the first quarter of 1889 the road did not even pay its interest charges, being several hundred thousand dollars short. The total net earnings for the three months ending March 31 were, for the Burlington proper and the Burlington & Missouri River roads, $1,579,941. The interest charges alone are approximately $550,000 per month. In addition to the interest charges, which have not been earned, the Burlington company is paying dividends at the rate of 1 per cent quarterly, which still further swells the expenditures above the net earnings.

While financial disaster follows the Burlington, the Union Pacific which pays better wages than was asked of the Burlington, shows a net increase for January of $172,000, over 1888. The Burlington system has deteriorated since the strike of its old employes, from the best dividend paying road in the west, to one that cannot earn its interest, and from one of the best manned roads in its engine department to the poorest, as their expense account shows. The following from the Aurora *News* of July 16. 1889, is significant: "Engine 339 of the main line was burned out at Mendota, Saturday, through the carelessness of the engineer and was immediately taken to Gälesburg for necessary repairs."

Retrenchment is apparent in the following: "A large amount of work continues to accumulate at the different departments of the car shops, especially in the car department and repair shops, where worn-out coaches and bad order cars of all kinds are rapidly increasing. Several tracks in the yards are also crowded with such disabled rolling stock."

When we look at the great depreciation in Burlington stock, and the immense direct lost the company has sustained, and from a surplus of two millions, to a borrower of ten, we wonder if the reader will think the Burlington, in defeating the Brotherhood, won the battle. They have run their own business, or rather, they have run other peoples', to suit themselves. They cornered the labor market in a vast territory, and then went on the principle that "Providence had sent a few men into the world, ready booted and spurred to ride, and thousands ready saddled and bridled to be ridden." The Burlington strike should be the last of its kind, but until railway managers realize their responsibilities to all shareholders, to the public, and the rights of the labor they control, we cannot expect such a blessing, labor will not meekly give up its rights and liberties, and until corporations shall "have dared to come up to the spirit of the pilgrim covenant of 1620 and shall declare that all men shall be consulted in regard to the disposition of their lives, liberties and property, strikes will remain possibilities. The Pilgrim fathers proceeded on the doctrine, that every man was supposed to know what he wanted, and had the right to a voice in the disposition of himself."

As these conditions have not materialized, the usefulness of organized labor is not over. Avoiding strikes should be one of their cardinal principles. Arbitration, the recognized mediator, and balance of justice, another. But the Burlington strike has demonstrated the fact that power is necessary to compel the use of these peaceful means. The Brotherhood should not forget, that evils which accrue to other laboring men, bear as heavily upon one as the other. In writing this book I have been actuated by a desire to soften asperity, and remove the causes of discord and doubt, that organized labor might come nearer together and practice the golden rule—"Do unto others as you would they should do unto you." Washington said "To prepare for war was one of the most effectual means of preserving the peace." As long as trusts and corporations exist, so long will legal or moral restraint be necessary. As there are no legal restraints, organized labor must protect itself. A part of the province of this work has been to show the conditions that have made the organization of labor necessary, but it has not been done with any malice or attempt to injure any party, and if the reader shall find anything commendable within these pages and the work shall tend to greater harmony among laboring men, and lead to more pacific relations between labor and capital, the compiler will feel that his first and only effort has not been without good results.

C. H. SALMONS.

C. H. FRISBIE.

SKETCH OF THE LIFE AND EXPERIENCE

OF

CHARLES H. FRISBIE,

FOR

FORTY-SEVEN YEARS A LOCOMOTIVE ENGINEER.

The author and writer of this short life-story first saw the light in Cortland county, New York, in 1822. My father was a farmer and a hotel-keeper. It was an old-time kind of a hotel, with a swinging sign, ample grounds, and a house that grew by additions. There was nothing small at an old style hotel but the prices. The customers were not the loafers of the town but were private travelers in their own carriages or on horseback, or movers, or drovers, or stage coach loads of passengers. There were no railroads then and farm wagons carried down to the city the products of the farm; or light teams of two horses, with light loads for short journeys, made the roads lively. The roads were for months impassable till a turnpike company elevated and leveled the road, put on gates, and charged toll of all travelers. Droves of fat cattle and sheep and hogs from western New York, walked to their fate in the city, two or three hundred miles away. Drivers were hired for a song, and the lazy herds would walk four or five miles a day, and would increase in weight on the journey, enough to pay the traveling expenses.

These country inns were usually five to six miles apart, and afforded a local market for hay and corn, but at what we should now call give away rates. Now, you can load a car with stock thousands of miles west and get to market quicker than you could then from western New York. People grew tired of the slow work and began to think of a more rapid transit. Then came the Erie canal from Buffalo to Albany with its 363 miles in length which cost nearly eight millions of dollars, built by the state, and a monument of the genius of Governor DeWitt Clinton, completed in 1825. When the ground was broken for that canal, on July 4th, 1817, my father often said he never expected that he or any of his children would live to see it completed. Yet they all did live to see it and many long years after. The writer of these lines lived to see it and, up to this writing, sixty-four years more. Many of us remember similar talk of the Union and Central Pacific railways. But no improvements in this country gave such a powerful stimulant to enterprise as the Erie canal. The immediate immigration to the state was immmense, new cities sprang up, and wealth poured in upon the people from every source. The lake crafts carried grain to Buffalo, and the canal boats took it to the sea coast, and the lowered expense of transportation lined the pockets of the farmer, and quickened trade of every kind.

Now, gentle reader, you have followed me along the uphill to boyhood. It is now 1837 and I am 15, and now let us strike a faster gait. Let us leave the creeping canal boat and go by steam. A horse railroad was finished at Quincy, Mass., about the same time that the Erie canal was completed, and, for the next fifteen years, a powerful head of steam in favor of railroads left canals far behind. About that time the New York Central was built from Albany by Schenectady and Syracuse to Buffalo. We did not build railroads then as we do now. Let us walk out along the track and see how they did it. The grading was done, then much as now. 'Now comes the track. Teams of two or four horses would draw from the sawmill, beams eight inches thick, and as wide as the tree would allow, and as near as may be to forty feet long. This was the foundation or mudsill. It was sunk even with the surface of the ground. These sills were laid along continuously, one on each side. Then come the cross-ties, split out of white oak with cavities to fit an eight inch wooden rail, then comes a three by two inch wooden ribbon and then on top of that an iron bar, one-inch thick by two and a half inches wide. Now on this cobble house you may bring on the cars, one by one, slowly, but, alas for the engineers and the firemen! the engines were mules, one, two, or three; according to grades, or length of train. That was my first engineering! I held the throttle of those four-footed engines for about a year. We thought the railroads would revolutionize the commerce of the world, and so they did but not till after the mules were sent to grass.

The first steam engine run in this country was built by Foster, Rastrick & Co., at Stourbridge, Eng., and was put on the Delaware & Hudson canal company's railroad in 1829. Mr. Peter Cooper built in Baltimore the first engine ever built and run by the same man, in America. This was on the Baltimore & Ohio in 1830. The supply of American built engines was slow, and many were brought from England. The three principal makers in this country were Rogers, Maqueen and Baldwin. Now, reader, you will see that I have got far ahead of the mules, and I will call a halt.

Step this way and look at my new engine, the Phoenix. George Howard of the Utica road is engineer. Then comes the Varrum, with Perk Howard at the throttle. The next was the Wyoming, built in the Auburn state prison. On board of her I had the honor to be extra fireman. Melank Mason was master mechanic, and Milt Alcott worked in the roundhouse. He was the man who built the first head light in the United States. The reflector was made of a kind of babbitt metal with sixteen silver dollars melted in it. It was about half as big as our present lamp. The first head light I ever saw was made of wood and resembled the shape of my mother's sun bonnet, only it had one glass in front. The back and sides were lined with tin, and the light was about a two candle power. A bright full moon would make it look sickly.

Now, reader, if you intend to stay by me, you will have to pull up your stakes and come along. We set out now from Auburn, on the New York Central, and at Albany take the steamer Alida for New York City, on which the fare—thanks to competition—is twenty-five cents. Let us take the Cortland St. ferry for Jersey City, and find the engine Phocion hitched to the

Philadelphia train, Howell Roe, engineer, Charley McCleary, fireman. I soon met with the old sweeper at the depot and learned that there was a fireman wanted for that train, and that Tim Smith was the boss. I found him. and in three minutes I had the first regular job I ever had on a railroad. Now; my overalls take their place, and I am assistant fireman on the engine Jersey City. All engines had names then, not numbers as now, and I was happy as a lark. The engineer got fifty dollars a month, first fireman twenty-five, and myself, the assistant twenty. Board was one dollar fifty a week, and cigars two for one cent.

The kind of engines used on the New Jersey Central road was the Baldwin make and the Rogers, both kinds from American shops. These ran between Jersey city and New Brunswick. From New Brunswick to Trenton they used English engines.

New Brunswick was the meeting place of the two different kinds or make of engine. It so happened that the Uncle Sam from the New Jersey road stood over night side by side with the John Bull from the Camden and Amboy road.

None of the engines, then, had whistles. In order to give a signal to apply the brakes, the engineer had to raise the safety valve, which made a noise similar to one you would make in driving a snooping cat out of mischief, and not much louder.

Every night after we had put our train away, we had to go on a side track to get water. Not a drop was there outside of the well, consequently it had to be pumped. In order to do the pumping we had to run the engine on a track over the well, and on a set of wheels, about the size of the driving wheels, which were connected with the pump. Then we would start the engine slowly, and that would turn the wheels connected with the pump, and we would wait until the tank was full. That was not very long for the tank was small and would run three cars about ten miles. After that we backed the engine over the Raritan river to the engine house, run the engine on the turn table, disconnect the tender from the engine, run the engine off the table, push the tender over upon a short side track, run the engine back over the table, push the tender upon the table, turn it the rest of the way around and push it into the house, then turn the engine and back her up to the tank, then fill the tank with wood, which was the best of Norway pine. That was the best wood I ever saw for generating steam, and was had in abundance at one dollar and a half a cord.

Now, after going through with all this process the night before, we went down in the morning and got the engine out and the train hitched on, ready for Jersey City. The engineer takes his seat on the right, the first fireman on the left, the second fireman, or wood passer, between the engine and the tank, standing of course, for there is only room for two on the engine. The brakeman always stood on the platform on the first car to give signal for brakes.

Now, it might be interesting to you, patient reader, to know what kind of coaches were used at that time. Well, many of them were four-wheeled, hung on what was called thorough braces. I will try and tell you A long time ago when stage coaches were young, the coach body swung on thorough braces. The thorough brace was made of several layers of strong harness leather, six or seven inches wide, and fastened to the back and forward bolster, one on each side. Then the body of the coach was set on these, and it hung in the middle. These strong straps served as springs and gave to the coach body an easy movement up or down, back or forward. When the coach went rapidly and suddenly over something either high or low, the passengers were often unseated, hit the ceiling with their heads, silently exchanged seats, or introduced to each other for the fortieth time, in a mode more speedy than polite, each one saying nothing but "Oh!" These coaches would hold only ten or twelve persons. They had to be hauled with horses part of the way over Bergen hill, a few miles west of Jersey City, a hill that has been tunnelled several times. When Bergen hill was passed so that engines could be used instead of horses, they used larger cars. Every seat was numbered and every car lettered, and your ticket called for a seat in a certain letter and number. The end doors were locked and the passengers entered a side door in the center.

The principal production of New Jersey, then, 1849, was Jersey lightning and buckwheat cakes. Jersey lightning was cider brandy, and the buckwheat cakes began soon after the first frost, and they never slacked up until the shad came in the spring. If you never had fresh shad for breakfast you have missed a good thing that never can be made up to you. The meal that working people made the most of was dinner, and it was an important matter, but they licked their plates for supper. I hope the New Jersey schools are better now than fifty years ago, for then, most of the fellows, in signing their receipts, made their mark when they receipted for their pay.

Our trains to New Brunswick were light, only two or three cars, all coaches, with but one freight train on the road. The engines were only fourteen by twenty inch cylinder; single driver. The two Philadelphia trains had larger engines, as they had five or six cars. Two of their best engines were built by Roger's, monsters for those days, six feet double drivers, cylinder thirteen inch bore, twenty-two inch stroke; the smaller engines had ten inch bore by twenty inch stroke. One of these large engines went with the train from Jersey city to New Brunswick, and on nearing the Passaic river the engineer saw that the draw was off, but he did not see the danger till he was within a fourth of a mile of it. It was too late to hold the train and down he went with the engine and baggage car. There was in the baggage car a deadhead who had left New Brunswick that very morning, getting on board a steamer in New York bay just in time to see the steamer take fire He leaped overboard and was rescued by his swimming to an island. He was picked up, and took that train for home and went down with the engineer. There were three draw bridges on that route, over the rivers Raritan, Passaic and Hackensack. I have known a fog from the ocean to last for three days, so dense that you could not see a signal fifty feet ahead.

After firing about three years I got to be extra engineer. Then I wanted to go home and make a visit and talk over the news. Now, friendly reader, pack your grip and come along, for I may stay some time. Now, we take the ferry for New York, the steamer for Albany, the cars for Auburn. There we found the cars running farther west, and hundreds of horses had left the stage coaches for eastern markets.

About this time there arose a great excitement about the Michigan Central railroad, and everybody with his dog was going there. This road belonged to a Boston company at that time, and was built to Kalamazoo, having a track of strap iron.

We now take a steamer for Detroit. There are three steamers in one line, London, Canada, and Atlantic; the last named is now at the bottom of the lake. She left Buffalo one night with one thousand persons on board, but she went down, and all on board perished, except two boys by the name of Becker, who floated off on a piece of the wreck. I met these boys more than forty years afterwards.

The same company afterwards built a floating palace, called the May Flower. She was magnificent, but she went to the bottom of Lake Erie three times and then staid there. About the last time that the May Flower went down I was given an engine on the Michigan Central, called May Flower, the very engine that gave name to the steamer, and she tumbled me all over the fields. That was the only engine in which I was ever hurt in forty-seven years of engineering. What's in a name? Nothing at all, perhaps, but all railroads have an engine on which bad luck rides oftener than on any other. I was going over the switch at Dexter, Michigan, when the bar that holds the rails in place, broke and let the May Flower down on the frozen ground and ice. She began to slew and started up street, and at about fifty feet from the track she turned up side down, and where was I? Under her, of course, caught by my left foot with steam blowing on it. But my foot was on the ice and the steam thawed it loose, when I crawled out with a scalded foot and all my bones unbroken.

Another time I started with the same May Flower engine, and when three miles out from Marshall, Michigan, I ran over an ox and threw the engine and train, every wheel, from the track. The engine rolled over twice and a half and lay on her back, fifty feet from the track, headed the opposite way. I looked around and found myself, and set up my underpinning, and on taking an inventory, I found one arm disabled, my face and hands scalded, and my shoulder and collar bone were broken. The fireman, poor fellow, fared much worse, and died in a few days. Now, tell me what's in a name? You may laugh, but I left the fated May Flower then and forever.

What did the company do about it? They paid my doctor's bill, they paid my full wages for the full year I was laid up. I never entirely gained the use of my right arm.

Now, reader, let me introduce you to officers of the Michigan Central. J. W. Brook, general superintendent; R. N. Rice, assistant superintendent; C. H. Hurd, general freight agent; three finer men never lived. Now let us go to the roundhouse to find S.T. Newhall, master mechanic, another of nature's noble men. All these men have now passed away. The death of S.

T. Newhall hastened the organization of the Brotherhood of Engineers. The man who took Mr. Newhall's place was an overbearing tyrant. To resist him, and to secure justice, the engineers organized what was then called the Brotherhood of the Foot Board. They hoped to have him removed but failed in this, but out of this society grew that noble institution, the Brotherhood of Engineers.

About the year 1850 my work called me to run through a region infested with hundreds of desperate conspirators. At that time the Michigan Central was not fenced, the country was sparsely settled, and stock running wild in the woods would often get on the track and get killed, and the company would not pay the damage. After much bickering without result, the settlers along a stretch of about twenty miles united to commit depredations on the company's men and property. They would burn timber on the track, and throw stones at engines and trains, and would fire guns at passing engines, so that we sometimes had to lie down behind the driving wheel guards to keep from being shot. In the night they would run a hand car just before us for miles, to delay us. They burnt a freight house eight hundred feet long in Detroit, the upper part of which was for storing grain. After a year or so, the company sent men to join them, as spies, and to give information. A conspiracy was hatched to burn a very large elevator belonging to the company, at Niles. One of the spies, on being initiated, was ordered to burn that elevator and a railroad bridge. The damage was averted by the information gained.

The company was about two years preparing for its first trial in the courts, and then they arrested about forty men all in one day. They were men who professed to be our best friends; they had ridden free on our engines, times without number. Some of them were in the employ of the company; one of them was a fireman on one of our engines. They took a change of venue for obvious reasons, and ten of them went together to the state prison, which broke up the conspiracy. The attorneys who did a good work for the company, and for morals, were Mess. Van Arman and Darius Clark; both eminent in their profession.

The Michigan Central was built from Detroit to Kalamazoo without any eastern outlet except the lake Erie. When navigation on the lake closed, in the fall, commerce was closed on the railroad. The engines were all laid up except enough to run two passenger and two freight trains. In my first winter I ran a freight, the next I ran a passenger train. Then the road was extended eastward through Canada to Niagara Falls, and there connected with the New York Central. I finally drifted west to the Burlington. That being a prairie road, there was but little wood along its line, but coal was abundant; the only trouble was that no one knew how to burn it, at least the method was very little known.

At the Burlington shops in Aurora, was a man by the name of C. F. Jauriet, master mechanic of that road, He was experimenting with coal burners, and he succeeded in making as nearly perfect a coal burner as there is in the United States to-day. He had the reputation of being the best machinist in the country. His firebox to-day is the most economical of any that I know of. At his time they had to use copper for fireboxes, for they found that steel would crack, though at this writing steel is used. His box would last ten and twelve years. He could hold his engines on the road three to five years. He well deserved the title of master mechanic, yet he never had credit from his employers for his skill or his success, but he was severely criticized and censured as being expensive, and ignorance or willfulness in high places allowed him to resign. How much the company lost by allowing such a genius to leave their service can never be known.

About this time coal was discovered on the line of the Michigan Central road near Jackson, Mich. It was pronounced unfit for use by Allen Sweet, master mechanic of that road. It so happened that while I was on a visit to Detroit, I saw Assistant Superintendent C. H. Hurd, of the Michigan Central, and I asked him how he got along with his coal burners. He said they were a failure, that the coal was no good. I then told Mr. Hurd, that I had used some of the coal on the Burlington road, and found it superior instead of inferior as Mr. Sweet had stated. Superintendent Rice was informed of what I had said, and in a conversation with him I suggested to him that he might exchange engines with the Burlington and get one of Mr. Jauriet's engines, which would very soon prove that I was right, that the fault was in the engines and not the coal. There had been a coal miners' strike in Illinois and the Burlington had from necessity got some of the Michigan coal, so I knew from experience that it was good, but Mr. Sweet had agreed to run the road for less money than his predecessor, and he could not do so and change his engines into good coal burners, and he did everything he could to prevent the success of the demonstation. Shortly after my return home, I was sent for by Mr. Jauriet, as Superintendent Hammond of the Burlington had instructed him to send one of his best coal burners to test some coal that they could not burn. Master Mechanic Sweet heard of this move and came to Aurora to see Mr. Jauriet and try to exchange engines without having the engine manned by a Burlington crew, probably thinking he could defeat the test, but Mr. Jauriet would not allow his engines to be condemned that way, and engine 34, with engineer and fireman John Smith and Henry Twist was sent; as neither of them knew the road I was sent to show them, when I was to return. At Chicago they gave us twenty-five double deck cars of stock, and they run us to Marshall, Mich., nearly two hundred milcs, then we took another train to Detroit, then commenced Mr. Sweet's effort to defeat the test. He had the engine sent to the dock, and the tank filled with dirty slacked coal, not a piece in it as large as a hickory nut. Engineer Smith naturally refused to go with such coal, as good coal was to be furnished. This refusal brought Mr. Sweet who said: That's the same coal that I burn in my engines, and if you cannot burn the same you had better take your engine back home. I said, Mr. Sweet do you pretend to say that your engines will burn that coal? "Yes sır, I do."

"I do not believe you can get steam enough with that coal to take your engine out of this yard." Mr. Sweet got very indignant, and said:" I want you to understand, you cannot come here and dictate to me what I shall burn in my engines. I will send you back home." He telegraphed to Chicago to have me recalled but they mistrusted what was the matter. An answer came to me, telling me to stay until further orders, and I staid until they were all satisfied the coal was good, which demonstrated the fact that Mr. Sweet, like many other officials, was working for himself more than for the company.

On my return to Aurora Mr. Jauriet sent me to Chicago to take charge of the engine house on Halsted street. I only staid there a short time. I longed for the free air of the prairies again, and on application for a change Floyd Cooly was sent to take my place and I went back on the road again.

I would like in my story to mention the names of a few prominent railroad officials with whom I have had more or less business. Some of them are yet living at the time of this writing, September, 1889, and a good many are not.

Edward H. Williams, once general manager of the Chicago & Galena Union. He was familiarly known as Doctor Williams. He was a man with whom it is an honor to have been acquainted.

John C. Gavitt was another, not only a gentleman, but a successful railroad manager.

E. T. Jeffery, who was born, not with a silver spoon in his mouth, but with a blackening brush in his hand. He is a skillful business man and a good judge of men. As a railroad manager he has no superior, and anywhere he is a perfect gentleman.

Thomas. J. Potter was another self-made man, of good judgment and of untiring industry. When he found that he could not agree with the general aims of a company, and could not change their plans, he would quietly and honorably retire with the good wishes and confidence of all parties.

Godfrey W. Rhodes was superintendent of machinery on the Burlington, a good business man, and in my opinion, a gentleman.

Henry B. Stone, the undeviating promoter of the Burlington interest in the office of general manager, was always with me attentive, polite, and cordial. I sincerely believe that if he had been allowed to choose his own policy rather than be obliged to follow the dictates of the directors, the C., B. & Q. railroad would have a treasury richer, by millions, than it is to-day.

Now, my clever reader, we have been friends together for many a trip, and I mean to take you into my confidence and introduce you to my wife, Mrs. C. M. Frisbie. As the age of a woman is always a secret I cannot tell you hers; but at this writing I am sixty-seven and it will take her ten years to get to the same point, but I'll never tell her age. I can tell a true story about my own little circle. One bright morning, thirty-nine years ago, a nice looking little youngster that had no age at all, came to my house and introduced himself as William W. Frisbie, the first of a series. He was very communicative, had a good deal of self-importance, but we took care of him, and at an early age we put him in charge of his father to become an engineer. I took this youngster with me to fire when he was yet a lad, and we worked on the same truck for seven years. He is at this writing, running a passenger train from Topeka to Newton on the Santa Fe railroad, and he is still at his post. I always taught him to shun saloons as he would vipers or scabs. I brought him up in the way he should go, and he went.

Now, if we stop and look about us a little, we shall see wonderful changes since 1837, when you first found me a boy of fifteen years. In that time, Queen Victoria reached the throne and has reigned during one half the period of the history of the United States. I was born in the administration of the fifth president of the United States, and of all our twenty-four presidents I have lived under twenty of them. In these forty-seven years of my engineering I never had a collision, but the engine of the general government has passed through fearful perils and met many an accident. We have had suspension of specie payments; sudden deaths in high places; infamous assassinations; marvelous discoveries of gold and silver; vast out-puts of petroleum; great extension of domain; many visits from impecunious princes of the earth, not omitting Kossuth with his $100,000 loan; brutal assaults within the federal buildings; the Dred Scott decision and Uncle Tom's Cabin, and the war that followed; the struggle between capital and labor; the nation embarrassed by its treasury surplus, and strikes without a parallel in their extent or in the intelligence with which employes have demanded what they saw to be their rights.

And now we come to the great railroad strikes that since 1877 have made inter-state commerce so uncertain, and which, during 1888, threatened all railroad systems, and actually unsettled one of the largest of them. This is not properly the discussion of a biographer, but it requires the broader sweep of the pen of the historian. That is the subject of all this book. Here the individual is lost sight of and the subject of the general good commands the attention of all.

Now, reader, come and see me; you will find my engine in the roundhouse, Aurora, Illinois, but the door is locked and the key is lost and I have plenty of time to talk. Bring your wife, or if you have none, bring your best girl, and let us spin the past over again, and map out the future. But don't all come at once. And here I conclude my biography as David Crockett closed his: "Dear reader, I bid you farewell and, as the fox said to the coon, we will meet again at the hatters.".